Oil and politics in the Gulf: rulers and merchants in Kuwait and Qatar

Why in recent years have the social and economic upheavals in Kuwait and Qatar been accompanied by a remarkable political continuity? In a region of revolution and coups, these particular monarchies have somehow survived. In her analysis of political change in the Gulf, Professor Crystal investigates this apparent anomaly by examining the impact of oil on the formation and destruction of political coalitions and state institutions.

This book contributes to a new theoretical subject in Middle Eastern studies, the distributive or *rentier* state, that is, to the question of how the availability of external revenues affects the internal politics of a state. It also adds to our understanding of state formation by highlighting the ways in which states and rulers structure the relationship between those with money and those with power, a fundamental political issue beyond the region. Partly based on a year's fieldwork in the Gulf and making full use of Arabic and Gulf sources, *Oil and Politics in the Gulf* goes far beyond previously published accounts of the region in its analysis of the effects of oil on domestic politics.

Cambridge Middle East Library: 24

The *Cambridge Middle East Library* aims to bring together outstanding scholarly work on the political, social and economic history, politics, sociology and economics of the Middle East and North Africa in the nineteenth and twentieth centuries. While primarily focusing on monographs by younger scholars based on original research, the series will also incorporate broader surveys and in-depth treatments by more established scholars.

Oil and politics in the Gulf: *rulers and merchants in Kuwait and Qatar*

Cambridge Middle East Library

Series list continues on p. 210

Oil and politics in the Gulf:
Rulers and merchants in Kuwait and Qatar

JILL CRYSTAL

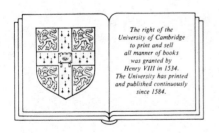

The right of the
University of Cambridge
to print and sell
all manner of books
was granted by
Henry VIII in 1534.
The University has printed
and published continuously
since 1584.

CAMBRIDGE UNIVERSITY PRESS

CAMBRIDGE

NEW YORK   PORT CHESTER   MELBOURNE   SYDNEY

Published by the Press Syndicate of the University of Cambridge
The Pitt Building, Trumpington Street, Cambridge CB2 1RP
40 West 20th Street, New York, NY 10011, USA
10 Stamford Road, Oakleigh, Melbourne 3166, Australia

First published 1990

Printed in Great Britain by Redwood Press Limited, Melksham, Wilts

British Library cataloguing in publication data
Crystal, Jill
Oil and politics in the Gulf: rulers and merchants in Kuwait and Qatar.
– (Cambridge Middle East library; 24)
1. Middle East. Petroleum industries. Political aspects
I. Title
338.2'7282'0956

Library of Congress cataloguing in publication data
Crystal, Jill.
Oil and politics in the Gulf.
(Cambridge Middle East library; 24)
Bibliography.
Includes index.
1. Kuwait – Politics and government. 2. Qatar –
Politics and government. 3. Petroleum industry and
trade – Political aspects – Kuwait. 4. Petroleum
industry and trade – Political aspects – Qatar.
5. Petroleum industry and trade – Social aspects –
Kuwait. 6. Petroleum industry and trade – Social
aspects – Qatar. I. Title. II. Series.
DS247. K88C79 1990 953. 67 89–9841

ISBN 0 521 36639 9

To Russell

Contents

Contents

Preface

This is a book about oil and politics. It analyzes the impact of oil on the formation, destruction and nature of political coalitions. It is also a book about money and power and about the ways leaders and economic elites, rulers and merchants, act to structure the relationships between those with money and those with power. Because the strategies rulers adopted have involved reaching out to the rest of the population for allies, this is also a book about elites and groups, albeit small groups. Finally, this is a book about state formation, about the state structures and institutions that emerged in the process of negotiating those relationships.

I began this book with a broad interest in delineating the realm of the politically possible. I was interested in how large economic transformations are mediated by preexisting structures – economic, political, social and cultural. I wanted to understand the extent to which these transformations removed everything in their path and the extent to which these economic forces were tamed and translated by the local structures in place. Oil involved just such a crisis. By providing revenues directly to the ruler, from outside the state, in dramatically large amounts, oil radically restructured economic and political life in both states.

I selected Kuwait and Qatar as the case studies for two reasons, first, in order to achieve as much comparability as possible and to avoid states with internal sectarian and regional conflicts severe enough to mask the unfolding of the initial processes associated with oil. In Kuwait and Qatar it was possible to control for these differences and compare similar variables over different cases in order to highlight general processes and to show that their critical similarities are rooted in one key variable – oil – and not in any particular historical idiosyncrasy. However, this book is also a comparison. In each state, oil intervenes in an ongoing process of state formation. While the general impact of oil is the same, the specific effect varies depending on the starting point, on the pattern of politics at the beginning of the process. This book not only explains general outcomes, but also allows us to understand differences in those outcomes. These two cases allow us to see the extent to which other variables, preexisting structures, affect political change, within the broad constraints set by oil. The different economic, social and political resources that existed in each state on the eve of oil tempered the impact of oil, producing slightly different outcomes. These cases allow us to focus on those factors that best explain the differences in outcomes, the variations on a theme.

When I began this project, there was almost nothing of theoretical interest written on oil and domestic politics. The most useful writings to me initially were studies of state building outside the region. These studies were most helpful in drawing my attention to the importance of revenue extraction and coalition building in state formation. They prompted questions about the nature of state formation in those cases where internal revenue extraction does not occur, when rulers of states once built on internally extracted revenues find themselves suddenly freed of that process by the availability of outside sources of revenues, rents. They also prompted questions about how rulers dealt with the sudden abolition of their historical need to depend on local elites to generate those internal rents and how they dealt with the alliances that had grown up in the context of this dependency. The answers to these questions form the core of this book. The book is thus a theoretical look at the inside of a *rentier* state, a look which is grounded in a careful examination of the historical and contemporary political processes that accompanied oil. In the course of writing it I have had the opportunity to watch and, in part, participate in the development of a new literature on and a deeper understanding of the properties of this *rentier* state.

In this book I also analyze political change in Kuwait and Qatar. The book is thus also a comparative historical political anslysis of two particular states. In order to study these states, it was necessary to examine the political processes surrounding oil in some detail. This was particularly challenging for Qatar which, with a few excellent exceptions (e.g. Zahlan 1979) has hardly been studied at all. For that reason it was necessary to work from primary source material. The study is based on a year's fieldwork in the Gulf and on two research trips to London's India and Foreign Office records.

In the course of the research I have incurred a number of debts. For financial support, I am indebted to the Social Science Research Council, which funded the work in the Gulf, to Harvard University's Center for International Affairs and Center for Middle Eastern Studies, which provided some support, and to the University of Michigan's Faculty Assistance Fund.

For intellectual support, I owe a debt to several people in the Gulf: Ahmad al-Anani, Shamlan Alessa, Abdul-reda Assiri, Jim Bulloch, David Good, Peter Kovach and Muhammad al-Rumaihi. Several people have commented on portions of the book: Al Badr Abu Bakr, Duaij al-Anzi, Eric Davis, Abdalaziz Fahd, Nick Gavrielides, Jim Hitselberger, Terry Karl, Thomas Philip, Roger Owen, Muhammad al-Sabah, Rosemarie Said, Hasan Saleh, Gary Samore, and two of my dissertation advisors, Samuel P. Huntington and Nadav Safran. Barbro Ek, the late A. J. Meyer, Sharon Russell, Tom and Diane Lander and Sam helped with the work in other ways. Two people have offered particular support from beginning to end – Gregory Gause who shared an office with this book for a time and who commented on it with enthusiasm and Lisa Anderson who offered extensive comments on drafts and read the entire manuscript, in different forms, at least twice.

For moral support I am grateful to Greg and Lisa, to my family, to my writing companions Majnoon and Bob, and to my husband, Russell Balch, to whom this book is dedicated, for his careful comments on the draft, for discussing the book with me, and for discussing anything but the book with me.

The Al-Sabah rulers of Kuwait

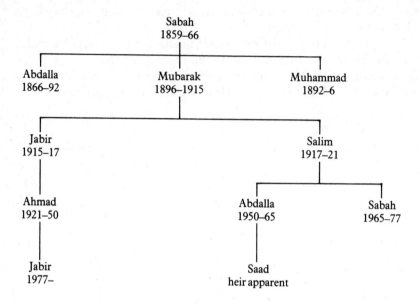

Sabah
1859–66

Abdalla
1866–92

Mubarak
1896–1915

Muhammad
1892–6

Jabir
1915–17

Salim
1917–21

Ahmad
1921–50

Abdalla
1950–65

Sabah
1965–77

Jabir
1977–

Saad
heir apparent

The Al-Thani rulers of Qatar

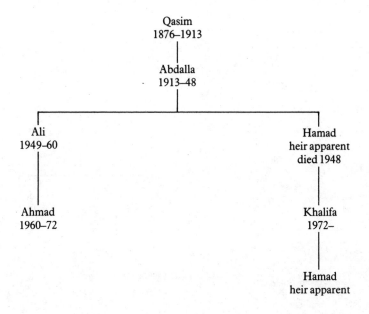

Qasim
1876–1913

Abdalla
1913–48

Ali
1949–60

Hamad
heir apparent
died 1948

Ahmad
1960–72

Khalifa
1972–

Hamad
heir apparent

1 State formation and oil

A few short decades ago Kuwait and Qatar were British dependencies, little known outside the Middle East. Today their oil resources and strategic location astride the globe's principal energy routes have brought them the attention of the world. In the intervening years Kuwait and Qatar have experienced a radical but apparently smooth transition from pearling to petroleum, poverty to prosperity. Oil revenues have fueled the development of new economic structures, new welfare systems and radically different and materially better lives for their inhabitants. Yet these rapid changes have been accompanied by remarkable political continuity at the apex of the systems: these two countries continue to be ruled through monarchical institutions of long standing. Despite the obituaries regularly written for these regimes, their rulers have survived the arrival and departure of Britain, the trials of independence, the challenge of populist Pan-Arabism and radical Islam and, finally, the demands of oil wealth.

This continuity has been achieved because of oil, not despite it. However, apparent stability on the system's surface has been accompanied by powerful transformations in the distribution of power just below the surface. The development of oil in the postwar years has led to the withdrawal from formal political life of the merchants, the group which historically pressed its claims most effectively on the state. Merchant claims have not been put forward because of a tacit arrangement between the rulers and the trading families: a trade of wealth for formal power. In effect, the merchants renounced their historical claim to participate in decision-making. In exchange, the rulers guaranteed them a large share of the oil revenues. Where economic elites once entered politics to protect their economic interests, after oil, merchants left the realm of formal politics to preserve those interests.

The merchants' withdrawal has also been accompanied by the unexpected development of new ties between the ruler (or Shaikh) and members of the ruling family (shaikhs) through new political and bureaucratic roles, and between the ruler and the national population, through social services and benefits. Oil revenues thus preserved continuity at the apex of the political system only by forcing the breakdown of the old ruling coalition and catalyzing the formation of a new pattern of political control. The political changes that

1

occurred – the breakdown in the old ruling coalition binding the trading families and the ruler and its replacement by a new set of elite arrangements – were not the result of idiosyncratic local factors, but a patterned, recurring response to oil. The same broad transformations that occurred in Kuwait also occurred in Qatar. Variations on the basic pattern appear in all the oil-dependent states. In Bahrain, Saudi Arabia, and the United Arab Emirates, the rulers have all gradually weakened their old economic allies and their depencence on those allies.

The new arrangements, however, are only transitional adaptations. Distributive policies designed to ensure domestic peace have inadvertently created relatively large and complex state administrations, distributive states, unusual in that they emerged from the imperative to expend rather than extract revenues. These bureaucracies are themselves now one source of change. As the state's role grows, so too does its power. As the state's scope grows, so with it grows the distance between the ruler and the population, as the popular perception of state services shifts from benevolence to entitlement. As the state's power expands, new actors appear who question the old arrangements. Finally, as oil revenues decline, the rulers' ability to keep the original bargain with the merchants declines, and they too begin to question the political arrangements prompted by oil. As their dissatisfaction grows, they are beginning to return to political life, through the back door of the bureaucracy.

Oil has set these transformations in motion. It has catalyzed the destruction of old political coalitions and the formation of new alliances. It has induced far-reaching changes in institutional structures. These two processes of regime change and state formation occur simultaneously and are causally related. The new distance from the merchants encouraged the rulers to build bureaucracies, a new arena for allies. The new bureaucracies, in turn, allow the merchants and other groups to eventually reinsert themselves into politics in a new way.

However, the processes induced by oil, although similar in each state, are not identical. The arrival of oil and the regime and state changes it induces do not occur in a vacuum. The nature of existing alliances and the nature of the state formation process already underway at the outset of oil encourage and discourage certain kinds of changes in regimes and institutions. Differences in the nature of state power and in the strength of the key actors and their potential allies on the eve of oil determine the particular balance of power and patterns of politics that emerge within the broad constraints set by oil.

Explaining regimes

These states and their neighbors defy most of the usual assumptions about how states are formed and how they normally behave. They are accidental states, owing their survival to regional upheavals, British policy, and political convenience. They are new and reluctant states: in the evening of colonialism they resisted British withdrawal. They are city–states, without peasantries, built on economies of oil and social structures of settled tribes and foreign laborers. They are, for the size of their populations, relatively large and complex distributive states, whose administrative structures have grown from the need to expend rather than accumulate wealth. Finally, they have been politically stable states.

Kuwait is notable both for its wealth and its stability. It has been ruled continuously by leaders from one family, the Sabah family, since it was founded in the eighteenth century. Since the death in 1915 of Mubarak the Great, Kuwait has been ruled peacefully by his direct descendants, all of whom have died in office of natural causes, no mean accomplishment for monarchs. There have been no civil wars, no coups. The old forms still seem to work.

Like Kuwait, Qatar has been remarkably stable. The ruling al-Thani family has dominated the country since the nineteenth century. Unlike Kuwait, Qatar has seen some seriously contested successions since oil: Abdalla to his son Ali in 1949, Ali to his son Ahmad in 1960, and Ahmad to Khalifa, the current ruler, in a bloodless coup in 1972. Yet despite these family divisions, the question of power leaving the al-Thanis has never seriously been raised.

Kuwait and Qatar have achieved this relatively smooth transition into the oil age despite the inarguable presence of the social forces that conventional literature suggests would normally promote instability. The modernization literature of the 1950s and 1960s posited an ideal-type dichotomy: tradition/ modernity (Lerner 1958; Rostow 1960; Deutsch 1961). States, these writers argued, moved from the first category (the entire Third World) to the second (an idealized version of the US) in a process sparked by capital and culture contact. This approach posited linear and inexorable connections between capital accumulation, economic growth, social mobilization, and increased participation. This literature had a powerful impact on thinking about the Third World in general and the Middle East in particular. Implicitly its assumptions continue to inform much, if not most, western writing on the region. Yet the framework was unable to anticipate the continued viability of the Gulf shaikhdoms. It would have predicted an increase in demands for formal political participation from newly mobilized groups rather than the withdrawal from politics which in fact occurred. In the Gulf where the key variable, capital, was available in abundance, modernization theories should have had the greatest predictive capacity. Yet here they failed most clearly.

In the late 1960s and 1970s the modernization literature came under attack by the dependency literature which introduced variables neglected by modernization writers: the international geopolitical and economic system (Frank 1967; Cardoso and Faletto 1979; Evans 1979). The power of this literature lay in the connections it drew between the world economic system, domestic economic structures, and form of rule. Other scholars have usefully applied this broad emphasis on international economic factors to the Middle East (Amin 1974;

Lackner 1978; Zureik 1981; Kerr and Yassin 1982; Ibrahim 1982; Ismael 1982; Waterbury 1984). In the Gulf the insights of the dependency literature allow us to understand the forces that shaped the region in the colonial era. Today these insights draw our attention to the importance of oil, the commodity which mediates the Gulf's integration into the world economy. However, like the modernization literature, dependency writing tends to rigid dichotomy (center/ periphery) into which the Gulf states do not neatly fit. The dependency litera-ture's teleological stress on economic dependency renders it less applicable to developing states with problems of excess capital.

To modernization writers, political life had its origins in economic forces; to dependency writers, in economic structures. Social structures such as class played a weak mediating role. Other writers, many looking at European state formations, focused on this mediating role. They sought the origins of political life in social structures, stressing the ways domestic social formations affect the nature of politics. States and regimes, these writers argue, are shaped by the economic interests they embody, with social formations and class alliances the intervening variables (Moore 1967; Tilly 1975; Stepan 1978). A few writers have analyzed state formation in the Middle East with attention to these categories (Batatu 1978; Nore and Turner 1980; Khuri 1980; Anderson 1986; Salame 1987; Beblawi and Luciani 1987).

These insights can be broadly applied to the Gulf. Before oil, politics in both Kuwait and Qatar were dominated by a ruling coalition between the ruler, or Shaikh, and the trading families. These merchant families were the link con-necting the monarch to the money he needed, money embedded in the sea rather than the land. Merchants extracted revenues from pearl divers rather than peasants, and gave a portion of these extracted revenues to the ruler through cus-toms dues, pearl boat taxes, and personal loans. Their political power grew from their economic strength. Their ordinary input into decision-making came from the social institutions of marriage (intermarriage between merchants and the ruling family was common) and *majlis* (regular social councils for airing grievances and concerns) which gave them informal but daily access to the rulers. Their independent strength lay in their control of the mobile pearling and nomadic workforce. In a dispute the merchants would simply leave for friendlier nearby ports, taking with them their pearl divers, a sizable segment of the popu-lation. To borrow from Hirschman (1970), the political choices the merchants faced were *Exit, voice and loyalty*. Potential dissidents could go along with things (loyalty), or they could speak their minds (voice) – and there is the memory of tribal councils – or they could leave. Until the early twentieth cen-tury, this kind of temporary exit was a powerful check on the rulers.

In the interwar period, a series of economic crises afflicted the Gulf: the crash of the pearling market with the invention of Japanese cultured pearls, the depression, World War II. In Kuwait these crises brought the merchants closer together. Kuwait already had a small cohesive economic elite with roots in the mercantile and pearling economy of the eighteenth and nineteenth century. This economic elite was also politically powerful. The same few families, often the same individuals, dominated public life.

In the interwar economic crisis, Kuwait's merchants returned to long distance trade and diversified, developing land on the Shatt al-Arab in Iraq. They were weakened economically, but they stayed. Their social and political cohesion grew as they formed alliances with ruling family dissidents. When their historical access to decision-making faltered, they were quick to organize – first through educational councils, then through explicitly political institutions such as the Kuwait municipality, secret meeting groups and clubs – and finally to protest, as they did in a brief rebellion in 1921 and through the *Majlis* Movement of 1938. Both movements, especially the latter, generated well organized and articulate political opposition: The 1938 movement produced a lively, though short-lived, legislative assembly. These moments of conflict were frequent and sharp enough to forge a conscious and politically organized merchant elite before oil.

In Qatar, however, a cohesive and organized grouping of merchants did not emerge. What set Qatar apart from Kuwait was the absence of an entrepôt economy. Qatar is a small, rainless peninsula, off the main trade routes. Ecology and location dictated for it a complete dependence on pearling. Because the population was not tied to fixed trade routes, but to the desert and the sea, a settled community emerged later than in Kuwait and, when it did, it was smaller and the trade sector smaller still. A national market did not appear in Qatar until the twentieth century. The different economy in turn affected the relative strength of social groups. The basic actors were the same – the ruler, his family, Britain, the merchants, the pearling workforce – but their size, strength, and consequently political role and bargaining power differed from that of their Kuwaiti counterparts. In particular the merchants were a weaker group. They were fewer in number and, completely dependent on pearling, had fewer economic options. Their control of the domestic workforce, which included a larger number of beduins with independent ties to the desert beyond Qatar, was weaker. One measure of the merchants' weaker control was that Qatar's pearl divers were, for the region, uniquely free of debt bondage. Finally, the merchants lacked a monopoly on trade, some of which was handled by foreigners, some by the ruler himself.

Because of Qatar's different economy, its society reacted differently to the pearl crash. The interwar economic crises which shook Kuwait almost destroyed Qatar. Where Kuwait's merchants, with more economic options, adjusted locally, Qatar's chose a still older response: exit. The economy turned inward and perhaps half the population, including many merchants, migrated. So, on the eve of oil, Qatar had no merchant class, let alone a politically seasoned class

5

that could challenge the ruler. Only two powerful merchant families remained, al-Mani and Darwish, and they were divided by competition for the Shaikh's favor. This put the Qatari merchants in a weaker bargaining position than their Kuwaiti counterparts. As a result they were unable to strike as strong a deal with the ruler after oil was discovered.

The impact of oil

Oil brought new forces which restructured political life. Within a few years of the postwar resumption of operations, oil revenues dominated both economies. The modernization writers were optimistic about this process: oil would bring needed capital which would finally spark sustained growth, and ultimately participatory political stability. Dependency writers were less optimistic; they pointed to the underlying similarities between oil and other commodities. Oil was a single export, a depletable raw material, and a commodity as dependent on unpredictable markets as any other. Oil would bring dependency and decline. Both predictions contained some truth. Oil did bring spectacular growth. Oil did bring dependency on volatile markets. But oil's transformations were more far-reaching than that. Oil produced a new kind of economy, built on rents – a rentier economy. Such an economy is heavily reliant on the export of a single raw material, the production of which requires little contact with the rest of the economy. Most critically for politics, these revenues, rents, are paid directly to the state or, in the Gulf, the rulers. One consequence of these revenues is to affect the independent power of social groups and to weaken the links between state and society. A second is to increase the power of the state (Mahdavy 1970; Delacroix 1980; Nore and Turner 1980; Skocpol 1982; Beblawi and Luciani 1987).

In the Gulf, the most important impact of oil and the rentier economy it produced was that it gave rulers direct access to external revenues, revenues generated outside the local economy. Where once these revenues had to be squeezed from the population, through the merchants, who in turn exacted a political price, the rulers now received revenues independently. There are always moments when the state develops a high degree of autonomy from its social bases. The Bonapartist state, where the bourgeoisie is unable to manage its own affairs, is the classic example. Writers focusing on the state as the mediator of domestic and international forces have analyzed particular circumstances in which states develop partial autonomy from their social bases (Nettl 1968; Huntington 1968; Anderson 1974; Trimberger 1978; Skocpol 1979). But oil-based states are unusual in that their higher degree of autonomy from other social groupings is not the result of a momentary crisis, but part of a structurally determined, ongoing process. This independence is almost uniquely peculiar to oil. Almost any other export – coffee, cotton – involves some accommodation between the rulers and the elite who control the workforce and extract surplus revenues. Oil does not. The elites on whom the ruler depends are not local, but rather multinational oil companies. The new revenues snapped the link binding the rulers to the merchants. The external nature of oil rents, the enclave nature of the industry, and the size of the boom spared rulers the need to extract, through taxation and repression, economic and social resources previously allocated through other (tribal, religious, but especially mercantile) networks of obligation, thus freeing the rulers from their historical, economically based dependence on the merchants.

In the long run oil also created new international interdependencies as these states came to rely on foreign markets for capital, labor, and goods, but these consequences were yet to be realized. Oil operations took place in isolated oil towns. The oil company presence seemed removed from the daily politics of the capital. The number of choices, the range of options that oil revenues created, the things that oil money could buy, these factors initially masked the growing dependency on foreign powers and markets.

The immediate consequence of oil revenues was the breakdown of the economic basis of the historical governing coalition – the alliance binding the rulers and the trading families – and the development of new and unstable arrangements which excluded the merchants from formal political life. Old alliances, forged in scarcity, did not hold up in an environment of abundance. The Shaikhs quickly came to rely on the oil companies for money and to use that reliance to distance themselves from the merchants. In the 1950s they settled the ruling families' merchant debts and lowered customs tariffs. No longer would the rulers or the state have to rely on port dues paid by traders. Rapidly the dependence of the rulers on the trading families withered.

The second consequence was that once oil dominated the economy, the merchants were no longer united by a common tie to the production process. Oil is an enclave industry involving few workers and generating few social and economic linkages. Oil altered the merchants' historical economic base, and with it the forces that had made the merchants a class. Yet the merchants, especially in Kuwait, maintained an unexpectedly strong corporate sense and continued to function, economically and socially, as a collective body. They did not simply disappear as a class.

Before oil, the merchants were a cohesive, self-conscious group because of their historical relationship to the (pre-oil) production process. Perhaps their group identity was simply a fading cultural remnant – the explanation that would flow from the modernization writing. But a vestigial merchant culture, developed out of the entrepôt economy that preceded oil, is alone insufficient to explain the highly successful reproduction of this class after oil. A fuller explanation lies in the fact that the merchants were bought off, by the state, as a class. State distributive policies not only favored the historic economic elites, but

7

favored them through mechanisms that perpetuated their group identity. Revenues were distributed not only through transfers but, indirectly, through the market. Even as the state expanded its economic activities, it preserved an enclave private sector, a playground for the merchants. Where merchants wanted to invest – trade, construction, services – the state stayed out, or offered encouragement. The mechanisms the state used were the preservation of an enclave (non-oil) private sector, legitimated by a free enterprise ideology, and direct aid and protection to merchants through grants of land, money, and monopoly concessions. In time this arrangement was institutionalized through protective nationality and commercial laws which restricted property and business ownership rights to nationals. The primary beneficiaries were the old trading families.

In Kuwait, the first crucial mechanism in preserving and augmenting the merchants' wealth was the land acquisition program. In the 1950s and 1960s land purchases were the single largest state budget items, exceeding development expenditures. Downtown land, largely owned (and assessed) by merchants was bought by the state at high prices, a fraction maintained for development purposes, and the rest resold at low prices, again to wealthy merchants. The net effect was a significant transfer of revenues from the state to the merchants. The government also made a tacit promise to keep members of the ruling family (Sabahs) out of business. It is not for lack of funds that few Sabahs appear in the historically merchant dominated Chamber of Commerce, or on corporate boards. Generally, their money has been invested abroad or, if at home, discreetly, through merchant fronts and partners. The government has also provided direct state support to the merchants. At first aid was *ad hoc*: the ruler helped individual merchants through preferential monopolies and dealerships, even personal loans. Later this aid was routinized: in the 1960s the government began to promote local trade through laws that restricted business and property ownership rights to nationals. Other laws gave Kuwaiti companies preferential treatment for state contracts. This economic nationalism largely benefited the established traders. The old merchant names soon came to dominate the boards of the family companies and shareholding corporations traded on the official stock market.

In Qatar a similar process occurred, but because the merchant community was smaller and weaker, because it lacked experience in political organization, it did not fare so well. In Qatar when oil arrived only two important merchant families remained and they were divided by competition. By the 1960s they were eclipsed by the ruling family and its new allies. By then there was no organized trading community left for them to turn to. In the following years oil prompted a deal with the merchants similar to that in Kuwait. Merchants received economic protection in the form of trade monopolies, agencies, and protective economic legislation. But while these laws, like Kuwait's, protected nationals, the ruler had more scope in determining which nationals to favor. When he turned to the merchants he could turn more often to families outside the old trading monopoly, tribal retainers tied to him through preexisting tribal patron-client networks. The merchants who rose to wealth were thus dependent clients of the ruling family. Because these families were newly rich and dependent, the ruler could more easily erode the original arrangement. In particular the ruler allowed ruling family members to invade the merchants' economic territory with increasing frequency.

The similarity between Kuwait and Qatar was that in both states the merchants were bought off collectively by the state. Because of this, they maintained some corporate identity, unifying economic interests, and an ongoing internal cohesion related to the economic structure. Social formations remained linked to a material base, although this was now through the means of distribution, not the means of production. Social mechanisms – marriage and *majlis* ties – reinforced this corporate sense.

Political arrangements

The rulers exacted a price for their economic largesse – political quiescence. In both states the transition to oil was accomplished through a tacit arrangement between the ruler and the trading families, a trade of formal power for wealth. In exchange for receiving a sizable portion of oil revenues, the merchants renounced their historical claim to participate in decision-making. As a result, trading families in both states rose economically, but declined politically. Their informal access to the top declined as the rulers turned more to family councils and as the ruling families themselves turned inward. Their formal access declined as old institutions faded and new ones emerged, dominated by the ruling families and their new allies. In Kuwait, for a time, the merchants held a vestige of formal influence through the National Assembly, but gradually the ruler came to contain even this institution through new allies. In both cases, this arrangement was a quiet agreement behind closed doors. Although its existence is commonly believed and some of its functions (allowances and private investment activity of the ruling family) are carried out formally, although secretly, through the palace, the arrangement was never public. In the Gulf the expressions of social power lie below the surface. Rules, while real, are publicly uncodified and social groupings sometimes lack clear institutional analogs. While not pacts, these arrangements bear a family resemblance to the more formal pacts that have emerged elsewhere (Lijphart 1969; Daalder 1974; Barry 1975; Linz and Stepan 1978; Karl 1981; O'Donnell, Schmitter and Whitehead 1986). They resemble, for example, the elite arrangements that occurred in Venezuela where, as Karl has argued, oil created the structural space that allowed the emergence of a reformist pact. As in the Gulf, oil removed the major

9

obstacles to alternative elite arrangements by destroying the political base for a conservative regime on the right (in Venezuela the landed elite lost their peasants, in the Gulf the merchants lost their pearl divers) and a radical regime on the left by isolating the more politicized oil workers and turning much of the indigenous workforce into a less volatile middle class. Oil predisposed the regime towards such an arrangement, but it could not guarantee its success. The smaller size of the Gulf states helped, as did the presence of a kinship system that guaranteed elite control of subelites, a low preexisting level of political mobilization, an institutionalized history of elite communication, political skill on the part of the leaders and a widespread belief in the system's legitimacy, coupled with an often threatening regional environment.

The merchants' withdrawal from public politics suggests that participation demands are tied to extraction of taxes and to the ability of those who mediate that extraction to influence the distribution of extracted wealth. Since in the rentier oil economies extraction of wealth from the population, by the state, does not occur, neither does the demand for political participation. The merchants' historical claim to participate, however, founded originally on their extractive capacity, gave them a sense of entitlement, and the ability to organize politically. The merchants were the one group in the early days of oil capable of sustained, organized, and potentially successful political opposition to the ruler. The rulers, recognizing this, offered them economic advantages. Since money was no object, it was easier for the state to buy them out than to repress them. As a result, the oil pact – this tacit trade of wealth for power – emerged.

Distributive policies

The arrangement with the merchants was not the only policy the rulers constructed to maintain domestic peace. They also formed new and independent ties with the national population below the merchants. Oil gave the regime the resources to develop new allies among the national population through distributive policies. Tribal distribution customs provided an indigenous rationale. The rulers have been careful to distribute revenues in politically useful ways. The benefits of oil have trickled down to all nationals, even the poorest. They are today healthier, better housed, better educated, and better fed than ever before, and they know that the state is directly responsible. For those old enough to remember, the pre-oil economy provides a comparison. For the younger generation, grounds for comparison are readily available in the Arab lands nearby and in the large foreign workforce at home.

Nationals are not only better off, they are reminded of it by strict nationality and commercial laws that bestow and withhold economic rights. The prosperity they enjoy is a direct result of state action in two areas: social services and employment. Nationals are entitled to free education, health care, and a variety of subsidized goods and services, including housing, as well as direct transfers of wealth. Any national can put some economic claim on the state. Nationals are also guaranteed state jobs and preferential treatment in salaries and position. Consequently, most nationals work for the state. Yet the majority are clearly underqualified or underutilized. Were their purpose primarily administrative, much of this staff would be superfluous if not harmful. State employment is but another means for distributing income to nationals.

These state policies exacerbated the political isolation of the merchants. Where merchants had once served as intermediaries, oil revenues now allowed the rulers to deal directly with the population, to implement distributive policies that bypassed preexisting alliance structures. By hiring nationals directly into the bureaucracy, the rulers deprived the merchants of a politically useful workforce. Nor were new ties likely to be forged between the merchants and other nationals because the bulk of the population benefited materially from this new state. Where elsewhere state formation has involved the state impinging on the population, here it was characterized by demands from the population on the state, demands from the poorest sectors for schools, hospitals, and services, demands the state met.

As the dependency literature predicted, oil meanwhile accelerated the decline of indigenous industries (a decline that had already begun with the pearling crash) and, by removing the economic incentive to revive these industries, hindered local industrialization. When the merchants lost the pearl divers, they lost their autonomous political clout, and they lost the ability to threaten to leave, taking with them a sizable portion of the population. Exit as a political technique was also weakened by the emergence of established borders, in large measure also due to oil. To the extent that exit remains an option, it functions as a safety valve for dissidents, a valve the state opens and closes. The merchants have no domestic constituency of their own, no independent economic power over significant indigenous social groupings. They do not even have the nuisance value that control of a popular following, a *street* in Middle Eastern parlance, would confer. The historic absence of an independent regional base has contributed to this weakness. Not only are the merchants directly dependent on the state for contracts, they wield little significant power apart from that granted by the state.

Centralization of power

Distributive and development policies rapidly increased the role and size of the state. In order to maintain control over this new state, the rulers turned increasingly to the ruling family, whose political functions now grew. Rulers chose their family, a group with a vested interest in monarchical rule, not only because it offered the most reliable set of allies, but also because it formed a ready-made protoinstitution – an institution in the making, a group with structured relation-

11

ships and rudimentary organization. Unincorporated, family members would also form the most likely source of opposition. Like the merchants, their historical sense of entitlement gave them a rival claim to power.

Because the rulers actively incorporated the ruling family into state positions, institutions grew up that were both bureaucratic and familial. Bureaucratic organization did not mean an end to other kinds of political organization such as those based on kinship, as many had predicted, because rulers were able to manipulate newly reinforced family ties to penetrate and control the new, oil-induced bureaucracy's top positions, centralizing decision-making. Political kinship, normally considered a traditional vestige, was in fact a response to the oil-induced bureaucratic state.

This political role for the ruling family was an important break with the past. Until oil, the ruling families were not cohesive political institutions. Family members were largely excluded from the Shaikh's decision-making. With oil, successive rulers strengthened family networks to provide more reliable elite recruitment pools for the increasingly large bureaucracies catalyzed by oil. The most distant family claimants were eliminated, the less distant received increased allowances, the nearer claimants sinecures, and the closest relatives high state posts. Gradually, by delegating responsibility the rulers came to share power with their brothers, uncles, cousins, and sons. As the ruling families became more cohesive and more powerful relative to society, the rulers became less absolute and less powerful relative to their own relatives. Today the organizing principle at the top of each system is political kinship. In both states, the ruler, or amir (the title taken on independence) controls politics and political institutions primarily through his family. Critical decisions are made by ruling family councils. Political continuity is maintained through a process of centralization and solidarity at the apex of the political system.

While the same broad processes occurred in both states, the different inherited political structures colored the way this transformation occurred. Key among these were institutions regulating succession. In the eighteenth century, Qatar had no enduring settlements and no central authority. Kuwait did; it was a well-defined unit with political institutions. By the eighteenth century not only had one family, the Sabah, emerged as clear rulers, but the family itself had developed greater internal discipline. Until the late nineteenth century, Sabah Shaikhs peacefully succeeded their fathers. Even before oil, Kuwait's political system was more stable than Qatar's. Succession was regulated, but the ruling family's political role was limited. Only a handful of family members held important political posts. As a political entity the family was decentralized and fragmented; in fact it was cracked right down the middle. It was early in this century that the most important Sabah family rift, the Salim–Jabir division, developed. But this rift was incorporated into a new succession pattern. The family worked out an arrangement whereby the ruler alternated between the

Jabir and Salim lines, excluding all others. In the 1930s oil exploration and the prospect of revenues catalyzed a change in the extent and nature of power wielded by the ruling family. Only then did the Shaikh begin to rely more heavily and in greater numbers on his relatives. By the time Kuwait received independence from Britain in 1961 the amir was quite dependent on his family. In Kuwait the ruler was, with oil, able to develop an already well disciplined ruling family into a more or less controllable institution. Corruption occurs, but no longer on the scale of the 1950s, when with the first oil-induced administrative growth a few family members were able to turn their ministries into personal fiefdoms.

In Qatar, oil catalyzed a similar process of centralization in the ruling family. But because of the weak family discipline, the absence of standing succession mechanisms, and the ruling family's larger size, the same techniques that worked for the ruler in Kuwait failed in Qatar. In Qatar a settled community and al-Thani rule appeared much later, in the late nineteenth century. Unlike Kuwait, succession was never regulated. Instead, a tradition of family-based factional opposition emerged. If the ruler was stronger relative to the merchants, he was weaker relative to his own, large family. Whereas in Kuwait Britain was content with a low domestic profile because domestic peace prevailed, in Qatar family differences caused Britain to play a direct role in assuring the throne. Internal dissent led the ruler to place different demands on Britain, demands for support in succession struggles. In Kuwait interwar politics revolved around the merchants and the Shaikh, with Britain a usually passive third player. In Qatar Britain played a more active role. When oil arrived, the Shaikh's rule was new, dependent on British support, and contested by his large family.

As in Kuwait, oil prompted the rulers to turn to the ruling family. In Qatar, however, oil revenues served to further divide an already contentious family. Repeatedly, ruling family members, shaikhs, turned their ministries into independent fiefdoms, launching pads for succession claims. The ruling family's size and the lack of an institutionalized succession mechanism have allowed grievances to fester to the point of explosion, culminating in a series of forced abdications: Abdalla to Ali in 1949, the first year of oil exports; Ali to Ahmad in 1960; and Ahmad to Khalifa in a 1972 coup. Today the amir continues to rely on immediate family (sons and brothers occupy all the key posts), but he cannot be sure of the extended family's acquiescence in his rule.

In both Kuwait and Qatar then, oil transformed political life by freeing the rulers from their historical dependence on the merchants. In each case it also precipitated similar policies – centered on distribution – and similar bureaucratic and familial institutions to reinforce the distance from the merchants and to carry out the new political functions. Regime change also prompted new directions in state formation. As bureaucratic growth proceeded, bureaucrats, many of them sons of once leading merchants, began to emerge who could develop their own ties with the population. As these independent ties took hold, the bureaucracy became a new arena for politics, a place for merchants and others to undermine the original pact. As the power of the bureaucracy and the bureaucrats grew, the rulers came increasingly to face problems of bureaucratic control and problems of loyalty, from their bureaucrats and from their citizens whose attachment to the regime was increasingly mediated by this often hostile bureaucracy. In both countries, oil bought the rulers a certain amount of political space, but it also set in motion a series of social structural and institutional changes that would have consequences of their own.

2 History's legacy: Kuwait and Qatar before oil

The one historical gift geography gave the tribes of the Gulf before oil was a gift of default: an outward orientation. Regional subsistence has always depended on the vagaries of long-distance trade routes. When trade was good, small settlements emerged to rival each other in carrying the traffic. When trade withered, routes shifted, or droughts deepened, then central regulation weakened, alliances changed, rivalries turned to war and tribes moved, with belongings and dependants, on camels and boats, up, down and across the Gulf. Until well into the modern period, the history of the Gulf has been one of ceaseless migration in search of trade and fresh water. As a result, the tribes of the region have always oriented themselves less to their original tribal ranges than to the fringes of the Gulf and the trade beyond.

Although Kuwait and Qatar were not populated by the ancestors of today's inhabitants until recently, transitory trade settlements there date back to ancient times. In Kuwait, ruins on Failaka island show settlements from perhaps 1000 BC. Archaeological evidence indicates that Qatar, too, was inhabited in prehistoric times; implements have been found dating back to 4000 BC. The Gulf's integration into the modern world economy began in the sixteenth century when the Portuguese captured several Arab ports, including Hormuz and Muscat. Portugal's presence meant a decline not only in their trading wealth but also in their political independence. Portugal armed its ships, built forts and established customs posts. Direct rule, however, proved costly. After local opposition made customs administration increasingly difficult, Portugal relented, settling into the policy of indirect rule its colonial successors would also adopt.

Portugal established European hegemony, but Portugal itself was not destined to Gulf monopoly for long. In the late sixteenth century the British arrived; in the early seventeenth, they established posts and settled down to trade. By the eighteenth century, when the migrations to Kuwait and Qatar were about to begin, Britain held the European monopoly on Gulf trade. The British presence consisted of only a few posts and East India Company ships, but it would soon provide the overarching structure that would dominate the rest. Britain was powerful in the Gulf, but not hegemonic. Local politics were still shaped by local players: the Ottomans, trying to extend central administration toward their outpost at Basra; the Persians, busy within their own borders; the tribes of the Arabian fringes – the Omanis, the "pirate" Qawasim and Bani Yas, the Bani Khalid, ranging from Basra to Qatar; and the Al-Saud of central Arabia, pushing their control eastward. The edges, and sometimes centers, of these fluid powers shifted constantly, as the constituent tribes migrated (often *en masse*, overnight) or switched alliances of convenience and calculation. All would share dreams of hegemony; none would succeed.

The Ottoman empire's local influence was limited by episodic wars with Persia and by its inability to control its own administrative periphery. The Ottomans touched the Gulf through their representative at Baghdad, who was himself rarely able to control his subordinates at Basra, who in turn were busy arranging shifting alliances with neighboring tribes. Persian aims were similarly limited. Invasions and a weak navy gave Persia little time for an aggressive Gulf policy. Inside Arabia as the eighteenth century opened, the tribes of the central Arabian province of Najd were settling their differences with the Bani Khalid in the eastern province of Hasa. In the early eighteenth century Bani Khalid power ran from Basra, through Kuwait, on down the coast to Qatar and into the Najd. Bani Khalid relations both with the Ottomans and with neighboring Arabian tribes were troubled.

On the fringes of the Gulf were several semi-independent clans whose tribal Shaikhs still enjoyed considerable autonomy. In the eighteenth century while Persia was weakened and Britain not yet at its zenith, these smaller groupings expanded to fill the vacuum of control over the Gulf's resources. In this period two new and different kinds of political units emerged. The first were small, mobile, transient groupings bound loosely to a tribal unit and tightly to a particular Shaikh. Rahma ibn Jabir, the "pirate" hero of Qatar, controlled such a unit. These organizations often faded with the death or fall of their leading Shaikh. A second type of political organization was the much larger tribal alliance. The most important were the Qawasim in what would become Trucial Oman (later the UAE) based in Ras al-Khaima and the Bani Yas based in Abu Dhabi. To Britain the Bani Yas and the Qawasim were the pirates of the pirate coast. These larger groupings were a new phenomenon. They were territorially based and sufficiently organized to build sustained, formally recognized war alliances, especially against Persia. Their separate identity was reinforced by the cultural expression of Sunni over Persian Shia Islam. In the eighteenth century the newly settled Bani Utub at Kuwait, Bahrain, and Qatar formed a third such protostate alliance (Sweet 1964). But as these alliances grew, Britain intervened to break them.

In the nineteenth century Britain came to dominate the Gulf. Its policy was directed by two related sets of goals: strategic and economic. The two went hand in hand; protecting strategic interests meant protecting the seas for maritime trade. Gradually, however, British strategic interests came to outweigh commercial concerns, particularly as trade was frequently interrupted by raids, plague, and internal unrest. The Political Agent in Bahrain, looking back from the early twentieth century wrote,

As the Indian Empire emerged, the importance of the Persian Gulf changed from that of a centre of trade with Persia and Turkish Arabia to that of a political and almost military outpost of India . . .

As time went on the Gulf became regarded more and more as the western frontier of India, and, owing to the infirmity of Turkey and Persia . . . we gradually assumed responsibility for security of trade, lighting, buoying and quarantine, and post offices and telegraphs. We took no territory for ourselves, but were jealous lest others would.

(Dalyell 1941: 58–9)

If Britain's concern with the Gulf derived from its concern with India, its concern with the small Gulf powers was more derivative still, stemming from its concern with European powers in the region, especially after France occupied Egypt in 1798. By the nineteenth century, European competition and local unrest had made Britain's presence a settled fixture of Gulf politics. Throughout the century the navy patrolled regularly.

A British political policy towards local powers evolved gradually in the nineteenth century to define and support the naval presence. In 1820 Britain signed a General Truce with the Shaikhs of the Oman coast and Bahrain, banning attacks on British ships. These treaties did not, however, keep the peace, so a second series of treaties followed in 1852. The political consequence of these treaties was to redefine and stabilize the identities of local political units. They forged the first link between political sovereignty (previously extended over tribes) and territory. The treaties also gave power and legitimacy to the particular signatory Shaikhs. Neither Kuwait nor Qatar signed these treaties – Kuwait, because it was not involved in what Britain considered piracy, Qatar because it was seen as a Bahraini dependency. But the treaties' ramifications were felt throughout the Gulf. Qatar and Kuwait were affected by the treaties' introduction of the international state system to the area. Inexorably, the Gulf shaikhdoms were either absorbed into other protostates or brought into the system as autonomous political entities. In the mid-nineteenth century, it was still unclear which course Kuwait and Qatar would follow. They were extended no consistent British policy. As a result, they tottered on the verge of absorption by two neighboring powers: the Ottomans and the Al-Saud. By the early nineteenth century the Al-Saud had defeated the Bani Khalid and exercised control over much of eastern Arabia, threatening both Kuwait and Qatar. But the Al-Saud were soon distracted by the campaigns of Ottoman Egypt's Muhammad Ali in western Arabia. The local significance of these campaigns was that for an important period in the first half of the nineteenth century Muhammad Ali, in combination with internal dissension, kept the Al-Saud from imposing hegemonic control over the Gulf. By the time that threat returned, the settlements at Kuwait and Qatar were well established.

The founding of Kuwait

Kuwait was founded in the early eighteenth century by clans of the Anaiza, a tribe from the Najd. Sometime in the late seventeenth century these clans migrated gradually from the Najd to the Gulf shores. In the course of these migrations, different tribal groups with different skills came together to form a new tribe: the families who moved together were not known collectively as Bani Utub until after the migrations. According to one local tradition, told to the Political Agent by Shaikh Abdalla, the Sabahs fled drought in the Najd in 1710. They migrated south, but finding conditions still bleaker, returned and now with other families migrated to Zubara, on Qatar's west coast. Conditions there were no better so they migrated again, this time north to Kuwait where, finding water, they settled. On the last leg of the journey they had *atabu ila al-shimal* (moved to the north). And that, according to one tradition, was the origin of the name Bani Utub. Another more romantic explanation for the name appears later, in the 1760s, to correspond with the emigration of one Bani Utub branch, the al-Khalifa, from Kuwait. A shaikh of the powerful Bani Ka'ab wished to marry reluctant Mariam, the beautiful daughter (sister, granddaughter) of Kuwait's then Shaikh Abdalla al-Sabah. The al-Khalifa, to avoid war, were prepared to hand her over (the al-Khalifa remember it differently). Shaikh Abdalla, of course, refused. With an invasion imminent, the al-Khalifa migrated to Qatar. Shaikh Abdalla then called the other notables before him and made them vow to defend Sabah honor. This vow was made on the threshold, *atiba*, of Abdalla's home, hence Bani Utub (Dickson 1956: 26–7). Whatever the truth, the name and the legends of the migration gave Kuwaitis the origins of a national identity in a unifying founding myth. During the migration the Bani Utub, clearly not sailors in Arabia, also learned to build boats and sail. This mobility was an important political resource. Migration would remain a factional political tactic for years.

When they arrived at Kuwait the Bani Utub found a small Bani Khalid settlement. Possibly the Bani Khalid had built the fortress there from which the name Kuwait, diminutive of *kut* or fortress, derives (Lorimer 1908–15, vol. 2: 1048). Even before the migrations, the Anaiza had stopped regularly at areas under Bani Khalid control and were probably on good terms with them when they arrived in Kuwait. Bani Khalid support contributed to Kuwait's rapid rise as a trading town.

The peace in the region dominated by the Bani Khalid, combined with the internal problems that kept other regional powers from interfering, allowed the

Bani Utub to develop their new maritime skills. The Bani Khalid were desert-oriented. Although they controlled the harbors and kept the peace, they did not trade much by sea. Kuwait had perhaps the best natural harbor in the Gulf. Its location also allowed it to benefit from the caravan trade to Aleppo and Baghdad, from the Shatt al-Arab trade, and from the smuggling trade into Ottoman territories (which Basra's high tariffs encouraged). The first known European traveler, who came through in 1758, Edward Ives, reported that caravans as large as 5000 camels and 1000 men passed through Kuwait (1773: 222). The relative self-sufficiency of the desert was now abandoned as the Bani Utub became linked to this trading network. Bani Utub trade included horses, wood, spices, coffee, dates and especially pearls: Kuwait was located within an easy sail of the pearl banks that stretched down the Arabian Gulf coast. In the summer boats sailed for pearls; in the winter they turned to entrepôt trade. Trade was good and the town soon flourished. The settlement was doing well when Ives passed through. By the early 1800s the traveler Buckingham wrote that Kuwait was:

chiefly inhabited by mercantile and trading people, who engage in all the branches of commerce carried on throughout the Gulf. The port sends out, at least, a hundred sail of vessels, large and small; and the people who navigate them . . . have the highest character for probity, skill, firmness, and courage.   (Buckingham 1829: 463)

Stocqueler, who visited in 1831, noted that,

Koete, or Grane as it is called in the maps, is in extent about a mile long, and a quarter of a mile broad. It consists of houses built of mud and stone . . . and may contain about four thousand inhabitants . . . A wall surrounds the town on the desert face, but is more for show than protection . . . It certainly is a commodious harbour for smallcraft.
                                                        (Stocqueler 1832: 18–19)

Pelly, the Political Resident, described Kuwait in the 1860s as "a clean, active town, with a broad and open main bazaar, and numerous solid stone dwelling houses stretching along this strand, and containing some 20,000 inhabitants, attracting Arab and Persian merchants from all quarters by the equity of its rule and by the freedom of its trade" (Pelly 1863: 73).

To organize life in a settled economy the Bani Utub developed new political, economic, and social arrangements. Tribal traditions were retained, but they were now placed within a more complex occupational and social stratification. Trade, the basis of the economy, became tightly, and hierarchically, organized. A division of labor appeared early on, certainly compared to Qatar. Divers were distinguished occupationally from ropepullers, captains or merchants. The proceeds from pearling and trade were then divided on the basis of occupation. At the top, a stratum of merchants soon became an elite. The Bani Utub formed their core.

Above the merchants, at the very top, were the Sabah family, who early on enjoyed some preeminence: soon after the colony was founded a Sabah became leader, ruling until his death in 1762. From Ives' account (1773: 222), the Sabahs were well established by 1758 and on good enough terms with neighboring tribes to offer Ives safe passage to Aleppo. Sabah power seems to have originated in political functions. One tradition has it that political preeminence went to the Sabahs as part of an explicit agreement: in 1716 the heads of the al-Khalifa, al-Sabah and al-Jalahima agreed to give the Sabah preeminence in government affairs, subject to consultation, the Khalifa the same in commercial affairs, and the Jalahima in maritime affairs (Ismael 1982: 23). Another local tradition has it that after reaching Kuwait the Bani Utub held a council and elected a representative to go to Basra to explain their peaceful intent to the Ottomans. The man chosen was a Sabah. Sabah diplomacy may also have been important with the neighboring tribes, especially as Bani Khalid power declined. Ismael says the Sabahs, because of their role in the caravan (as opposed to sea) trade, developed closer ties with the desert, and as a result became the tax collectors there, in this period an important revenue source. Abu-Hakima (1965: 54) links their rise to their administrative functions. Control of a harbor doubtless helped, as a port required more state administration and also increased the Shaikh's power by giving him access to resources independent of the desert, hence some independence from tribal alliances. The port also gave the ruler a territorial base. Compared to the predominantly pearling communities down the Gulf, Kuwait's entrepôt economy was oriented to fixed land and sea routes. As the nomads became sedentary and deserted grazing for ship-building, pearling, and long-distance trade, people became linked to the land, the settled became ascendent over the bedu, and the stakes of politics changed. The political unit was slowly tied to the land, the idea of a people to a place. This, too, enhanced the Shaikh's power.

The common element in all these accounts is that the basis of Sabah power was, from the start, political. The Sabahs were not the most pious or learned, the most warlike, the most skillful sailors, or the wealthiest. Their currency was diplomatic and negotiating skill. In this they differ from Qatar's al-Thanis, who were leading traders from the start. By the late eighteenth century, the political hierarchy in Kuwait was well established, the merchants deferring to direct orders from the Shaikh. By the nineteenth century not only was the ruling Sabah much stronger than a desert Shaikh, he was also capable of naming his son successor. Beginning with Shaikh Abdalla (1762–1812), four sons peacefully succeeded their fathers and a fifth his brother: Jabir (1812–59), Sabah (1859–66), Abdalla (1866–92), and Muhammad (1892–6). The Sabahs had made the transition from tribal Shaikh to territorial protector, from leader to ruler (Lienhardt 1975; Peterson 1977; Wilkinson 1983). Sabah rule was legitimated by a tribal ideology, as Ismael (1982: 18) puts it, of genealogy. To this they grafted a founding myth, which included an identity (Bani Utub) and a pantheon of heroes (and at least one heroine). This Sabah preeminence departed significantly from inherited political institutions, where a leading Shaikh ruled with only limited and contestable power. The right of a family to rule, although respected, was historically limited. An individual Shaikh's right to rule and to pick his successor was still more constrained. The primary political role of Shaikhs was to mediate relations between clans. Internally their role was, historically, limited.

At first Bani Khalid power gave Kuwait the breathing space to settle and grow, providing the Bani Utub with a political and economic umbrella. But in the early eighteenth century the ruling Bani Khalid Shaikh died and a long succession crisis followed. This, coupled with growing Al-Saud power, led to the gradual weakening of Bani Khalid control. The Bani Utub responded by arming ships and building fortifications. By 1820 Kuwait could generate an armed force of 5–7000, which it used as necessary (Lorimer 1908–15, vol. 1: 1006). Kuwait also relied on the goodwill of neighboring tribes, secured through alliance, marriage, and tribute. Then, as today, the backbone of Kuwait's military policy was a foreign policy of calculated neutrality, tilting towards but never wholly siding with whatever power seemed most useful, while keeping channels of communication open with all parties. The new demands for diplomatic and military leadership that arose with the Bani Khalid decline helped secure the Sabah's leading position.

Sabah family rule, though well established, remained limited until well into the twentieth century. This was because the merchants, owing to their financial power, could still check Sabah designs. The financial influence of the merchants came from their control of trade and imports, duties on which sustained the Shaikh. This influence could be subtle and it could be overt. The ultimate tactic the merchants had at their disposal was secession. Mobility was originally acquired from the desert migrations; it became politically important when it was transformed into secession, by clans or protoclan segments. Because wealth was embedded in movable property, because refuge was tolerated by neighboring Shaikhs, because Britain intervened only when important interests were at stake, secession was a powerful tactic. Merchants could now leave with ease because during the migrations they had learned to sail. Because rulers knew segments could leave, merchants could use their voice. A large secession could reduce the shaikhdom's economic and military power and create a refuge of future dissidents.

Shortly after Sabah's death, a turning point in Kuwait's history occurred. In 1766 the al-Khalifa and, soon after, the al-Jalahima, left Kuwait, *en masse*, for Zubara in Qatar. Why they left is unclear. Perhaps they hoped to corner more of the Gulf trade by striking out on their own. Perhaps it was a quarrel based on external politics. Kuwait's growth had attracted the concern of neighboring tribes, whose attacks were beginning to harm trade. Perhaps it was a succession dispute; the al-Khalifa may have hoped to succeed the Sabah. Whatever the reason for the break, it was reparable. Relations between the Sabahs of Kuwait and the al-Khalifa of Qatar (and later, Bahrain) remained amicable. If the al-Khalifa left for trade, there was enough for all. The disagreement was soon left behind and both families benefited from their continuing alliance. By the 1790s the Bani Utub of Qatar, Bahrain, and Kuwait formed a larger trade and war alliance similar to the Bani Yas and Qawasim. Domestically, the al-Khalifa and al-Jalahima had clearly been among the top contenders for power. Their emigration left the Sabahs in undisputed control. By the end of Abdalla's long reign (1762–1812) Sabah rule was secure. Throughout the nineteenth century internal politics were stable.

In foreign relations, Kuwait in the nineteenth century was a vulnerable but still largely independent shaikhdom, affected directly by three powers: the Ottomans, the Al-Saud, and Britain. Kuwait began the century as a nominal Ottoman dependency, linked administratively and economically through Basra. On the other side, Kuwait's relations with the Al-Saud ranged from correct to hostile. As Bani Khalid power and protection waned, Al-Saud power grew. Theirs was the threat that made Kuwait look elsewhere, to the Ottomans and Britain. As the nineteenth century opened, Kuwait's relations with Britain were just beginning. Unlike the Qawasim down the coast, Kuwaitis were not, to Britain's mind, pirates. Kuwait's location near Basra, however, gave it peripheral but increasing importance to Britain, for whom it was an easy retreat from that occasionally troubled port. Kuwait also served as an early warning of the rising and waning fortunes of the Ottomans, the Al-Saud, and other Europeans. Even though Britain found it unnecessary to interfere in Kuwait's affairs, it monitored them closely.

Kuwait's first official contact with Britain had occurred in 1775 when first plague, then the Persians, struck Basra and East India Company personnel made arrangements to have their mail sent from Kuwait (Lorimer 1908–15, vol. 1: 1002). The East India Company also sent a ship to Kuwait to evaluate it as an alternative port for Basra and the captain noted its excellent harbor. Although no action was taken, these inquiries forged the first political link between Britain and Kuwait. From then on, relations were generally good, but for some time limited. When Stocqueler visited Kuwait in 1831 he was told no Europeans had been there for years (Lorimer 1908–15, vol. 1: 1008). Britain had as yet no enduring interests in Kuwait.

The reign of Mubarak the Great (1896–1915) forged the critical alliance between Kuwait and Britain. In the late nineteenth century, resurgent Ottoman power coupled with rising Al-Saud power drew Kuwait closer to the Ottomans. This took the form of political recognition, diplomatic aid, military support, and closer economic ties. The new relations with the Ottomans received official sanction in 1870 when Abdalla was given the title of provincial governor. The Sabah attitude towards the Ottomans was flexible, with political distance and proximity a function of need. These links curtailed, but did not sever, relations with other powers, especially the Al-Saud and Britain.

This began to change as the century closed. When Shaikh Muhammad came to power in 1892, disagreements soon arose between him and his brother Mubarak. Muhammad dealt with this by busying Mubarak with affairs outside the capital, sending him off to Hasa with an Ottoman force, and out to the desert to restore order among the tribes, but providing him with no funds. Mubarak, after repeatedly requesting money from his brother, finally decided on a plan of his own. In 1896 he summoned his sons, Jabir and Salim, and some supporters and rode to Kuwait, secretly entering the Shaikh's house. There he killed Muhammad and his brother Jarra. In the morning, Mubarak announced that his brothers had died, and that he ruled in their stead. Perhaps, as Lorimer (1908–15, vol. 1: 1016) suggests, Muhammad had been unpopular. There was apparently no resistance to Mubarak's accession.

The most radical change Mubarak initiated was to realign Kuwait's foreign policy from the somewhat pro-Ottoman orientation of the last few decades to a solidly pro-British stance. Although the immediate catalyst came from Mubarak as a result of disagreements with the Ottomans over succession, the new alignment was forged in the context of Britain's growing hold on the region. When Mubarak turned away from the Ottomans in search of allies, only Britain was there.

The realignment did not occur immediately. The Ottomans felt Britain was behind the murder, while Mubarak remained suspicious of Britain for giving his ousted relatives sanctuary in India. Later the Political Agent at Bahrain wrote, "not unnaturally Mubarak suspected that we did this merely in order that we might have someone handy to install in the Shaikhdom if it suited us to do so later on, but the years passed by and there grew up a strong friendship and trust between Mubarak and ourselves" (Dalyell 1938: 353). For a time, Britain wavered. It had no interest in unnecessarily antagonizing the Ottomans, but it soon became clear that the Ottomans would not accept Mubarak. Meanwhile, Mubarak himself was requesting a closer relationship with Britain, to prevent an Ottoman attack. Britain relented, and in the end decided to draw Kuwait into the trucial system. In 1899 the Political Resident arrived and signed a treaty to that effect in which Mubarak pledged not to cede, sell or lease any territory to any other power without British consent. In an accompanying letter Britain assured Mubarak of its good offices towards him and his heirs and agreed to pay him 15,000 rupees (rs) on the condition that he adhere to the treaty and keep it secret (treaty and accompanying letter in Lorimer 1908–15, vol. 1: 1048–50).

The treaty soon became an open secret and the Ottomans moved to test its limits. Mubarak watched closely to see what steps they would take, and how

Britain would respond. The first Ottoman protest had already come with the Political Resident's arrival, when the Ottoman sanitary agent, with few rules at his disposal, declared the landing a public health violation. When an Ottoman attack seemed imminent, Britain sent ships to Kuwait and Mubarak was reassured. Mubarak's concern with British support was also tied to trouble from Arabia with Ibn Rashid (his opponent, Ibn Saud, was living in Kuwait). Against this threat, Britain also armed Mubarak's fort at the desert village of Jahra. In the course of these threats and attacks, from the sea and the desert, Britain became increasingly drawn into protecting the shaikhdom. The secret treaty became a standing obligation. In 1904 Britain appointed its first Political Agent, Knox. The British now had a domestic political presence. Mubarak's policies thus also inaugurated a new phase, perhaps unintentionally, in Kuwait's domestic politics, involving a larger British local presence.

On consolidating power, Mubarak also moved to exercise control over a greater portion of the wealth Kuwait's trade generated. By the early twentieth century, Kuwait had grown dramatically. Lorimer (1908–15, vol. 2: 1051) put the population at 35,000 at the turn of the century. Trade and pearling were at the heart of this growth. In 1905–6 Kuwait's 461 pearl boats employed 9200 men. Secondary industries, especially boatbuilding, grew up around this trade. In 1912–13, for example, 120 pearl boats were built (GB, Admiralty 1916–17: 286). Business was thriving. Because Mubarak's military ambitions in the desert required substantial funds he introduced a series of new taxes: an import tax, a pearling tax, a house tax, a pilgrimage tax. To the dismay of the merchants, he even introduced price controls (Harrison 1924a: 152).

In 1909 the merchants expressed their opposition. In protest over new and what they considered extortionate demands, the richest pearl buyers led a secession to Bahrain. They were joined by a number of large traders, as well as rank and file staff and seventeen ships. The Political Resident described the importance of the act,

In the case of Koweit it will be far more serious as the whole of the available wealth and capital in Koweit is derived from the pearl industry. The four Towashes [pearl buyers] concerned represent some 25 to 30 lakhs of rupees in capital and probably have some financial hold direct or indirect over some 250 to 300 boats and perhaps 6000 to 8000 men.

It can be imagined what effect the displacement of this large amount of capital and population (for the men would follow their leading Towashes very shortly) would have on the commercial prosperity of the port of Koweit.[1]

The merchants' opposition was carefully organized. They carried out the protest with planning and stealth, arranging beforehand to secret their valuables aboard their ships. They made sure they had backing. Hilal al-Mutairi, for example, one of the richest merchants and a leader of the uprising, promised supporters he would forgive their debts and destroy his books in front of them if they remained with him.[2] Mubarak was forced to retreat. The merchants' revenues were critical to his rule and the merchants had popular support. In the end he conceded and canceled the taxes. The boats came back; the last holdout, Hilal al-Mutairi, returned in 1911 to a cordial welcome by Mubarak.[3] The Political Agent wrote, "the Shaikh is said to have become very tame and courteous after the trouble of the Towashis and pearlers and is now ever ready to listen to reason and to help."[4]

This act of secession ended one era and began another for the merchants. It was both the last time the merchants would use secession as a political weapon and the first of several times in the twentieth century that they would organize politically in opposition to the Shaikh. It was the last large-scale use of political exit and the first experimentation with new political methods. The secession also involved a clearer statement of loyalty to Kuwait than had occurred before, the first hint of a local political identity. The traders had left because they feared bankruptcy; but they wanted to return – they specifically told the Political Resident that they had no desire to leave, emphasizing that they were all Kuwaitis by birth and family tradition.[5] The enduring political consequence of the rebellion was to leave the merchants more organized politically.

Another inadvertent consequence of Mubarak's new taxes and policies was to create the basis for the first state administration. To handle the taxes, Mubarak introduced a new customs administration. Mubarak's British alliance catalyzed Kuwait's first social services. Knox and his medical officer, who ran a small dispensary, formed the embryo of a protectorate administration. In 1911 Mubarak allowed the Arabian Mission of the Reformed Church in America to work in Kuwait. They built a hospital and opened a school for boys and a night school for men, teaching English and typing. Graduates went on to head Kuwait's first public works, health, and customs departments. One consequence of these services was to precipitate community action by the merchants for the provision of community services. The missionary presence catalyzed the merchants to start an alternative school, the Mubarakiyya. This in turn prompted the leading Shias, not a part of the Sunni merchant elite, to start *their* school. Opposition to the clinic's foreign ownership similarly inspired the Kuwait Benevolent Society to establish a dispensary, although it soon closed (Mylrea 1917: 125–6; Calverley 1962: 41).

The economic consequences of the rebellion were mixed. In winning, the merchants succeeded in retaining their economic power. However, Mubarak did not relent completely. Despite opposition, he succeeded in raising some new taxes. Ismael argues that this money was used in the long run to finance Bani Utub merchants, who formed a middle stratum of petty merchants distinct from the larger, regionally oriented Ottoman merchants of Basra. With Mubarak's support the Bani Utub merchants became increasingly separated from their regional ties and dependent on the Sabahs and, through them, Britain. Mubarak's policies were thus a crucial link in the integration of Kuwait's economy into Britain's economy. After Mubarak, Britain gradually came to dominate both long-distance trade to India and Africa and local trade to Basra, relying on steam power and fire power. Bani Utub trade was relegated to subsistence goods for the city, desert trade, and limited shipping. Mubarak weakened regional rivals, the Ottoman merchants, through customs and supported the Bani Utub by transferring taxes to them through liberal loans. The Bani Utub merchants used the loans to buy Ottoman ships as they went into debt. The position of the Bani Utub merchants was constrained, but within these constraints, encouraged. In the long run, though, the bulk of the profit went to Britain for imported goods now carried by steamer (Ismael 1982: 55–7).

However, the Kuwaitis never completely abandoned long-distance, let alone regional, trade to Britain. Europeans used large ships that could approach only a few ports. Because of this and the Arabs' familiarity with the waters, Britain relied heavily on smaller Arab boats and on local pilots, especially through the Gulf to Basra. In the course of the eighteenth century in response to the European presence, the Gulf Arabs also gradually improved their boats (Bowen 1949, 1952; Villiers 1969). Into the interwar period Kuwaiti merchants were still sailing to India and East Africa. Finally, the merchants themselves clearly did not perceive any alliance with the Shaikh. The early twentieth century is marked by explicit and repeated political opposition to his rule.

By the end of Mubarak's rule, then, Kuwait had an economic and social structure that reflected a century of pearling and trading. Its political structure consisted of a ruling Shaikh, whose preeminence was secure, but constrained by the merchant elite, tied to the economy of pearling and trade. To this Mubarak's policies added the first hint of a larger state administration and a larger national political identity. In terms of the ruling coalition, the Shaikh's pre-oil efforts to centralize power provoked an organized response from the merchants that left them in better shape politically to face the Shaikh after oil. In terms of ruling institutions, the changes Mubarak introduced precipitated the nucleus of a new state bureaucracy.

The founding of Qatar

Qatar's modern history dates from 1766 when segments of the Bani Utub clan in Kuwait, the al-Khalifa and al-Jalahima, left Kuwait for Zubara, on Qatar's western coast, where they founded a settlement. Qatar's history before that is obscure. The peninsula's dry interior had no real settlements at all but was worked from time to time by nomadic tribes. The only settlements that existed when the Bani Utub arrived were small, poor fishing villages oriented towards the sea or towards the desert of their tribes' original ranges. These settlements were ephemeral. Often populated by clans made temporary refugees through tribal disputes, the towns of Qatar could disappear overnight as their few families packed belongings on camels or boats and headed for the desert or the sea.

When the Bani Utub arrived, the Bani Khalid probably exercised some weak, and fading, control over Qatar. Possibly the al-Khalifa secured their blessings before settling. The largest village, Huwaila, was inhabited by distant kin of the Bani Khalid. Nonetheless, the Bani Utub had trouble with this settlement and rapidly built a wall and forts to defend Zubara (Abu-Hakima 1965: 70). Two smaller towns also existed, Doha and Fuwairat, inhabited by different tribal factions, among them the al-Thani clan. Tradition says the al-Thani had migrated from central Arabia to eastern Qatar in the late seventeenth or early eighteenth century.[6] Some time before 1766 they moved to Fuwairat; later they would move to Doha, the capital. If the al-Thani were important before the Bani Utub arrived they were soon overshadowed by the new settlement at Zubara.

Zubara quickly flourished as a pearling center and, because of its ties to the Bani Utub at Kuwait, as a trading port. This mercantile success brought Zubara to the attention of Persia and Muscat. In response to attacks from these two powers in the 1770s the Bani Utub of both Zubara and Kuwait, with the help of some Qatari tribes, attacked and captured Bahrain in 1783. With the conquest of Bahrain, most of the al-Khalifa left to settle there (where they rule today). They retained, however, a toehold at Zubara.

The al-Khalifa departure changed the course of Qatar's political history. When the Bani Utub left, they took with them the political and trade ties to the large Bani Utub alliance in the north and the political institutions that went with that alliance. Consequently Qatar did not develop the centralized authority and strong leaders that characterized its neighbors in Kuwait and Bahrain. By the time the Bani Utub left, Britain was also much more powerful locally than it had been when Kuwait was settled. Because of this new regional constellation of power and because of Qatar's poorer resource base – poorer harbors, inhospitable climate – no central authority succeeded the Bani Utub. Instead, Qatar was dominated by a series of mobile and transitory Shaikhs.

The most famous of these Shaikhs was Rahma ibn Jabir al-Jalahima. Almost immediately on arriving at Zubara, hostilities developed between the al-Khalifa and the al-Jalahima. The two clans set their differences aside to conquer Bahrain, but new disagreements arose from the conquest and the al-Jalahima returned to Qatar. After their return, a succession struggle developed between Rahma and his brother Abdalla. Abdalla lost and took refuge at Muscat. Rahma stayed and developed the village of Khawr Hasan into a base for operations against Gulf (mainly al-Khalifa) ships, soon acquiring a reputation as one of the most notorious pirates of the Pirate Coast. Until his death in 1826 Rahma held his own by shifting alliances with the Al-Saud, the Qawasim and Muscat. When

27

his fortunes fell, he moved his families to new locations. His rule reflects the local politics of the period, characterized by frequent exit, violence, and shifting alliance. After Rahma, Qatar lacked any one powerful figure or consistently dominant city. Bahrain exercised some influence over Zubara, and occasionally over other settlements. Britain recognized Bahrain's sovereignty, but also responded to local truce violations as it saw fit. In 1821, for example, just after the first series of treaties, the East India Company destroyed Doha for violations of the trucial peace, prompting the temporary migration of 300–400 residents. In 1823 when the Political Resident visited Doha, he found the town unaware of the 1820 treaty, which their Shaikh had not signed, even though they had just been punished for violating it (Lorimer 1908–15, vol. 1: 793). In general, the peninsula's settlements and alliances were highly fluid.

Kuwait in the late nineteenth century was, by local standards, flourishing. This was hardly the case in Qatar. Palgrave, who visited Qatar in 1863, left a picture of life there:[7]

To have an idea of Katar, my readers must figure to themselves miles on miles of low barren hills, bleak and sun-scorched, with hardly a single tree to vary their dry monotonous outline; below these a muddy beach extends for a quarter of a mile seawards in slimy quicksands, bordered by a rime of sludge and seaweed. If we look landwards beyond the hills, we see what by extreme courtesy may be called pasture land, dreary downs with twenty pebbles for every blade of grass; and over this melancholy ground scene, but few and far between, little clusters of wretched, most wretched, earth cottages and palm-leaf huts, narrow, ugly, and low; these are the villages of . . . Katar.

(Palgrave 1865: 231)

Qatar's economy was based on the sea. As Muhammad al-Thani told Palgrave, "we are all from the highest to the lowest slaves of one master, Pearl" (232). In the summer the pearl fleets deserted the villages, leaving a guard to watch for attacks and, if necessary, warn the fleet to return and defend the coast. The small economy of trade was handled by outsiders, as Palgrave's description of the major towns suggests. Bida (today a suburb of Doha), the home of Muhammad al-Thani,

owns a long narrow and dirty market-place, where some Bahreyn shopkeepers and artisans ply their business on a small scale; for the rest, Bedaa' consists of a mass of little narrow dingy houses, separated by irregular lanes. The total amount of its inhabitants when on land, which is not often the case, reaches about six thousand; a few colonists from Hasa come hither to try their fortune and grumble at the country . . . If we go down to the beach, we find there line on line of huge black boats, whose grooved edges show where the divers' cords have been let down.

(236)

Doha, he said, was about half Bida's size: "the houses of Dowhah are even lower or meaner than at Bedaa', and the market place is narrower and dirtier. Two castles overtop the place: one stands on the neighboring cliff, the other within the town itself" (237–8). Then comes Wakra, about the size of Bida: "under the patronage of its chief, several small traders and artisans from Bahreyn have established themselves here; and Wokrah has on the whole a thriving look" (238). Finally, "further down the coast towards the east begin the settlements of Benoo-Yass, an ill-famed clan, half Bedouins, half villagers, and all pirates" (234).

The political picture Palgrave draws is one of terrible insecurity. The villages "are each and all carefully walled in, while the 'owns beyond are lined with towers, and here and there a castle 'huge and square' makes with its little windows and narrow portals a display of strength" (231). And further on,

> But if the people of Katar have peace within, they are exposed on the land side to continual marauding inroads from their Bedouin neighbors, the Menaseer and Al-Morrah. The former of these tribes is numerous and warlike . . . Hence the necessity for the towers of refuge which line the uplands: they are small circular buildings from twenty-five to thirty feet in height, each with a door about halfway up the side and a rope hanging out . . . At times the Menaseer, emboldened by impunity (for the people of Qatar have no great pretensions to warlike valour) attack the main villages, and carry off more valuable booty than kine and sheep. Hence the origin of the strongholds or keeps within the towns themselves, and of the walls which surround them. (233–4)

There is little information on internal authority or on the al-Thanis' rise to power. Probably they, like other clans, balanced secession with fragile alliances: the family moved to Doha from Fuwairat (where they were when the Bani Utub arrived) in the mid nineteenth century. Probably, too, they manipulated matrimonial alliances: the daughter of Muhammad al-Thani who later signed the 1868 agreement with Britain married an al-Khalifa. Muhammad al-Thani had sufficient power to collect tribute from the surrounding towns. Palgrave writes,

> From each other, indeed, the men of Katar have, it seems, little to fear. Too busy to be warlike, they live in a passive harmony which almost dispenses with the ordinary machinery of government. Ebn-Thanee, the governor of Bedaa', is indeed generally acknowledged for head of the entire province . . . Yet the Bedaa' resident has in matter of fact very little authority over the other villages, where everyone settles his affairs with his own local chief, and Ebn-Thanee is for those around only a sort of collector-in-chief, a general revenue gatherer, whose occupation is to look after and to bring in the annual tribute on the pearl fishery. (232)

This tribute (although the bulk went on to Bahrain) was one source of income. Muhammad al-Thani was also a successful merchant on his own account. Palgrave describes his visit to his castle,

> a donjon-keep, with outhouses at its foot, offering more accommodation for goods than for men. Under a mat-spread and mat-hung shed within the court sat the chief, Mohammed-ebn-Thanee, a shrewd wary old man, slightly corpulent, and renowned for prudence and good-humoured easiness of demeanor, but close-fisted and a hard customer

at a bargain, altogether he had much more the air of a business-like avaricious pearl-merchant (and such he really is) than of an Arab ruler. (237)

In addition to pearls, he also traded dates (he lodged his guest in a date ware-house). Finally, he also performed religious functions, serving as prayer leader in the larger mosque.

Muhammad al-Thani, then, was a man with some local political, economic and religious power who protected his position with intelligent alliances. But he was not the only local power and his influence did not extend much beyond Bida. Although the chief of Doha was a "small sub-collector" to al-Thani, Wakra was ruled by an unrelated Shaikh (238). The al-Khalifa also exercised some limited influence around Zubara and among some of the tribes. The al-Thani did not enjoy undisputed recognition, either with the tribes inside Qatar, or with the forces outside.

The dispute that produced Britain's first recognition of the al-Thanis and of Qatar as a semi-independent political unit had its origin in Bahrain. In the 1860s tensions between the al-Khalifa and residents of Qatar grew strained over a series of smaller disputes (Zahlan 1979: 41–2). In the tense atmosphere disagreements soon escalated, culminating in 1867 in an attack by the al-Khalifa, allied with forces from Abu Dhabi, on Qatar. In the attack, the forces destroyed Doha and Wakra. Pelly, the Political Resident, responded to the attack by demanding reparations from the offending Shaikhs. However, lacking navel reinforcement from India, he was powerless to intervene. In 1868 the tribes of Qatar rallied and attacked Bahrain. Over 1000 people were killed and 600 ships destroyed in this attack (Pal 1945: 72). This confrontation demanded British attention; it was the most flagrant violation of the 1835 maritime truce in years.

Until the 1867 attack Britain had paid little attention to Qatar, which it regarded as a Bahraini dependency and, through Bahrain, bound by earlier treaties. Clearly this arrangement was not working. Following the 1868 attack Pelly visited Qatar, met the leading Shaikhs and signed the Treaty of 1868 (Zahlan 1979: 144–7) with Muhammad al-Thani. In the treaty, Muhammad agreed to renounce maritime warfare, to submit disputes to Britain, to maintain a correct attitude towards Bahrain's new Shaikh, to refer differences to the Resident and, finally, to return to Doha and live peaceably. Pelly also assigned a fine to Bahrain and set Qatar's future tribute to Bahrain. These arrangements shed some light on the decentralized authority in the peninsula. The tribute was divided by tribe, suggesting this was still the most important political division. Muhammad al-Thani was to collect the largest share from specific tribes, apparently under his jurisdiction (Zahlan 1979: 43).

The treaty marked the first British recognition of Qatar and particularly of Muhammad al-Thani, the signatory Shaikh. The treaty did not formally acknowledge Qatar's independence – in fact it recognized its tributary ties to

Bahrain – but the effect was to mark off and recognize Qatar as distinct and partially autonomous from Bahrain. The treaty laid the juridical basis for Britain's later acknowledgment of Qatar as an autonomous political unit and, through recognition, gave special standing to the al-Thani family, who would thereafter rule Qatar.

Barely had Muhammad al-Thani been accorded British recognition when the international environment shifted again. Until World War I, the only other major power exercising influence over Qatar was the Ottoman empire. Britain never officially acknowledged Ottoman sovereignty, but tacitly accepted it when necessary to avoid open confrontation. Until World War I, Britain watched affairs in Qatar with mixed interest, dealing sometimes with the al-Thanis, sometimes with the Ottomans. As a result, the Ottoman presence preserved Qatar's independence, by minimizing, although not entirely eliminating, British and Bahraini intervention, giving the al-Thanis the chance to consolidate local power.

In 1871 the Ottomans occupied Hasa. Several factors entered into the al-Thani calculations regarding the acceptance of limited Ottoman sovereignty. Their immediate concern was probably with the recent al-Khalifa claims. In the past, the Al-Saud presence had provided some protection or at least counter-balance to these claims. Perhaps the Ottomans could do the same, or better yet, free the al-Thanis from both sets of claims. In the hinterland, Qatar was already being used as a base for Al-Saud raids on Ottoman troops in Hasa. Ibn Saud had alienated some of the peninsula's settlements with his demands for tribute and supplies. Then too there was Britain, constantly busying herself with Qatar's coastal waters. Finally, there was the indisputable fact of the Ottoman presence. On the other hand, Britain had recently recognized the al-Thanis; something might be made of this. In the end, Muhammad al-Thani chose to side with Britain and refused the Ottoman flag. His son Qasim, however, welcomed the Ottomans. Muhammad was getting old (he died in 1878); the Ottomans chose to ignore him in favor of his son.

Under the umbrella of the Ottoman occupation, Qasim tried to extend his authority inside the peninsula focusing on, first, the nontribal elements (Indians) in the areas he controlled and, second, on the settled areas outside his control such as Bahraini Zubara in the north. Finally, Qasim tried to eliminate Ottoman control itself. Qasim's concern with the Indians grew from their competition in the pearl and date trade. His eventual ouster of the Indian community allowed him, and his family, to become locally important merchants. Because the Indians were British protected subjects, Qasim had to proceed carefully. In the 1870s and 1880s, he took every opportunity, formal and informal, to harass the Indians. He raised their taxes. He encouraged his tribal supporters to attack Indian ships and shops. He closed their businesses. He did everything but obtain Ottoman support, although this too he tried. The British supported the

Indians to a point, in some cases demanding compensation. However, by the 1880s the Indians had had enough and, with British aid, left. The incidents had, for Qasim, served to test the limits of aid and coercion from both the Ottomans and Britain. Qasim eventually got what he wanted but in the process learned the Ottomans would support him only so far; the British tolerate only so much. The long-term consequence of these incidents, however, was that it left Qatar, alone in the Gulf, with no sizable Indian trading community (Lorimer 1908–15, vol. 2: 1535). It also left the al-Thanis with a trading niche from which they could become important local merchants.

Outside Doha, Qasim's control was weak. He faced several secessions from tribal factions, major raids, and continuing trouble with dissidents from Abu Dhabi. In all these conflicts, the Ottoman forces again failed to back him. The lesson Qasim learned was how little aid their garrison would offer him against enemies internal and external. Qasim also tried, and in this almost succeeded, to end Bahrain's serious claims to the peninsula, although the issue would continue to resurface. In 1878, after repeated Bahraini claims to Zubara and more interference, Qasim, in alliance with Bahraini dissidents, attacked Zubara with a force of tribal supporters, destroying the settlement. Zubara ceased to be, and that was more or less the end of Bahrain's claims.

These incidents convinced Qasim that the Ottoman occupation was a liability. In 1875 when the Resident visited Doha, the al-Thanis told him they were tired of the Ottomans, but feared saying so. They said the Ottomans insisted the shaikhs consult them on every matter and demanded large sums of money (Lorimer 1908–15, vol. 1: 804). In the 1880s relations between Qasim and the Ottomans deteriorated, as Qasim threatened resignation in an unsuccessful attempt to block the Ottoman expansion. A showdown was inevitable. It came in 1893 when an Ottoman representative from Basra came to Doha and Qasim, fearing arrest, refused to meet him, sending his brother Ahmad instead. When the Ottomans arrested Ahmad and twelve Doha notables, Qasim appealed to Britain and even Bahrain for protection. The Ottomans sent troops. In the ensuing battle Qasim's forces managed to defeat the Ottomans. By capturing Doha's well, Qasim was able to force the release of his brother and the notables. The victory, although shortlived and partial, improved Qasim's strength among his followers and deepened his hostility towards the Ottomans. The Ottomans reinforced the garrison and sent an assistant, but abandoned plans for direct administration. The century closed with the situation thus, the al-Thanis anxious to expel the Ottomans, and increasing their appeals to Britain.

Throughout the occupation, Britain maintained a close interest in Qatar, but limited its interference for fear of antagonizing the Ottomans, whose rights it nonetheless did not acknowledge. Britain did intervene directly when it felt important issues had arisen such as the rights of its Indian subjects, incidents of piracy, and major truce violations. Britain also episodically protested official references to Qatar as an Ottoman dependency. It did not, however, respond to al-Thani appeals for protection, appeals that increased in the 1890s. Given the general maritime peace prevailing, Britain had no incentive to upset the status quo, beyond occasional protests. It would take the war to change the balance of its interests.

Conclusion

If we compare Qatar's history to Kuwait's at this point, the differences are large. The complete dependence, from the beginning, on pearling and trade produced in both countries a few leading trading families. In Kuwait, however, the unifying migration, the early sedentarization, better location, the large size of the settlement, the dependence on entrepôt as well as pearling trade, the relative independence and the earlier political stability created a powerful and cohesive class of merchants. Kuwait entered the twentieth century with a settled and organized merchant class; Qatar did not. In Qatar, the political fragmentation and smaller size produced not only fewer and weaker merchants, but also a less clearly defined division of labor between the political and economic elites. Because the trade was dominated by foreigners, their elimination left a vacuum that the ruling family could enter.

In the eighteenth century Kuwait was already a political unit. Qatar was not, it had no central authority. The peninsula consisted of a few sleepy fishing villages governed informally by local Shaikhs, transitory nomadic camps, and two recent and growing settlements tied to Bahrain. While violence, consensus, and matrimonial alliance played an important part, secession was still the most important political tactic, certainly the best recorded. Not until the late nineteenth century did Qatar have permanent settlements of some importance, even a degree of central authority, and a history of its own. Politics were fragmented by impinging outside powers: Britain, the Ottoman empire, Arabia, Oman, Bahrain. Until the 1860s Qatar's history was dominated by Bahrain, first by the al-Khalifa struggle with Rahma ibn Jabir, then by Bahraini claims and succession crises. As a result of its role in these conflicts, Qatar, first viewed as a Bahraini dependency, came to British attention, resulting in the treaty of 1868. After that, the al-Thanis gave the peninsula a political center, but their story was largely determined by the new Ottoman occupation.

The era of the Ottoman occupation, down to World War I, coincided with Qasim's rule, 1876–1913. This long reign, however, masks significant internal family dissension. Qasim had succeeded his own father peaceably, but not without disagreement – Muhammad refused to fly the Ottoman flag to his death. After Qasim's accession, competition developed with his brother Ahmad who served Qasim as mediator with the Ottomans. After Qasim fell from grace, Ahmad was named provincial governor. But tension continued. In 1905 when a representative of Ibn Saud visited near Qatar, Qasim sent him a letter of welcome and gifts; Ahmad warned him not to cross the border (Lorimer 1908–15, vol. 1: 835). The struggle ended abruptly in 1905 when Ahmad was murdered in ambiguous circumstances. When Qasim died in 1913 he was succeeded by his fourth son, Abdalla. Abdalla inherited the family disputes, stemming both from his twelve brothers and his cousins, the sons of Ahmad. From his father, Abdalla inherited the entire Qatar peninsula, the consolidation of power that was the consequence of Qasim's reign. He also inherited, in the treaty of 1868, the basis for later British recognition.

For Kuwait, the establishment of a settlement occurred in the eighteenth century in, compared to Qatar, a smooth manner. Within a few decades of the founding, a Sabah emerged as paramount Shaikh. This Sabah preeminence became monopoly when the al-Khalifa and al-Jalahima left for Zubara. By the eighteenth century, Kuwait had well established patterns of authority and succession. Legitimacy had passed from the family to the Shaikh, succession now went from father to son. Kuwait's location allowed the early development of a settled trading community. The Bani Khalid decline left a vacuum that Kuwait could fill. In this vacuum the Bani Utub alliance developed. When the alliance broke down, under British pressure, the Bani Utub at Kuwait and Bahrain inherited its institutional legacy, including a well defined and coherent economic and political elite, and this contributed to the earlier institutionalization of power.

To reiterate, in Qatar this institutionalization of power did not occur. There the Bani Utub elite migrated and the smaller transitory Shaikhs such as Rahma left no institutional legacy. This contributed to Qatar's weaker development as a state. The pearl-based economy, located off the main trade routes, encouraged mobility which the presence of many rival tribes exacerbated. As a result, Qatar lacked a settled community until late in the nineteenth century. One index of this difference is that Qatar lacks a founding myth, while Kuwait has a detailed legend of its own origins. As in Kuwait, family power was finally monopolized partly by default when the major contenders, the al-Khalifa, the al-Jalahima, and other tribal segments left the peninsula, while the al-Thanis stayed. But instead of a powerful Shaikh emerging, different family factions developed.

Because the institutionalization of power occurred later in Qatar, it occurred in a new international environment and was therefore more closely connected to the problem of acquiring international recognition. Both countries' histories were shaped by the international environment. External forces determined that these particular settlements would become states, and to some extent that their leading families would become ruling houses. Fortuitously caught on the fringes of expanding and contracting empires – Ottoman, Saudi, British, and others – Kuwait and Qatar and their ruling families survived down into an age when the norms of the international state system and oil revenues would provide them with new defenses. Location and chance, a series of accidents, allowed these states to survive into the oil age. Had the Ottomans and the British not held back the Saudis, Kuwait and Qatar might today be part of that state. Had they been swallowed by the Ottomans, as for a time it seemed they might, they might have become successor states. But the last pulse of Ottoman energy reached them too late to have an enduring effect. Instead their borders were determined, after the elimination of contending regional powers, largely by the extent of the Saudi reach, mediated by Britain. In this process, rulers were acknowledged and, in Qatar, finally entrenched. When the international music stopped the al-Thanis were sitting on the right chair – Doha. A coincidence of timing placed them in the right position to receive Ottoman and British recognition. This recognition, in turn, allowed them to consolidate power internally. International recognition occurred at roughly the same time – both countries were affected by the same broad international configuration – but because it occurred in Kuwait after, and in Qatar before the consolidation of internal power, its domestic significance was different. Because the Sabahs had already secured power at home, they were able to a certain extent, to negotiate with, rather than submit to Britain and the Ottomans and maintain a higher degree of autonomy. In Qatar, Britain played a larger role from the start. In Kuwait, the rulers had developed patterns of politics and succession which Britain had no interest in challenging. In Qatar no such patterns existed when Britain finally arrived in World War I. Instead of a strong leadership institution emerging, the power of the family factions to challenge the rulers became partially institutionalized.

3 Kuwait on the eve of oil

In the interwar period, Kuwait's merchants crystallized into a new political force. By the early twentieth century the merchants had gradually evolved into a homogeneous and unified economic and social elite. Their political power, which flowed from this economic and social power, was institutionalized in a series of informal and semiformal mechanisms – marriage and *majlis* – that granted them access to the palace. In the interwar period, a combination of severe economic pressures and political opportunities, including open divisions within the ranks of the ruling family, led the merchants to reorganize politically, culminating in a briefly successful demand for parliamentary representation in the *Majlis* Movement of 1938. Up to this point the struggle between the rulers and the emerging bourgeoisie was following a classic pattern. Then, just when the merchants' political influence was at its peak, oil arrived. This new economic force transformed the emerging struggle between the merchants and the ruler and gave rise to a new pattern of politics.

The merchants' interwar political interventions were failures in that they did not secure enduring, formal access to decision-making. However, these acts, in conjunction with the disputes within the ruling family which they helped fuel, had unintended consequences. In terms of alliances, the political action of the 1930s reinforced a sense of community among the merchants. Later in the century this corporate sense was crucial in helping merchants pass on to their children and grandchildren privileged access to the new oil-generated wealth. In terms of state formation, political action permanently affected the idea and form of political opposition in Kuwait. Where opponents had once migrated to other Gulf ports, the interwar merchants chose to stay and confront the ruler. This choice helped entrench new ideas of the state and loyalty to it. The particular tactic the merchants used, the legislative assembly, later became enshrined in the national myth. Political action also changed the way the ruling family organized power and in so doing changed the relationship between the ruler and the state. Finally, political action led to the creation of new state institutions: not the parliament opponents had intended, but rather the precursors of today's ministries. Thus it played a formative role in the administrative development of the state.

Economic structures

Well before oil, clearly by the first decades of the twentieth century, Kuwait had a narrow and well-established elite: wealthy trading families who were linked by marriage and shared economic interests. They were long-settled, urban, Sunni families, most of whom claimed descent from the original thirty or so Bani Utub families.[1] In a mosaic society stratified by origin, sect and historical occupation these families formed a homogeneous elite: sedentary not nomadic, Sunni not Shia, *asil* (original, i.e., noble descendants) of the first migrants. They married each other and, sometimes, the Sabahs, whom they considered their peers. The patriarchs of these wealthiest families were merchants by trade, men who had acquired their fortunes from pearling, shipbuilding, and long-distance commerce. They were a cosmopolitan elite. Most had traveled extensively, to India, Africa, even Europe, where they sold pearls. They educated their sons abroad more than other Gulf Arabs (al-Hatim 1980: 58). Western visitors noted that they used typewriters and European office systems and followed European culture with curiosity. Lindt, writing in 1939, described his wife's visit to a Kuwaiti household: "she showed her hostess a photograph of our children, and, 'In the name of Allah,' said that silk-robed, henna'd lady, 'thy daughter is the image of Shirley Temple'" (1939: 622). The richest were in general trade, with ten of them worth 25–500,000 rs (Lorimer 1908–15, vol. 2: 1055). By one estimate, the al-Ghanims and al-Hamads were, before the 1940s, worth millions of rupees (Abu-Hakima 1972: 37).

The accumulation of wealth that set these families above the rest had occurred well before the twentieth century opened. The structure of both the trade and pearling industries strongly encouraged concentration of wealth and accumulation of profit at the apex of the system, in the hands of a few merchants. Workers were tied to the system through the structure of financing, the lack of alternatives, and force. Each worker received a percentage of the total catch, a prorated share based on occupation. After each dive, oysters were tossed on a collective pile, to be opened only at day's end. Since no diver knew which oysters were his, there were no windfall profits, but there were losses. As these accumulated, divers became tied to specific captains. Debts were heritable, so dependency gradually increased. Later, with oil, it took the intercession of the ruler himself to arrange the transition from this payment system to wage labor. The Pearl Divers Law of 1940 (Ismael 1982: 161–71) which collected and codified customary arrangements stipulated that seamen who took government or oil company jobs were to pay the chief of divers 15 per cent of their monthly salary (presumably until the debt was repaid). Eventually most divers were caught in a virtually inescapable system of debt-bondage. The diving law suggests how often coercion was invoked to keep the system operating. Several articles stipulated the action to be taken when the crew refused to obey commands: when they failed to appear before the season to service the boat, when they were absent without excuse, when they failed to obey the captain, when they stayed behind in port, when they escaped frequently, etc. Towards the top of the system were the traders who moved the goods: the broker (*dallal*) and the middleman (*tawwash*) who bought pearls from the returning ships (Lorimer 1908–15, vol. 1: 2220–93; Villiers 1948; Bowen 1951; 1951a; Dickson 1956: 463; al-Naqeeb 1978; Baz 1981: 87–99; Ismael 1982: 61–4).

Above the divers, pullers, and various seamen were the captains who were in turn tied to the merchants in a similar system of advances and debts. Merchants normally financed trips with straight loans to captains. If the boat sank, the captain absorbed the loss. These obligations were also detailed in the diving law. For example, article 34 states,

> [In the case of] every merchant who advances a loan to a diving captain [in anticipation of the] diving harvest and the captain was not able to gain enough to make payment . . . the merchant has no right to demand payment from property. But he takes all the seamen and the ships. And if this does not satisfy all the loan, he can then take property, with the exception of the captain's private dwelling. (Ismael 1982: 167)

The highest categories were not mutually exclusive. Members of the same families, often the same individuals, were frequently general traders, ship-owners, shipyard owners, and pearl brokers. The typical merchant family had offices run by sons in major ports along the route, with a head office at Kuwait or Basra. Villiers described the al-Hamad family, owners of the dhow he sailed on in 1938,

> Two younger brothers, Ali and Abdulla Abdul-Latif al-Hamad, were looking after the family business over an area from Jidda, the port of Mecca, to Berbera in what was then British Somaliland, and from Adis Ababa in the interior of Ethiopia to Mukalla and al-Shihr in the Hadhramaut. It appeared that their influence reached into every port small and large on both sides of the Red Sea and down the coast of Africa as far as Arab ships could sail (which was as far as the NE monsoon blew) and, with other brothers and close relations they looked after Arab trading points in India, Iraq, Iran, Asir, the Hedjaz, and much of Saudi Arabia. (Villiers 1969: xvi)

In the summer the fleets would dive for pearls in the banks of the Gulf. In the winter boats would trade local and distant ports. Ships picked up dates at Basra and sailed them to India or East Africa, making two Indian or one African trip a season. From India and Africa they brought back shipbuilding materials. This trade dominated the pre-oil economy. The only other economic activity of any importance was some marginal agriculture in villages such as Jahra and a small service sector in Kuwait town catering to local and beduin needs: smiths, textile workers, food workers, and retailers (Lorimer 1908–15, vol. 2: 1054).[2]

In the interwar period, this entire structure underwent radical change as a result of a series of crises. The first came in the early 1920s with the Saudi embargo of Kuwait, following the failure to reach an agreement on transit and import duties. Shaikh Ahmad complained to Dickson, the Political Agent, "to such an extent had trade between Nejd and Kuwait been interfered with that my revenue has been reduced from its former figure by 70%. This too has been brought about by Bin Saud's siege operations which have been going on without interruption from the year 1340 (1921) to the present time [1929]."[3] The embargo, which lasted until the late 1930s, was accompanied by raids from Ibn Saud's Ikhwan supporters (and rebels) and regular forces. The second crisis came in the late 1920s with the development of Japanese cultured pearls. Competition virtually destroyed the local pearling industry, the basis of the entire Gulf economy, by driving down prices. Dickson counted over 700 pearl boats in 1921; by 1933 he counted 320. In 1939 Villiers counted 100 to 150 (1969: xx). By the 1940s the number was down to 40.[4] The pearl slump was followed by the last crisis, the world depression.

Merchants coped with these crises in a variety of ways. They had responded to other crises by diversifying. In 1907–8, for example, drought and a poor pearl season had led many pearlers to try using their boats to import fresh water from the Shatt al-Arab in Iraq.[5] Now Kuwaiti merchants again began looking for new income sources. Many returned to long-distance trade. In 1939 Villiers wrote that pearling was depressed, but that new deep-sea boats were being built at the rate of two or three a month (1969: xx). Long-distance trade grew even more dramatically during World War II when British steamers were recalled for the war effort. Some Kuwaitis, in partnership with Iraqis, even tried to start a steamer company to compete with the British.[6] Some traders diversified into real estate, especially date palm land on the Shatt al-Arab, turning their trade interests from Arabia toward Iraq. A political turn toward Iraq would soon follow. Many made windfall profits from smuggling. In various ways the merchants built new niches for themselves during this period of economic turmoil. They were weakened but, most importantly, they survived. After the war, when oil revenues began pouring in, they were particularly well placed to reap the benefits.

Social stratification

The merchants at the apex of the economic pyramid were distinguished from their fellow Kuwaitis not only by wealth and influence but also by social origins. The leading trading families were a homogeneous lot; Kuwaiti society as a whole was not. Politically salient sectarian and ethnic cleavages defined a number of relatively autonomous social communities within Kuwait. These communities and cleavages in turn reinforced the homogeneity and isolation of the old Sunni Najdi elite. The most important cleavage was sectarian: Sunni–Shia. Kuwait's

Shia community consisted of four groups: descendants of the putative original inhabitants of Bahrain; emigrants from eastern Arabia's Hasa province; Arab Shias who had migrated to Persia from Arabia and back (there were also Sunni Arabs from Persia); and, largest, Persians originally from Iran. The latter often spoke Persian and maintained family and business ties with Iran. Yusif Bahbahani, for example, a member of one of the more prominent of such Kuwaiti Persian Shia families operated a business in the 1930s ferrying Iranian corpses to Iraq, via Kuwait, for burial on holy ground.[7]

The size of the Shia community is hard to estimate. Until late in the century the distinctions among various Shias were inconsistently drawn. Estimates vary in part depending on which Shias the observer counts. At the beginning of the century, the Political Resident estimated there were about 1000 Shias.[8] Lorimer (1908–15, vol. 2: 1051) wrote that the Persian Shias:

do not inhabit a separate quarter but are scattered through the town; nearly all of them are permanently settled at Kuwait, nevertheless they go and come freely between Kuwait and the parts of Persia to which they originally belonged. Persian merchants are about a score; over 100 Persians are shopkeepers; 200 of the remainder are penniless labourers who live from hand to mouth.

Under Ahmad, the Shia community grew. The Political Agent wrote in 1921,

I estimate that there are at present about 10,000 persons of Persian origin in Kuwait town; many of these, however, have been settled here for two or three generations and have presumably lost their Persian nationality. As there is no form of registration it is impossible to say how many actual Persian subjects there are; the number is probably over 6,000 though I doubt if 5,000 could . . . prove their nationality.[9]

In 1933 Dickson estimated the Persian community, which, however, he said was growing rapidly, at about 10,000.[10] There were a dozen or so Persian merchants and several shopkeepers, but most Shias were laborers. In 1938 Fowle put the entire Shia community at 18,000.[11] By 1952 the Shia population had grown to 30,000 (Dickson 1956: 40).

The Sunni–Shia division was more than religious. It was economic. There was a sectarian division of labor – the local water-carrying trade, for example, was exclusively in Shia hands.[12] It was social – the communities did not intermarry and they organized social services such as schools separately. It was also political. Unlike the Sunnis, who enjoyed a series of informal but direct links to the ruler, the Shias could only make their case to the Shaikh indirectly, through his secretary, Mulla Salih. In the 1930s even this line of communication would come under attack by the leading Sunni merchants, increasingly seen by the Shia community as actively and partisanly Sunni.

The final important social dichotomy was between long-settled families and tribal families, clans still predominantly nomadic in the early part of this century. This distinction was not as sharp as the sectarian rift, as Lindt observed in 1939: "as most of the influential families of the town have sprung from Beduin tribes and as they have maintained contact with the life of the desert there is not that deep cleft between town-dwellers and nomads which is so great an obstacle to national unity in other Arab countries" (1939: 625). There was less tension between the beduin and the settled families because there was more social and political interaction. The beduin were then, as today, a second stratum, a recruitment source for the leading families. Besides the Shia and tribal families, other minorities included Jews (100–200), blacks (over 400, two-thirds slaves), and communities formed in the few geographically isolated areas, such as Failaka Island or Jahra.[13]

Pre-oil politics and the merchant elite

In 1915 Mubarak the Great died. He was succeeded by his son Jabir who ruled for just over one uneventful year until on his death in early 1917 his brother Salim succeeded him. Salim's rule was also brief, and troubled, first by his disputes with Ibn Saud and the Ikhwan, second by a British war blockade imposed in 1918 to prevent supplies from reaching Turkey. These problems, deeply felt in Kuwait, produced some unity in adversity, some support for Salim in his brief rule. Then in 1921 Salim died. On his death the crisis consensus evaporated. No sooner had he died than a group of notables under Hamad al-Saqr, a leading merchant, organized themselves into a council and submitted a petition to the ruling family demanding their right to advise on the administration of the country and, specifically, on the succession. The council comprised twelve notables, representing the east and west sides of town. Hamad al-Saqr, the council chair, soon became the most prominent political figure outside the Sabah family in the interwar period, the leader of the opposition. He was a merchant by trade, from an old Najdi, Sunni, *asil*, Bani Utub family of captains and shipyard owners which had grown wealthy through commerce. Hamad himself was wealthy enough to buy one of Kuwait's first cars. When Hamad died in 1930 his son Abdalla Hamad became the opposition leader. In the 1930s Abdalla served on the merchant Education Council and was active in the revival of the Ahliyya Library, established in 1922 as a meeting place for students and intellectuals. In 1938 Abdalla served in the Legislative Assembly (al-Hatim 1980: 66–7, 143).[14]

This interwar opposition was something new. Before this century the political technique merchants most often used to express opposition to the ruler was simply to leave. But in the twentieth century the merchants began to abandon emigration in favor of new political institutions. Mubarak's reign had seen in the pearl broker revolt of 1910 the last large-scale political use of exit and the first experimentation with new institutions. Now the 1921 council demanded, first, that the ruling family select Salim's successor from among three contenders they had approved: Ahmad Jabir, Hamad Mubarak and Abdalla Salim. Failing this, the council threatened to appeal to Britain.[15]

After consultation the family selected Ahmad Jabir, who would rule until his death in 1950. This choice by the family was a watershed, although it did not seem so at the time, in that it established a new succession pattern, the alternation between the Jabir and Salim lines, an alternation that continues today. Ahmad, on receiving the family's nomination, called a meeting of the local notables and promised to consult them on all important matters and to work with the new council. For a short time, he did. But within two months the council collapsed, falling victim to internal dissension (al-Hatim 1980: 53–4).[16] The council did not succeed in injecting the merchants into formal, institutionalized decision-making in any enduring way. It did, however, leave a highly organized and politicized merchant community. In the following years the council members remained politically active. The 1921 council was a dress rehearsal for the Legislative Assembly of 1938.

Britain meanwhile watched the events leading up to Ahmad Jabir's accession with detached curiosity. Because of Kuwait's late entry into the trucial system, its distance from the trucial "piracy," and the minor leverage it enjoyed through playing off Ottoman Iraq and Arabia, it maintained greater independence. Only occasionally did Britain intervene in politics in any decisive way. By the early twentieth century its goals were clear: to secure the route to India and to keep out other European powers. As long as domestic politics remained contained, as long as disagreements did not bring in other powers, Britain was content. Because Kuwait had the institutional mechanisms for settling succession and other crises, Britain could and did remain in the background.

In the interwar period Britain's formal presence grew. The Anglo-Turkish Convention of 1913 recognized Britain's treaty relations with Kuwait and stipulated that Kuwait's territory, although nominally Ottoman, was to be autonomous. Still the relationship remained ambiguous. As one observer described it, "it is a tribute to the elasticity of British policy that it is almost impossible to find a constitutional term to express the relationship between these states and Great Britain" (Lindt 1939: 620–1). Certainly Britain did not establish a complex administration. From 1904 on it sent a Political Agent to Kuwait, but by the 1920s the western population still consisted only of the Agent, the agency doctor, a few American missionaries, and dependants.[17] The Political Agent did not have the formal status of advisor and his advice, although taken seriously, was not always taken. Even Britain's formal jurisdiction was narrower than in the other Gulf states, with local courts responsible for most Muslims (Liebesny 1956; Monroe 1964; Khuri 1980).

Britain did have an interest in foreign policy, in regional affairs. Normally this did not affect Kuwait greatly. The one exception was the issue of Kuwait's borders. Unlike other nearby states, Kuwait had had a well-defined territorial nucleus since the eighteenth century, but its borders, the nomadic areas, were unsettled. As Britain now began the process of incorporating Kuwait into the international state system, borders naturally followed. Barely a year after Ahmad's accession the border issue arose at the Uqair Conference of 1922, convened by Britain to settle the borders of Saudi Arabia, Iraq and Kuwait. According to Dickson, present at the conference,

Sir Percy took a red pencil and very carefully drew in on the map of Arabia a boundary line from the Persian Gulf to Jabal 'Anaizan, close to the Transjordan frontier. This gave Iraq a large area of the territory claimed by Najd. Obviously to placate Ibn Sa'ud, he ruthlessly deprived Kuwait of nearly two-thirds of her territory and gave it to Najd.

(Dickson 1956: 274)

To the south and west Britain created two neutral zones where it suspected the existence of oil. Kuwait, which had no say in the matter, lost substantial territory and the accompanying tribes. In the end its borders were set by the reach of other powers: the British and the Saudis, determining and foreshadowing Kuwait's future in the international arena as a small and weak state.

The ruling family

Within the broad constraints of this British presence, ruling family disputes flourished. The intrafamily politics of Ahmad's reign were dominated by his rivalry with the sons of Salim. The tension began with the accession. When Ahmad came to power in 1921 on the death of his uncle Salim Mubarak, Salim's oldest son Abdalla (one of the three Sabahs acceptable to the merchants' council) hoped to succeed his father.[18] Eventually on Ahmad's death in 1950 Abdalla did become ruler, but in 1921 he was passed over in favor of his cousin. This set the family rivalries for the next several decades.

The trouble between Abdalla and Ahmad began almost as soon as Ahmad took power. The Political Agent summarized the opening stages of the conflict:

There appears to have been rather a serious quarrel between 'Abdullah as-Salim and the rest of the Subah family. As I reported at the time he had hopes of succeeding his father. Since Ahmad's return and recognition as Shaikh he has been "assisting" him and got a good deal of power into his own hands, which Ahmad with his easy-going nature allowed him to do. He seems to have been trying to discredit Ahmad and issuing orders etc. not as Ahmad's deputy but in his own name. Recently he drafted a scale of salaries for all the members of the Subah, including Ahmad, in which he allotted himself nearly as much as Ahmad, and considerably more than Hamad or any of the others . . . There was then a stormy scene between 'Abdullah and the rest of the family at which Jabir as-Subah did some very plain speaking as is his custom and since then 'Abdullah has not appeared in public at all.[19]

In the 1930s the disagreement reemerged. Abdalla was now backed by his two brothers, Fahad and Sabah Salim. Together these dissidents were able to form a solid opposition because of their control of two crucial institutions of the small state: force and finance. Sabah ran the police; Fahad, the treasury.

Ahmad's supporters came from two family factions. The first was his immediate family: his brother Hamad, who ran the municipality, and his sons Abdalla, in charge of the citadel, and Muhammad, who handled his affairs in Basra. The second and more powerful cluster of relatives included Ahmad's second cousins, grandsons of Mubarak's brother Abdalla (who ruled from 1866 to 1892). This faction included such powerful figures as Ahmad's brother-in-law, Abdalla Jabir, who headed justice, education, a small police force, and land customs. Ali Khalifa ran the armed forces and was governor of Kuwait town. His brother Abdalla Khalifa was port director. Other shaikhs allied with the ruler included his uncles Hamad Mubarak, who sometimes officiated for Ahmad, and Abdalla Mubarak, assistant governor to Ali Khalifa.

Completing the palace clique were Ahmad's supporters outside the family: his secretaries, Mulla Salih and Izaat Jaafar, and a few loyalist merchants, such as Khalid al-Zaid. Salih, originally a trade agent in Iraq, was secretary to Shaikhs Mubarak, Jabir, and Salim before Ahmad. Under Ahmad he was also Gulf Oil's powerful local agent, active in the concession struggle with the Anglo Persian Oil Company. Salih and his son and successor Abdalla Salih had as their chief rival Jaafar, the ruler's social secretary, newsreader, and companion. Egyptian born, Syrian educated, Jaafar had also served in the Turkish army. Jaafar had his hand in everything in Kuwait. He was a go-between in reconciliations between Fahad al-Sabah and the ruler. He was involved with oil negotiations over the neutral zone. He lived at the palace and was close to Ahmad's sons Jabir and Sabah when they were young. Jaafar also had extensive commercial interests.[20] Now Jaafar and Salih joined forces with the Shaikh against the merchants and their allies.

The merchant opposition

The interwar period was a time of severe economic dislocation for the merchants. By the 1930s the turmoil of the 1920s – the decline of the pearl industry, the world depression, the conflicts with Ibn Saud, the loss of the tribes – were beginning to take their toll. When the ruler responded to this growing economic crisis with new taxes in the early 1930s and with a toleration for the heightened corruption of ruling family members in state institutions, the merchants felt squeezed (al-Rumaihi 1975: 33).

Then oil arrived. Oil negotiations had begun in 1923. In 1934 Kuwait signed the first concession agreement and in 1936 the Kuwait Oil Company (KOC), a joint holding of British Petroleum and Gulf, drilled its first well. In 1938 it discovered oil. These revenues, and the promise of more, sharpened cleavages both within the ruling family and between the Shaikh and the merchants. The ruling family began questioning the size of its allowances. Merchants began asking for a say in the distribution of the new wealth. Ahmad placated the ruling family by raising their allowances. He offered the merchants no such largesse, in fact he raised customs taxes (al-Sabah 1980: 3).

The merchants' response was both hostile and political. Their historical sense of political entitlement, founded originally on their financial interdependence with the rulers, led them to believe they had a continuing right to a say in the distribution of state wealth. Their historical access to decision-making was reinforced by their still recent experience in opposition in 1921. They were also developing a new sense of themselves as modern political actors, experimenting with local institutions such as the municipality and various councils. Now the historical basis of the merchants' power was threatened by the new oil revenues. In the long run the ruler's new fiscal independence would free him from the merchants by allowing him to buy the merchants out of politics and by enabling him to develop new allies in the national population and a new administrative network based on the ruling family. In the short run however the merchants, still organized, continued to demand their historical say. Left to itself, merchant opposition might simply have faded as it did in 1921. But this time merchants also received support from the dissident faction of the ruling family led by Abdalla Salim.

Merchant opposition began to assume an organized form in the 1930s. It began with a set of economic and political grievances. It took shape as the merchants learned to turn newly developed institutions to political ends. It grew as the merchants turned to allies inside the country – dissident branches of the ruling family – and to what they hoped were allies outside – Britain and Iraq.

The first political institution the merchants developed was the Education Council in 1936. Education was an area where the merchants had practical experience. At the beginning of the century the only schools in Kuwait were small Quran schools and an American Mission school. These schools carried a heavy burden, as the local interest in education was strong. In 1938 the Political Agent wrote, "as education goes in the Arabian Peninsula, the standard is quite high. At least every boy, and nearly every girl, goes to school, if only a Koranic school."[21] Still, those wanting non-Christian education beyond basic literacy had to study abroad. To remedy this situation the merchants founded the Mubarakiyya school in 1912, followed in 1920 by the Ahmadiyya school, funded by merchant contributions.[22] The economic problems of the 1920s however affected the school and in 1931 it was forced to close when there were no longer funds to support it. In order to reopen the school and expand education the merchants established the Education Council in 1936, which organized the hiring of expatriate teachers, the opening of new schools and the systematization of the curriculum (al-Shihab 1980: 72).

The most important new institution of the 1930s, however, was the municipality. The inspiration for it came from a leading merchant, Yusif Isa al-Qinai,
who was also a force behind the Education Council.[23] In 1928 on a trip to
Bahrain he had observed the Manama municipality, established by Britain in
1919, and returned home to write about it. He and his coauthor Abdalaziz
al-Rushaid, owner of the magazine *al-Kuwait*, also took the idea to the other
merchants. In 1930 al-Qinai raised the idea with the Shaikh, who agreed to the
project. The municipality opened in 1930 (al-Jasim 1980: 1–42; al-Shihab 1980:
53–60).[24]

The municipality's responsibilities, laid down in a basic law of 1932, included
a broad mandate for health and social affairs. Initially the municipality's practical functions consisted of supervising and cleaning the market. Its tasks soon
expanded to include supervising traffic, zoning, housing, roads, school support,
a variety of public health functions, and rudimentary planning. Its geographical
range expanded to include outlying villages. The original staff of directors, a
clerk, a few tax collectors, market cleaners, and guards grew to include book-
keepers, auditors to watch the tax collectors, and other employees. By the mid-
1930s the municipality was spending 45,000 rs a year on staff (particularly
guards), road repairs, construction, engineering, irrigation and sanitation.[25]

Two attributes distinguished the municipality from previous institutions.
First, it was financially independent of the ruler. Its revenues came from small
taxes on imports and businesses, and rents.[26] Second, it was an elective institution, created by merchants and more or less operated by them. The municipality's decision-making authority was its board of directors. The chairman was
from the ruling family, but all other members were merchants. The board was
elected every two years by the notables from a list drawn up by the municipality.
In 1932 this electorate numbered 250. Elections were taken seriously. Counting
the ballots alone took several hours. When it was done, results were prominently
posted on a board in the market (al-Jasim 1980: 36). The elected board members
were predominantly Najdi, Sunni merchants, many of whom were active in
other political forums such as the Education Council. Board members were, as
al-Jasim described it, the conscious segment, those who traded and bore the
financial burden of customs taxes and who raised contributions in times of
economic crisis (1980: 34).

Elections were first held in 1932 and then every two years until 1954 when a
new municipality law was introduced. Although the electorate was small, the
elections were hotly contested. Election irregularities were common enough to
elicit complaints, yet limited enough to preserve a high level of support among
the merchants. For example, in the 1936 election twenty candidates ran for
twelve seats. Two of the candidates, Sulaiman al-Adasani and Abdalla
al-Humaidi, filed complaints with the director, asserting that ballots hadn't
reached all their supporters. The director investigated and reported that some of

the supporters hadn't registered their names in the election books, others the ballot distributor had been unable to locate (al-Jasim 1980: 36).

In the late 1930s merchant opposition to the ruler began to coalesce. It appeared in these new institutions. In 1937 the first hint of the *Majlis* Movement appeared in the municipality. Several municipality members, supported by members of the Education Council, began calling for administrative reforms. When the Shaikh responded by dismissing the Education Council, municipality board members resigned in protest. When the municipality director appointed replacements, two of them refused to serve. In March 1938, as preparations for new elections began, the ruler declared the resigned members ineligible (al-Jasim 1980: 38). By then however the locus of opposition had shifted to the new Legislative Assembly. The Education Council and, especially, the municipality had meanwhile given the merchants a forum for political organization and experience in standing up to the ruler.

The *Majlis* Movement of 1938

The merchants' grievances grew from their economic problems and focused on achieving the kind of political input that would enable them to address those problems. The uprising began in early 1938 when a group of merchants met secretly to draw up a list of reforms which they then circulated in leaflets and anti-government wall-writing. Some merchants began calling for Ahmad to step down in favor of Abdalla Salim. These actions were accompanied by the simultaneous appearance in the Iraqi press of articles criticizing the Kuwaiti government.

On the opposition side were most of the leading merchants, backed by dissenting members of the ruling family led by Abdalla Salim and his brothers. The merchants also drew on popular demands for an improvement in basic social services – education, health care, development – and a limit to corruption.[27] On the other side stood the Shaikh and most of the ruling family, the palace supporters (including the ruler's private secretaries), a few leading merchants, and many of Kuwait's Shias.

The government responded quickly. In March the ruler arrested a dissident, Muhammad al-Barrak, accusing him of propaganda and intrigue.[28] On being beaten he released the names of three other dissidents, all leading merchants, headed by Yusif al-Marzuq.[29] Al-Barrak's treatment crystallized growing opposition. Yusif al-Marzuq approached the British requesting British nationality. When the request was refused, several merchants took this opportunity to leave for Iraq.[30] The merchants who stayed put together a delegation and petitioned the ruler to form an elective council. Meeting in Yusif al-Marzuq's home in June 1938, they drew up an electorate comprising notables from the heads of 150 leading families. They then elected a Legislative Assembly of fourteen. The members were well-established Najdi, Sunni merchants from trading families long in Kuwait.[31] They included the four board members who had resigned from the municipality in 1937 when the trouble first began. The merchants then asked Abdalla Salim to head the Assembly.

Following the election the dissidents, led by Yusif al-Qinai organized themselves into Kuwait's first political party, the National Bloc. The goals they outlined were to support the Legislative Assembly, spread cultural consciousness, and kindle the spirit of nationalism (*qawmiyya*) among Kuwaitis. To this end, they distributed pamphlets and organized a large rally at which speakers spoke, readers read the Quran, and one dissident recited a poem directed against Salih (al-Hatim 1980: 198).

By July the opposition's complaints had crystallized into a series of concrete demands. On 4 July 1938 representatives from both sides met and, to pacify the notables, the Shaikh dismissed Khalid al-Zaid, the merchant who had sided with the Shaikh in his dispute with the municipality. An angry crowd burned his car (Khalid was later rewarded for his support – he reappears in the early 1950s as chairman of Kuwait's first national bank; al-Hatim 1980: 185). Two days later the ruler consented to the Assembly.[32] The new Assembly then prepared a basic law.[33] This law extended the Assembly's control over key state institutions (budget, justice, public security) and stated the Council's intent to improve services in education and public works. The law was also a participatory document. Article 1 referred to "the people" in their elected representatives as the source of authority. On that authority, it assumed the right to legislate on financial matters (excepting the private property of the Sabah), justice, public security, education, health, development, and foreign policy (although it separately assured Britain of its willingness to cooperate). When at first Ahmad refused to sign the law, the bloc protested and Ahmad, faced with a united front, finally agreed.

The Assembly lasted six months. In its brief life it introduced a number of reforms. Some were economic; all were designed to increase public support.[34] For the traders, the Assembly canceled all export duties, the tax for beduin and villagers on goods from the city, and the import tax on fruits and vegetables. It reduced rents and market taxes. It canceled monopolies. For the consumers, it introduced market regulations forbidding the adulteration of butter and the sale of bad produce. It permitted public radio playing. The Assembly also built a new land customs house and repaired the old sea customs building. It opened three new schools, including one for girls, formed a new police force, built a new port police building, laid the foundations for a new government building and introduced a number of court reforms. It dismissed and replaced several corrupt officials – customs officers, judges, municipality members. To handle these new functions, it created new departments, the most important being the finance department, which it placed under Abdalla Salim.

The Assembly also introduced a number of decrees directed at the ruling family. It began by attacking the ruler's closest associates, his personal sec-retaries. In a concession, Ahmad replaced Salih with Salih's son Abdalla. The Assembly also directly attacked many Sabah privileges, suggesting not only the degree of privilege the family enjoyed, but also the resentment these privileges engendered, particularly when they infringed on the merchant's realm of trade. While the Assembly did not touch Sabah private income from Iraqi date gardens, it forbade tribute taking from butchers and fishermen. The Assembly forbade Sabah monopolies on shop building and certain commodities. It forbade discounts to the ruling family. It forbade the forced use of free labor by the Sabahs. Finally, the Assembly attacked state income. It canceled the pearl tax to the ruler. In the past, the ruler had distributed customs revenues. In October, the Council began collecting and distributing the revenues itself, paying the Shaikh and ruling family their allowances.[35] The Council also extracted a promise from Ahmad that he would turn the next oil check, for December, over to them.

That was where Ahmad drew the line. On 17 December he dissolved the Assembly. The members did not accept the dissolution without a fight. As Ahmad collected his supporters, the Assembly members locked themselves into a fortified building, accompanied by their guards and supporters. This was a strategic error. Although Abdalla Salim tried to negotiate a settlement, in the end the matter was settled by force. The ruler called in his beduin supporters and the forces of Ali Khalifa.[36] Outmanned, the Assembly conceded defeat. To be sure, the ruler finished off the affair by closing the local arms shop.

For a time Ahmad still tried to hold on to the form, if not the substance, of parliamentary opposition. He ordered new elections held, using a larger electorate of 400. The elections, held 24 December, brought in an enlarged Assembly of twenty, including twelve from the first Assembly.[37] Ahmad then submitted a constitution to the Assembly that would have significantly enhanced executive power.[38] When the Assembly refused to ratify it Ahmad dissolved the Assembly a second time, in March 1939. The Assembly responded by refusing to hand over accounts and records. At this juncture a Kuwaiti dissident, Muhammad al-Munayyis, a small grain merchant and erstwhile water carrier, returned to Kuwait from Iraq, gave a moving speech to the Assembly members and handed out leaflets declaring the ruling family deposed and calling on Kuwaitis to resist, assuring them of the Iraqi army's imminent arrival.[39] When al-Munayyis was promptly arrested, two of his supporters, Yusif al-Marzuq and Muhammad al-Qitami, tried to obtain his release and a fight ensued. In the struggle al-Qitami fired on the police, but missed; they returned the fire, killing al-Qitami and wounding al-Marzuq, as well as a nearby shopkeeper. The fight quickly escalated, Ahmad's military and tribal supporters joined in, and Ahmad intervened personally to restore order, sustaining a slight injury in the process. He was able to restore order only by promising to try al-Munayyis immediately.

That same day al-Munayyis was tried, convicted, and executed. Ahmad then began obtaining Assembly members. When he found one member, Sulaiman al-Adasani, in possession of a letter, signed by other Assembly members, addressed to Iraq's King Ghazi, requesting Kuwait's immediate incorporation into Iraq, that was the last straw. Ahmad ordered the members jailed (al-Hatim 1980: 221).[40] Other dissidents, Abdalla al-Saqr at their head, had already seen the direction the rebellion was taking and fled to Iraq. The uprising was over.

It was a sign of the political novelty of the uprising that Ahmad was forced to build a new jail to house the dissidents, Kuwait's first political prisoners. The old one had rarely held more than one prisoner and Ahmad's efforts to persuade India or Bahrain to take the dissidents failed.[41] Yusif al-Marzuq, wounded in the foot, stayed for a while in the Mission hospital, but was jailed on his release.[42] The remaining dissidents fled or were jailed. In March Ahmad formed an appointed council with more Sabah representation and after a decent interval this body was allowed to fade into oblivion.

Despite frequent petitions from their wives and mothers to the ruler and the Political Agent, the prisoners stayed in jail until 1944 when Ahmad declared a general amnesty.[43] Those in jail were released; those abroad could return. Soon most did. When British forces occupied Baghdad in 1941 to oust Rashid Ali, some of the dissidents, many of whom had been loosely tied to the Rashid Ali movement, began drifting home to a warm welcome.[44] There were three exceptions: Abdalla Hamad al-Saqr, Rashid Abdalghafur, and Muhammad al-Barrak.[45] Later, in 1946 al-Barrak and Abdalghafur were deported to Kuwait from India, for offenses there. Both were arrested on their return but later released. Abdalla al-Saqr alone died in exile, in India. Sentenced to prison in absentia for his part in the uprising, Abdalla had fled to Iraq where he developed business interests in Basra and political interests in the Rashid Ali revolt. Soon after the affair ended Ahmad and Saudi Arabia also worked out an agreement to end the Saudi embargo. Trade resumed and the merchants retreated to economic life.

The Assembly failed for two reasons. First, the merchants were unable to cash in on the initial support of Iraq and, especially, Britain. Second, the merchants were unable to put together a durable domestic opposition coalition, one that extended beyond the Bani Utub elite. Although the source of the movement was primarily internal, its initial growth benefited from the hope for support that many merchants placed in Britain and Iraq. The Political Agent in Kuwait was on good terms with the merchants who were, as the British records attest, an excellent source of information. The merchants originally believed they had a nod of support from deGaury, the Political Agent, whose relations with the ruler were tense and who initially encouraged both the notables and the ruler to form an Advisory Council. Fowle, the Political Resident, also had initially supportive comments:

His Highness will appreciate that since in these days, popular and democratic movements exist in most countries all over the world, it is not surprising if one should now be starting at Koweit. Experience has shown that the best way to deal with such movements is not mere repression which cannot be continued indefinitely as the movement gets stronger, but the maintenance of law and order combined with a sympathetic guidance.[46]

In June 1938 the Political Resident advised Ahmad to form a council such as the one that had advised Mubarak from among the Sabah and leading notables. In the early months of the movement merchants approached Britain collectively for a more formal statement of support and, individually, for possible asylum. In October 1938 the Political Resident visited Kuwait and made a point of meeting each council member. When instead of an advisory council, an elected council emerged, one that began to take a greater interest in political matters closer to Britain's heart, such as oil and foreign policy, Britain reconsidered and began backing the ruler. By July the Resident was suggesting that Britain should try to keep a balance between the ruler and the Assembly. He voiced his worry that the Assembly, although pro-British for the moment, might easily become more nationalistic. Feeling however that some reform was not uncalled for, either for its own sake or to forestall further trouble, Britain continued to give qualified support to the protesters. In October 1938 the Resident wrote that he felt the Assembly was there to stay and that there were no grounds for British inter-ference. When Ahmad informed the Political Agent in December of his inten-tion to dissolve the Assembly, deGaury told him only that he should risk no failure. In December when the first Assembly was abolished, two members, still hopeful, approached the Political Agent for support. His answer was evasive. But the India Office felt the Assembly was acquiring too much power and expressed its hope that Ahmad would rein it in.[47] After the dissolution, the Resident wrote, "balance of power as between Sheikh and Council has been readjusted in favour of the former which suits us."[48]

One important outcome of the *Majlis* Movement was thus to turn the leading merchants away from Britain. As they turned from Britain they assumed a more nationalist stance, precisely as the Resident had predicted, and began seeing more connections between their opposition to Britain and that of other Arabs. In the 1930s Britain could assume Kuwait's relative indifference to, although not isolation from, events in the Arab world. In the interwar period the origins of Kuwaiti domestic politics – the changing of leaders, the setting of domestic policy – lay in the distribution of power inside the shaikhdom. Domestic politics were largely shaped by domestic actors, with little foreign intervention. Kuwaitis noted with concern the growing problems in Palestine and followed with interest events in Egypt. But this was foreign news, not something to weigh in considering local matters. In 1938 the Political Agent wrote, "the reactions to the publication of Palestine Royal Commission's Report were very mild in

Kuwait. The man in the street (or rather in the dhow or Bedouin market) knew and still knows nothing about it. The very limited literate and wealthy class took more interest."[49] Kuwait showed little beyond curious concern for the Arab world, except where it intruded directly, through Saudi Arabia first and then Iraq. By the late 1930s this was changing. The first to change were the merchants. It was the leaders of the opposition – Yusif Isa al-Qinai, Ahmad al-Humaidi, Muhammad al-Ghanim, who established committees to collect funds for Palestine (Zahlan 1981: 3). By the early 1940s many wealthy, educated Kuwaitis had become both pro-Arab and anti-British. The Political Agent attributed it to Britain's Palestine policy and the general wave of Arab nationalism, especially among the young and the students.[50] But disenchantment with Britain's Kuwait policy also played a role. In the following decades, as Britain began to pose a threat to their economic interests, the merchants would become still more hostile.

After Britain, the merchants' next hope for outside support lay with Iraq. Merchant ties with Iraq had grown steadily in the 1920s as the Saudi blockade limited links with Arabia (al-Rumaihi 1975: 33). Political and cultural shifts followed. But as the merchants looked to Iraq, the Shaikh looked increasingly to Arabia where Ibn Saud, though suspicious of Ahmad, was far more hostile to the opposition movement.[51] As the rebellion gestated, Ahmad grew increasingly pious in public. Where before he had worn European clothes, encouraging Kuwaitis to do the same, he now began publicly extolling Arab dress and its role in preserving religion.[52] In the cause of virtue he forbade women's evening excursions outside the town wall, in keeping with pronouncements of Ibn Saud. These excursions were a source of income for taxi drivers, their abolition a precipitating factor in the 1937 strike, Kuwait's first, led by the taxi driver, Muhammad al-Barrak, who was beaten and imprisoned for his role, leaving him apparently more inclined to oppose the government (al-Hatim 1980: 150). Ibn Saud wanted nothing to do with a reform movement in Kuwait, particularly one with echoes in nearby Dubai and Bahrain.

Iraq, however, was interested. Iraq had a standing claim to Kuwait based on the assertion that it had inherited Ottoman title to the area. The reassertion of this claim in the late 1930s stemmed from both a general, growing sense of Arab nationalism and from specific disputes with Iran over the Shatt al-Arab, Iraq's channel to the sea. Kuwait offered an alternative to the port of Basra.[53] The Iraqis were also concerned about the smuggling of arms and other goods into Iraq from Kuwait. In 1938 the Iraqi foreign minister in a speech before Parliament referred to Kuwait as an inseparable part of Iraq, Iraq's natural outlet to the sea.[54] The fact that oil had now been found in Kuwait heightened Iraq's interests, as did the fact that Kuwait's Shias, potential supporters of Iran, were opposed to the merchants.[55] Iraq tried to take advantage of this anti-Shia sentiment among Kuwait's Sunnis. Iraqi press reports, for example, complained of the number of Persians in the Kuwaiti police force (although, as the Political Agent noted, no one on the force was even remotely Persian).[56]

In the early 1930s the Iraqis first tried to win the Shaikh over, arguing the Saudi threat, and causing the Political Agent some concern.[57] When that failed, they tried appealing to Britain. Iraq pursued its interest first through direct petitions to Britain for the cession to Iraq of some, or all, of Kuwait's territory. Through 1938–9, Iraq's foreign minister, Tawfiq Suwaidi, pressed Iraq's case on Britain.[58] The Iraqis also tried to nibble at Kuwait's independence indirectly. They suggested that Britain extend the Iraqi train line through Kuwait and construct a port there.[59] The British response was cool. The border issue had been settled at Uqair. Britain had nothing to gain by relinquishing its position in Kuwait, particularly to an unstable Iraqi government.

When these efforts failed, the Iraqis tried to press their claim through more covert attempts at destabilizing the Kuwaiti government. They tried their hand with the opposition, working with the many Kuwaiti merchants who traded and smuggled, owned land, and studied in Iraq. These merchants needed little prompting. Many Kuwaiti families (the Political Agent estimated thirty-five) owned land in Iraq.[60] Certainly some – the Political Agent thought perhaps dozens – actually favored annexation. Abdalla al-Saqr, Muhammad al-Barrak, and others prominently associated with the uprising visited Basra and Baghdad regularly, meeting with prominent nationalist politicians and newspaper editors.[61] At the height of the rebellion, many left Kuwait for Iraq. Abdalla al-Saqr's ties were particularly strong. He owned substantial estates in Iraq.[62] Early on, he had taken Iraqi nationality for his family. There were even rumors that Iraq had promised Abdalla al-Saqr the future Kuwait seat in the Iraqi parliament in exchange for his support. There were also rumors that the Iraqis had promised him (and Yusif al-Ghanim) contract work on the Kuwait port. When the movement was over, al-Saqr moved to Iraq with many supporters.

The Iraqi press also actively published anti-Kuwait propaganda, articles with titles like, "Why is Kuwait not annexed to 'Iraq?" By the mid-1930s, Shaikh Ahmad was complaining bitterly to Britain about such coverage.[63] As the 1930s went on, this press activity grew, until by 1938 it was quite insistent.[64] The newspaper reports encouraged rumors already flying around Kuwait. The second Assembly considered the constitution amid rumors of an Iraqi battalion on the border.[65] Baghdad Radio added its contribution, listing the shortcomings of Kuwait's ruler and calling for rebellion and annexation. These broadcasts were immensely popular in Kuwait, with people filling the cafes and delaying prayers until after the broadcasts.[66] In May 1938 Ahmad visited Iraq in an effort to halt the articles, but to no avail. After that he simply banned Iraqi papers (al-Rumaihi 1975: 35). Iraq's support, however, while highly verbal was little more than verbal. It offered no forces against those of the Shaikh.

In the end, neither Iraq nor Britain would offer the merchants much practical support. Iraq was unwilling or unable to offer more than this verbal support. When the ruler turned against his opponents Britain did not intervene because of the Assembly's growing interest in foreign affairs (including relations with Iraq), because of the Assembly's direct contacts with the oil companies, and because Britain belatedly realized the continuing nuisance that a democratic, potentially radical, movement could pose.

But foreign powers no more lost the movement than they had instigated it. Ultimately, the merchants failed because they could not put together a strong domestic coalition. The Assembly generated internal opposition among those groups not represented by the 14 members or the 150 families. The most important group was the Shias, who opposed the Assembly from the start. They appealed to the Assembly, Britain, and the ruler for representation on the Assembly and councils and for their own schools. For a time the Shias found some support in Salih, the Shaikh's secretary. When he responded to the Assembly by trying to organize a counter bloc based on Shias, the Assembly called for his dismissal. When the merchants attacked him personally, Shia concern deepened. A period of tension followed and then the ruler backed down and agreed to sacrifice Salih, sending him off on indefinite leave (after the rebellion was over, he returned) and replacing him with his son Abdalla, who was not much more popular.[67] Abdalla's sole defender in the Assembly was Yusif al-Marzuq, who owed him money. For his support of Abdalla, al-Marzuq was expelled from the Assembly.[68] As for Abdalla, he turned increasingly to his commercial interests: he was the ruler's representative with KOC, the Sulphur Company and the Electric Company, board member of the Water Company, consultant to the Imperial Bank of Iran, and agent for Middle East Airlines. When Abdalla died in 1955 his son Badr replaced him as state secretary and oil company representative (Abdalla's daughter meanwhile married Ahmad al-Khatib, in the 1950s and 1960s the leader of the nationalist opposition).

As the Shias became more beleaguered, they turned to Britain. In 1938 the Political Agent received citizenship applications from 4647 Shias.[69] The Assembly responded to this news by announcing that anyone applying for foreign nationality would be liable to deportation, a curious ruling since many Assembly members were hedging *their* bets with Iraq, but one which only served to heighten Shia fears. The Political Resident met with the Assembly to suggest some concessions as a safety valve, but the Assembly was adamant. When these avenues failed, the Shias took to the streets, demonstrating for the Assembly's abolition (al-Rumaihi 1975: 39).

The merchants alienated other supporters besides the Shias. Some merchants as well as ruling family members were hurt by the Assembly's cancellation of some market monopolies. They lost one town's pivotal backing by banning the sale of their tomatoes. In December 1938 critical military support for the ruler came from the town of Qasur, which specialized in pitted tomatoes. Two weeks earlier the Assembly had banned the sale of pitted tomatoes along with bad and unripe tomatoes. The Political Agent wrote that the Assembly also lost some popular support through the threat of a census (a step toward more accurate taxation) and by forbidding dancing and drumming within the city walls (a move aimed at the ruling family).[70]

The merchants were also unable to hold onto the faction of the ruling family that, for a time, allied itself with them. They were able to take advantage of the long-standing dissent of one branch of the family, led by Abdalla Salim, who had long nursed hopes of becoming Shaikh. Abdalla was able to build on support from others in the family in part because of their dissatisfaction over allowances.[71] The merchant opposition had emerged in the interstices of this royal dispute, as dissident shaikhs reached outside the family for support. Without the encouragement of the Salim branch, the opposition would not have achieved so much. Yet in the end Abdalla was unwilling to risk a complete break with the ruler. Without the support of his forces, without British support, the Assembly lacked any credible defense, whereas the ruler still controlled the beduin forces. At the first show of arms the Assembly surrendered.

Finally, in the case of both internal and external allies, a new force was beginning to make itself felt. Oil was beginning to work a sea change in Kuwaiti politics. In 1935 Ahmad received 475,000 rs from KOC for the concession. In 1938 his annual revenue from KOC was 95,000 rs.[72] Oil was not by any means the best source of revenue; it was still far below customs duties, which brought in 200,000 rs from a total income (state and private: the distinction was not yet clearly drawn) of 828,400 rs. But neither was it insignificant. And it was growing.

Oil informed Iraq's claim to Kuwait. If Britain was interested in ensuring that the opposition did not go too far, it was also because of its new but growing concern for the oil company's stability of operation. The Political Resident's main expressed concern when he met the Assembly in October 1938 was that they had begun to address KOC directly. He told them clearly that this was a matter between the Shaikh, in whose name the concession was held, and the Company.[73] When Ahmad agreed in 1938 to turn over the entire oil check to the Assembly, the Resident was surprised at his equanimity. It was, he suspected correctly, a sign that Ahmad had no intention of allowing the Assembly a long life.[74] Ahmad understood quite clearly the impact of oil. So did Abdalla; if his faction of the ruling family would not risk a complete break with the ruler, it was in part because the family, long a disparate group of relatives, was beginning to close ranks, the better to protect their new monopoly on oil. If the merchants rebelled against these changes, it was in part because of a dawning understanding that oil would deprive them of their critical role in providing revenue, and with that cost them their power.

Conclusion

The interwar period and the *Majlis* Movement left two important legacies. The first was coalitional, the second institutional. At the beginning of the century the merchant community in Kuwait formed a small, close-knit, homogeneous elite, an aristocracy of wealth, status, and power. Fifty years later, on the eve of oil, the merchant community in Kuwait still formed a small, close-knit, homogeneous elite, an aristocracy of wealth, status, and power. In one way, nothing had changed. Yet in a period of significant socioeconomic transformation this continuity is remarkable. The resiliency of this elite, its ability to survive decades of depression and reproduce itself, is worth noting because the process would repeat itself, with some variation, in the following era, with oil. In the interwar period the merchant elite demonstrated an ability to adapt to political changes. In the beginning of the century, the merchants' access to decision-making was primarily informal. Their influence on the policies of the ruler was casual and left no written record. The most common kind of informal influence was proximity: the influence of those with everyday access to the ruling family through marriage, friendship, and court presence. Here a distinction exists between those with consistent and historically precedented access and the isolated individuals who, as in any court, managed through talent, wile, or luck to gain access to the ruler. Abdalla Salih held that sort of tentative power under a series of rulers. The Political Agent explained why:

the strength of Abdulla Mullah [Salih]'s position is that everyone in the town hates him. For that reason he is invaluable to the Ruler who is thus assured that he will not gang-up with any possible usurper. The present Ruler [Abdalla Salim] hated Abdullah Mullah during his predecessor's reign and tried to oust him then but when he became Ruler himself was wise enough to see the value of Abdullah Mullah.[75]

More important in the long run were those families who had structural proximity, who enjoyed established patterns of marriage and *majlis*. This was the kind of influence the leading merchant families enjoyed, families like the al-Ghanims, privy to the ruler's oil negotiations, bankers to his relatives, and married into the ruling line.

Predictable access came from two primary sources: the merchants' control of the labor force and of the sources of revenues. Control of labor meant control of large segments of the population. Before oil, the merchant elite even organized military levies, as in 1920 when the leading merchants supplied a quota of men to guard the town wall at night.[76] Control of labor meant in turn control of the ruler's subjects. Until the complete integration of Kuwait into the international state system later in the century, emigration was always an option for the politically dissatisfied. As the mutiny of 1910–11 shows, the threat of leaving Kuwait with the workforce in tow was powerful. The merchants also exerted influence through their wealth. This took two forms: direct loans and customs revenues. Even as late as 1938 the ruler's chief revenue source was customs taxes, revenues that existed only because of the economy of trade, and most importantly, revenues that could only be tapped via the merchants.

On the surface, the relationship between the ruler and the merchants did not change dramatically in the interwar period. Politically it was one of counterbalance; economically, one of dependence. The old power relationships had not yet shifted. Shortly after Ahmad's reign ended, the Political Resident wrote:

1951 may be one of the last years in Kuwait in which, except in the material and commercial fields, there is no change whatsoever to record. The old medieval framework of society – the shaikhs, merchants, and the poor – prevailed. The nexus between them was intact. The Shaikhs borrowed money from the rich merchants and intermarried with them, living on the remnants of the tradition of what would now be called the protection racket.[77]

This all began to change with oil and the shift was now beginning.

The coalitional legacy of the *Majlis* Movement was that it left Kuwait's merchant community at a peak of political organization just at the moment when the historical economic base of its political influence was about to be removed by a new, outside revenue: oil. Indeed, the impending oil revenues were one catalyst to the *Majlis* Movement – others included the economic dislocation of the preceding decade and divisions within the ruling family. The interaction in 1938 was a harbinger of political changes to come: the merchants demanded a say in the distribution of the new revenues; the rulers, realizing the merchants could no longer compel such input, refused. The merchants, however, fought back politically. It was fortunate for them that they did, because, after oil, when the rulers no longer needed the merchants at all economically, it was the rulers' memory of the merchants' oppositional potential that persuaded them to buy the merchants out of politics rather than simply drive them out. In the first years of oil the merchants were, as the rulers would realize, the one group capable of sustained, organized, and possibly successful opposition. In Qatar, where there was no *Majlis* Movement, where the merchants could not organize politically, they did not fare nearly as well with oil. In Kuwait, instead of emigrating, instead of relying wholly on informal access, instead of acquiescing, the merchants tried to formalize and institutionalize their access to the ruler and to the decision-making process. The act of defiance also streamlined and homogenized the community, turning it into the most coherent and organized political force in Kuwaiti society. Their reluctance to bring other groups in, a reluctance that cost them some support in 1938, was perhaps in the long run a strength, since it preserved their political identity. As a result, legitimate opposition to the ruling family became identified with, and more or less the sole preserve of, a small segment of Kuwait society.

A concomitant legacy of the 1930s thus was ideological. The 1921 and 1938 councils, dormant for two decades, reemerged at independence transformed, a part of the national myth. Today the interwar assemblies are invoked by National Assembly supporters as proof of Kuwait's traditional democratic spirit. Well before the twentieth century Kuwait already had a founding myth, a well-defined legend of its own origins. In the interwar period the symbolic and practical concomitants followed. To the myth of the nation was now grafted this myth of a long tradition of merchant equality and democratic opposition. It was a merchants' myth, that the ruling (not royal) family had come to power almost by accident when the others left it behind during the pearling season to watch over the city. Despite the fact that it was a counter myth, it was also an integrating myth because as it developed it came to accept the state of Kuwait as a basic premise. If there was any doubt, it was settled with the failure of the 1938 uprising and, in particular, with the defeat of those who favored integration with Iraq.

During this period opposition within the ruling family also jelled into the two factions that appear traditional today: the Jabir and Salim lines. Out of this a new relationship between the ruling family and the trading community was forged: a tacit alliance between the merchants and the Salim branch. This appears not only in Abdalla Salim's support of the 1938 rebellion, but in his own initiative later, as amir, in creating the National Assembly. A new tradition created in this period was the introduction of a new succession pattern. The nineteenth-century passage of power from father to son gave way to an alternation between these two lines. In retrospect we can today date the beginning of the alternation from Ahmad's time, but it didn't seem that way then. Some of the most powerful forces – Abdalla Jabir, Abdalla Mubarak – were of neither branch.

The second legacy of the interwar period was institutional. Although the Assembly itself didn't last, it catalyzed the formation of new state institutions. First, the rivalry between the merchants and the ruling family generated the shortlived Assembly and the Education Council, and the longer-lived municipality. Second, the popular demands from the uprising, coupled with the ruler's need to expand his support base, given the merchant opposition, led to a small expansion of rudimentary social services. By the early 1940s, 25 per cent of customs duties were earmarked for education, health, and municipality.[78] Finally, intra-ruling family rivalry led to the expansion of the two pillars of the modern state: the fiscal and coercive apparatus, as Abdalla Salim took control of finances and the security forces became institutionalized.

Just as the Education Council of 1936 was prompted in part by the arrival of the American missionary school, so too the Council provided the impetus for the creation the following year, of an education department, responsible for overseeing the Education Council's functions, building schools and recruiting foreign teachers (al-Shihab 1980: 72). The state carefully took over the associated institutions that had served as a merchant base, such as the Ahliyya Library, founded by the al-Saqrs, where in the early 1930s dissidents would meet. This was the first formal assumption by the state of the welfare functions that today constitute the bulk of its activities. Health care likewise developed. Until the 1930s health care was provided by the American Mission Hospital. In 1936 the government opened its own one-doctor clinic and pharmacy; in 1939 it created a health department which provided free service.

The municipality, which outlived the troubles of the 1930s and continues in an altered form today, was part of the process that politicized the merchant community and which gave merchants their first experience in local government. At first the municipality was eclipsed as an institution by the 1938 Assembly, which in its short life formally assumed many of the municipality's functions. The existence of the Assembly also changed the composition of the municipality as protesting board members abandoned the municipality in 1938 for the Assembly. When the ruler encouraged this turnover, banning members from belonging to both institutions, one consequence was to open the municipality up to new membership (al-Jasim 1980: 58). This new membership allowed the municipality to survive the 1938 uprising.

The finance department was also one important outcome of the struggle between Abdalla Salim, the department's first director (1937–50), and the ruler. Until the Assembly, the ruler drew no formal distinction between his funds and state revenues. Salim had introduced fiscal reforms: he abolished some export duties, established a uniform import tax, and appointed an inspector to watch over the customs master and Salih. The uprising forced further administrative reform. In 1938 a new finance department was created and placed under Abdalla Salim's control. After the rebellion, the finance department stayed, with Abdalla Salim in charge. In the following years oil revenues accelerated this trend towards more explicit financial organization. With the ending of the Assembly, Abdalla used this department to retain some political independence.

The next institution to emerge in a new form from the trials of the 1930s was the security apparatus. Following the *Majlis* Movement, the government began to draw more formal distinctions between internal and external security. Until 1938 there were various small forces: a night guard, the ruler's palace bodyguard, tribal forces. The 1938 uprising brought home to the ruler the importance of internal security, while Iraq's predatory tendencies made him think more deeply about external security. In 1938 a police center was established under Sabah Salim, assisted by his nephew, Saad Abdalla (today heir apparent), and their merchant allies – Ghanim al-Ghanim and Muhammad al-Qitami. When the uprising ended, al-Ghanim had fled to Iraq, al-Qitami was dead and Sabah and Saad held on to the police force. The uprising also prompted Ahmad to build a new prison for the dissidents. After 1938 the security needs of the oil companies accelerated this trend.

External security developed more slowly. In earlier days, alliances had been Kuwait's first and last defense. Standing forces were small. In the 1930s Ahmad's force consisted of only 300 foot soldiers who served as his personal bodyguard, night watchmen and messengers.[79] In a crisis, this system could raise a force of 2000 beduin and 3000 townsmen (Dickson 1956: 42). These alliances were carefully maintained by tribal liaisons (Abdalla Salim played this role under Salim and Ahmad) and by tribal payments. There were also sanctions: tribes dependent on trade with Kuwait could be banned. Kuwait and Britain adapted their relationship to this tradition of alliance. Britain used her forces against the Saudi Ikhwan on behalf of Kuwait in 1921 and 1928–30.[80] There were, however, no border police and no standing security system outside Kuwait town. State authority didn't extend much beyond the city walls. In the 1930s a regular force began to develop. As the oil operations got underway, the company hired guards. Ahmad occasionally sent *ad hoc* forces to the villages in trucks provided by the oil company. Ahmad also bought armored cars to expand his force (al-Salim: 145). At the end of 1938 a small public security department was established under Shaikh Ali Khalifa (later Abdalla Mubarak) to handle borders and travelers. In 1942 a US observer noted that police posts, manned by relatives of the ruler, managed the outlying areas, but that effective state control did not run much beyond twenty-five miles outside the town (Declassified documents 1977: 12). In all, the coercive apparatus, both external and internal, was small, but growing.

The administration of justice, a branch of the coercive structure, also changed in the 1930s. Until the mid-1920s, the ruler himself played a highly visible role in the court system. In the early 1930s a new court system was created. More important cases were handled by Abdalla Jabir, with commercial matters forwarded to merchant arbitration courts, sea matters to a captains arbitration court, and other matters to the appropriate guild committee, personal status and religious matters to the religious courts of the appropriate community (Sunni or Shia). This new court system was widely disliked. Corruption in justice was one of the chief causes of public resentment. Abdalla Jabir, for example, was known for arbitrarily reversing decisions, for having men beaten for failing to respond quickly to his summons, and generally for his corrupt manner.[81]

By the end of the 1930s, then, two institutional changes were beginning to occur. First, old functions of the state (justice, finance, coercion) were being institutionalized, although they were still controlled by members of the ruling family, even if by rival factions. Second, the state was taking on new welfare functions – education and health. Prerogatives of both the ruler (defense, finance, justice) and the private sector (health, education) were assumed by the state. In the process protoministries were created: the municipality, finance, education, health, and security. These were important changes on the eve of oil, but they left open the question of whether, in the new oil era, the old rulers would be able to manipulate these changes – coalitional and institutional – to coopt and create allies with an independent stake in their regimes' continued existence, or whether their expenditures would only serve to antagonize old opponents and create new ones.

4 Kuwait after oil

In the decades since oil, Kuwait has experienced remarkable political stability. This stability has been achieved by a complex – and precarious – redistribution of power within the shaikhdom, a process which involved the eclipse of the merchants as a major political force and the ruler's replacement of his merchant allies with a strengthened ruling family and with supporters in the larger national population. These alliances, between the ruler and his family, and the ruler and his new popular base, were established in the 1950s and reshaped in the post-independence period to accommodate the political transformations which growing oil revenues, independence, and the policies of the 1950s themselves catalyzed. The strategies worked; continuity was maintained. In the process, however, Kuwait's rulers were forced to contend with new problems associated with the bureaucratic growth which accompanied the expansion of state services and with the growing interest of Britain in Kuwait which accompanied the development of Kuwait's oil industry.

The rise of the ruling family

Historically, Kuwait's ruling family was a weak political institution. The ruler relied on his family as little as possible, preferring court favorites and merchants. Early in the century, Lorimer (1908–15, vol. 2: 1074–5) observed Mubarak's rule to be "personal and absolute . . . The heads of his departments are mostly slaves; his near relations are excluded from his counsels; even his sons wield no executive powers . . . In the town the smallest disputes, whether civil or criminal, are settled by the Shaikh himself." Under Ahmad, power was still highly centralized. The Political Agent described his style of rule: "there is daily every morning the usual Arab Assembly of the Ruling family and notables but it is very brief, and the Ruler does not obtain its consent to, or opinion upon, administrative decisions, or consult or frequent the company of his family."[1] Under Ahmad only a handful of family members played important political roles, for example Abdalla Jabir, who ran the municipality, a police force, and land customs. A few others had to be reckoned with from time to time because they were powerful in their own fiefs. Ahmad relied less on family members than on his private secretaries Jaafar and Mulla Salih (and later his son Abdalla) who had served before him as secretary to Shaikhs Mubarak, Jabir, and Salim. As a political entity the family was decentralized, fragmented, and politically isolated.

In the 1930s organized political opposition, then oil revenues, catalyzed a change in the extent and nature of power wielded by the ruling family. Only now did the ruler begin to rely more heavily and in greater numbers on his relatives. The first phase in the development of the ruling family as a centralized political institution was the *Majlis* Movement of 1938. The 1938 movement both convinced Ahmad of the unreliability of the merchants and placed his family, in particular his relatives on Abdalla Salim's side, at center stage. The Political Agent summarized the change in a letter to the Political Resident in 1939,

you will remember, as you often remarked to me, that the Ruling Family here, unlike those of other Arab states, were allowed to take no part whatever in Administrative affairs . . . Since the 18th of December the Subah family have taken up superior posts in all departments of the Government, including security, sea and shore police, the control of the arms reserve, the city police etc.[2]

The 1938 rebellion also convinced the Shaikh of the need to have exclusive control over the family; the 1939 Constitution which the Assembly refused to ratify included a provision that the ruler alone could deal with the ruling family's differences and interests.[3]

For the ruling family, the outcome of the 1938 rebellion was a division of state responsibility along the Jabir and Salim lines, a division between the ruler, Ahmad, and the partisans of Abdalla Salim. The Shaikh kept his position as ruler and overseer of politics. Abdalla Salim came to handle day to day matters in the key areas of finance, customs, supplies, and police. To assist him, his brothers Fahad and Sabah Salim gradually moved into new state positions. Each faction kept to its own division, more or less, and peace and prosperity reigned.

The movement thus produced a division of labor at the very top of the family. This politicization then trickled down to the rest of the family. Oil accelerated the process. With oil revenues, family members became more vocal. They began demanding higher allowances until in 1940 their protests succeeded in winning family allowance increases of 40–50 per cent (in some cases up to 250 per cent) from the ruler.[4] This money in turn set off a flurry of land speculation. Ahmad saw an opportunity and used land claims as a way of rewarding and consolidating his family. Many shaikhs took land with his direct consent.[5] Where before rulers had intervened, Ahmad permitted rents to rise so as to allow his family, the largest, often absentee, landowners to profit.[6] In 1948 the Political Agent wrote:

A curious outbreak of land claiming by the Shaikhly family, reminiscent of gold staking in the past, is now taking place in Kuwait. Owing to the building now beginning outside the walls, part of the desert have [*sic*] ceased to have a marginal value and began to appreciate in price. H.H. the Shaikh apparently mentioned that he would not mind some of the family taking up some land outside the walls if they thought it worthwhile.[7]

They did. Land markers appeared all the way into the Neutral Zone. The process continued unabated into the 1950s. In 1952 the Political Agent observed, "one activity is in full swing – land grabbing, mainly by the Shaikhs – the Al Subah are without peers, even in the Gulf, in the exercise of rapacity and selfishness. They are marking out large areas of desert with the object of claiming huge sums in compensation when the land is required for town-planning."[8] Sabah Nasir staked out large plots, subdivided them and gave them to his beduin followers so that, as the Political Agent observed, "should the Shaikh find it necessary to revoke these grants, the resultant unpopularity would fall upon him."[9] Several plots were then sold to merchants. Abdalla Mubarak, the last living son of Mubarak the Great, and an increasingly important political player, also did quite well, fencing in large tracts of land.

The ruler rewarded his family not only with land, but with lucrative administrative positions. In the 1940s, new departments sprang up as a result of war controls: water, food, clothing were all rationed. While smuggling had been more or less a merchants' preserve, corruption increasingly became a shaikhly preserve. By the end of the 1940s the family was both richly rewarded and deeply divided. Then in 1950 Ahmad had a fatal heart attack. So tense had family differences become that the Political Agent anticipated a serious struggle between the heir apparent Abdalla Salim (in Oman at the time), Abdalla Mubarak, and the sons of Ahmad – perhaps a violent struggle. In anticipation the British called military forces towards Kuwait and gave thought to flying in troops.[10] It was the closest they had come to the direct intervention that characterized British policy further down the Gulf. However, Abdalla Salim was fully confident that the family would close ranks behind him and he proved correct, returning to Kuwait and peacefully succeeding Ahmad.

At Abdalla's inauguration there was money for all and more to spare. Revenues had risen from $760,000 in 1946 to $16,000,000 in 1950 (Khouja and Sadler 1979: 26). At first his accession caused no radical break with the past. He had been ready for the post since the near-coup of 1938 that left him in charge of finance. He had also served as director of customs, the 1938 Assembly and, during the war, food supply. He needed that government experience now.

Abdalla spent his first years negotiating with the oil companies. Ahmad, in his last years had tried to alter the 1934 oil agreement that set Kuwait's revenues. Now, both the success of other oil-producing states, especially Saudi Arabia, in obtaining 50-50 profit-sharing agreements, and the accession of Mossadegh and production declines in Iran, prompted Abdalla to reopen negotiations. In April 1951 he approached KOC for an increase in the 9 cents per barrel royalties. In November they signed a 50-50 agreement. British difficulties in Iran, where

Mossadegh had nationalized oil facilities, helped Abdalla's negotiating position. Both the example of a British setback and the new importance of Kuwait's oil, now that Abadan production was down, gave Abdalla leverage, which he recognized and used.[11] Kuwait's production rose as Abadan's declined. In 1951 KOC broke its production record, producing over 500,000 barrels a day (b/d).[12] In 1953 Kuwait hit a new export record of 1 million b/d.[13] An increased share of profits and increased production led to a rapid rise in revenues.

When it came to spending the revenues, however, Abdalla had to face his family. In Ahmad's last years, as state income rose, shaikhs had succeeded in turning administrative fiefdoms into virtual empires. The largest belonged to Fahad Salim and Abdalla Mubarak. These empires had, by the 1950s, reached the point where Abdalla could no longer tolerate them. The leading shaikhs were notorious for their expensive entertaining at home and, increasingly, abroad. Corruption had gone so far that few funds were actually reaching development projects. Abdalla now began the process of consolidating the family into manageable factions in order to control development spending. It was the first step towards institutionalizing the family's political functions.

Abdalla began by giving money to his closest relatives. The first official acts were ones of calculated largesse: raising the allowances of junior, then senior Sabahs. By 1951 the civil list included 200 to 300 shaikhs.[14] In 1950 Abdalla also made a large payment to descendants of Mubarak's murdered brothers, closing a debt from the last century and preparing the way for the return of this branch to Kuwaiti politics.[15] In the following years the brothers' descendants would come to be useful administrative allies. Their sons and grandsons would go on to become cabinet ministers, ambassadors, and high-ranking defense department officials.

The next step was to institutionalize this largesse. Abdalla insisted that British contractors take Kuwaiti partners, many of whom came from the ruling family. Several shaikhs rapidly became multi-millionaires. Abdalla Jabir, in charge of school contracts, did well, as did Fahad Salim, Abdalla Mubarak, and others at the top. The family was also rewarded with new markers of status. By the end of the 1950s a Sabah could be easily distinguished from his wealthy merchant neighbors by the two gold ribbons on his cloak or the flag in his car (Abdou 1958: 18).

While remunerating the key factions, Ahmad also streamlined the family and downgraded the marginal factions. Any opposition was suppressed. One prominent case was that of the al-Maliks, a family that claimed to be a distant Sabah branch. The al-Maliks had moved to Kuwait from Saudi Arabia, where Fahad al-Malik had been a bodyguard to Ibn Saud. In Kuwait Fahad began acting like a shaikh. He used the special flags on his car that only the Sabah used. He began claiming desert land, like a shaikh, erecting buildings without permission and, in one case, tearing up a Kuwaiti's deed to the land. Finally, a land claim of his was formally contested and the ruler's court ruled against the family. When al-Malik now insisted the family was Saudi, the ruler ordered them to leave Kuwait. Fahad refused and the ruler's forces, under Abdalla Mubarak, took over. Through relatives in the police the al-Maliks had armed themselves and fortified their property. The security forces responded with artillery and large guns, shelling the compound and killing eight (Johnson 1957: 55).[16] Fahad himself was captured and executed, as was his brother Salim, a storekeeper in the state armory and the source of the family's weapons. The al-Malik affair was a clear warning to other family factions, that claims could not be pressed in this manner, that the Shaikh would be the final word on who had rights to shaikhly perquisites. On this the leading shaikhs were in unusual agreement: Abdalla, Fahad, Abdalla Mubarak, all supported the course of action toward the al-Maliks. As Fahad al-Malik had claimed to be both a Sabah and a Saudi, it was also a message that nationalism was beginning to matter; one had to choose. Nationalism was if anything more important to the ruling family who, increasingly wealthy, could only claim to be equal to other Kuwaitis in this national sense. As the family became more clearly defined, with formal allowances and hierarchical ranks, it had begun to turn inward, rejecting historical intermarriage with the merchants and beduin (Gavrielides 1987: 161). As society became more hierarchical, politically and economically, Kuwaiti heritage became one of the few areas where the ruling family could claim to be equals.

Finally, the last step the ruler took to control the family was to institute administrative reforms with the aim of both bringing the family into government positions and overseeing their power once there. Gradually, by delegating responsibility the ruler came to share power with his relations. This process centralized decision-making in the family, fusing shaikhly and bureaucratic political forms. The ruler achieved continuity at the apex of the political system by manipulating both the administration and the ruling family. To accomplish this dual process of family centralization and control Abdalla had to turn to Britain, which was anxiously waiting for just this opportunity.

Britain and the bureaucracy

Until Abdalla's rule Britain had been a shadowy presence in Kuwait. From Mubarak's time on the Political Agent was a background figure, setting the limits to political disputes, but playing only a small domestic role. When Kuwait was threatened from outside, as it was from Saudi Arabia in the 1920s, Britain did intervene. But even in Kuwait's most troubled moment, the 1938 uprising, Britain's involvement was largely confined to keeping a close eye on matters. The British administrative legacy was so weak that years later when the opposition leader Ahmad al-Khatib criticized it, he had to resort to blaming the British for the administrative damage done to Kuwait by Egyptian advisors, originally tutored in British ways (*Foreign Broadcast Information Service, FBIS*, 12 February 1985: C1).

Oil increased Kuwait's importance to Britain, and with it Britain's interest in expanding control. In the early 1950s, Britain tried to expand its role through advisors. The effort, however, failed. Britain was never able to convince Abdalla to take on a senior advisor; the junior advisors that were pressed on him eventually quit in frustration. In the end, Britain had to fall back on the Political Agency as its line of communication and to a lower level of involvement. Britain's efforts were largely limited by the internal cohesion of Kuwait's ruling family and the ruler's control of other political factions. As in Qatar, Britain was able to move with greatest ease when internal political troubles created an opportunity, a crack. In Qatar these opportunities were frequent. In Kuwait, these cracks were fewer, and sooner sealed. One inadvertent consequence, however, of Abdalla's efforts to control both his family and Britain was the emergence of new state structures.

Britain's interest in Kuwait began to grow in the early 1950s. In 1953 the new Political Resident received explicit instructions on Kuwait,

During the last three years Kuwait has become of prime importance to the United Kingdom and to the sterling areas as a whole. It is now a major source of oil supplies and an important element in our balance of payments . . . H.M.G. can no longer afford to confine themselves to the role authorised by the treaties and agreements in force and sanctioned by usage but must also interest themselves in all matters which affect the political and economic stability of Kuwait or which may affect the interests of the United Kingdom in the widest sense. This new conception of the role of H.M.G. in regard to Kuwait entails a change in the nature of the advice to be tendered to the Ruler and in the channels through which that advice is communicated.[17]

Specifically this included reorganizing the administration, especially the financial administration, placing British advisors and personnel, and watching the interests of the oil companies. The Political Agent's post was upgraded, staff was added, and the Political Agent was given a direct line of report to the Foreign Office. The intent to meddle could not have been clearer.

Britain had already pressured Abdalla's predecessor, Ahmad, to accept advisors, but except for a medical officer and a few police officers for expatriates, Ahmad had refused. In 1949 he told the Political Resident he would hire advisors only on direct orders, which Britain did not issue, the Resident conceding to the Foreign Office that advisors appointed against the Shaikh's will could hardly function effectively.[18] The Political Agent wrote home in frustration, "they are anxious to adopt and absorb western ideas and inventions which they think may be beneficial to Kuwait while rejecting any but strictly technical guidance on how this may best be done," an attitude he characterized as xenophobic, but one which served Kuwait well.[19]

At Abdalla's accession in 1950 the British presence still consisted of the Political Agent and his assistants. Britain's primary local function was handling expatriate legal matters and liaison work with KOC. Britain was so anxious to change this arrangement that it raised the question of advisors with Abdalla within days of Ahmad's death. At first Abdalla resisted, saying the Political Agent was the only advisor he needed.[20] But then in October 1950, to the Political Agent's surprise, Abdalla suddenly agreed to hire advisors. The reason for this reversal lay with Abdalla's family. Abdalla had one aim in accepting British advisors: countering domestic pressure from his relatives, especially Abdalla Mubarak and Fahad Salim. As the ruling family began to assume more government positions, it became more powerful relative to the rest of society. At the same time, the ruler became less powerful relative to his own relatives. It was this family trouble that compelled him to allow in the British advisors that Ahmad had for years refused. Administrative initiatives were Abdalla's response to family pressure.

Abdalla Mubarak and Fahad Salim were particularly strong forces. Both had passable succession claims. Both had clienteles within the administrative departments they controlled. Fahad, Abdalla's half-brother, headed the municipality and the health department. Because Fahad was anxious to expand his patronage network by bringing work to more Kuwaiti contractors, he wanted to restrict the five British firms that dominated development, and this put him in conflict with Britain and its advisors. Abdalla Mubarak was the last living son of Mubarak the Great. In the 1940s he developed his power base as head of security in the city. By the late 1940s he had extended his power into the desert.[21] At this juncture he began to pose a possible succession challenge to Shaikh Abdalla. In the 1950s, Abdalla Mubarak managed to turn what had been an auxiliary police force into a small army. Abdalla Mubarak also officiated as acting ruler in the Shaikh's absence. Britain considered him heir presumptive. By the late 1940s, both Fahad and Abdalla Mubarak were pushing Shaikh Ahmad, and after him Shaikh Abdalla, to the limit. Abdalla hoped British advisors would contain them both by limiting their administrative reach.

In 1951 the first advisors arrived: Crichton in finance, then Hasted, an engineer, in development. When Crichton arrived he took on a financial department with few books and no supervisory or allocatory responsibility. Hay, the Political Resident, described the administration in the 1950s:

The system of Government is patriarchal and the high offices of State are held by members of the ruling family, each of whom conducts the affairs of the department entrusted to him with the minimum of financial or any other control by any central authority. In fact, each of these Shaikhs is a law unto himself, and there is much in the administration which depends on their relations with each other, their presence or absence from the state and the willingness of the Ruler to control their activities . . . It is difficult for Westerners to realize the power which a few individuals in Kuwait have to interfere arbitrarily in the daily details of administration. (Hay 1959: 101)

Each department, financially independent, answered directly to the ruler and received lump sums at his discretion. Some departments even had their own bank accounts. The three concerned with development – health, education, and municipality – were somewhat more organized. They received fixed customs shares (a practice established under Ahmad) supplemented by occasional grants from the Shaikh. Education and health also submitted annual financial estimates.

Crichton began his efforts to estabish central financial control over this administration by trying to deprive department heads of their autonomous budgets. He also established a Development Board of advisors and department heads to oversee state spending and start on a master city plan. The Board was hardly off the ground before Fahad objected in every possible way. He forbade his people to attend Board meetings. He canceled major projects midstream, such as the ruler's new hospital.[22] He got into fistfights with the Board's notable supporters.[23] He developed outside allies, using his municipality post to lower rents and raise salaries.[24] Crichton's work was blocked. Hasted, too, crossed the shaikhs. He came up with a development plan, exceedingly ambitious, if not extravagant, which relied heavily, almost exclusively, on the five large British firms which dominated development work, and their select local contractors, to the exclusion and dismay of most of the merchants and of Fahad and Abdalla Mubarak. Fahad responded to Hasted's appointment by bypassing him, hiring a Syrian engineer, Jabri, for development work.

The early 1950s saw open warfare between Abdalla's British advisors and Fahad. In 1952 the entire British medical staff threatened to resign, and the head physician vowed not to renew his contract if it meant continued service under Fahad.[25] The ruler's advisory health department committee resigned as a result of Fahad's activities. This prompted the ruler to fire Fahad, only to relent and reinstate him. The British were outraged – they wanted Fahad banished from Kuwait.[26] Their advice on Fahad, however, met with evasive answers from the Shaikh, who had hoped Britain would solve the problem.[27]

Abdalla was caught between Fahad, who wanted the advisors out and his men in, and the Political Agent, who wanted Fahad out and his man, a senior advisor, in. In frustration, Abdalla himself finally threatened to resign, prompting an abdication crisis in the early 1950s.[28] Britain had no way of countering this sort of threat. In May 1952 the advisors conceded defeat and suggested dissolving the Board. The Shaikh acquiesced. He cut a deal with the most powerful shaikhs. First, he turned development functions over to the municipality, under Fahad. Then in a formal reconciliation, he made Fahad director of the Board. Rather than blocking his strongest opponents he now settled for containing them, allowing them into his new administrative organizations.

By the early 1950s, then, Abdalla had succeeded in consolidating the ruling family and bringing it more prominently into politics. He had tried, but failed, to use Britain to control his relatives in the state administration. He spent the rest of the pre-independence period using administrative reforms to try to contain his family directly, both to allow him more control over the state machinery and as a response to growing opposition to shaikhly corruption in the national population, among groups he was courting through social services and jobs. In 1954 Abdalla created a High Executive Committee to propose government reorganizations. The Committee was a tame body, composed of shaikhs and loyal supporters, but even its protests were too much for Abdalla Mubarak and Fahad. One of the Committee's first acts was to assert that land outside the town was state land. Fahad and Abdalla Mubarak both had large desert claims (Abdalla Mubarak claimed the land under the new airport) and would have none of this.[29] When the Committee continued to cross Fahad, reversing many of his development decisions while he was abroad, Fahad simply reversed their reversals on his return. Abdalla Mubarak, for his part, stated simply that he would not have the Committee investigate his security department and left for Lebanon. Rather than take him on directly, the Committee tried to bypass him, setting up, for example, an independent, but stillborn, prison department. Abdalla Mubarak was no more amenable when in the country. The story is told that a Committee member informed Shaikh Abdalla that Abdalla Mubarak had refused him information on his department's affairs. The Shaikh replied, "why did you insist? Now you will have to leave the country for five or six weeks" (Smith 1957: 166). But on the whole, the Shaikh's problems with Abdalla Mubarak were not as great as those with Fahad. Abdalla Mubarak's attention was devoted to developing his police force, a goal that overlapped to some extent with Britain's. There were differences of course: Britain wanted British officers, to which Abdalla Mubarak, after some resistance, agreed. Abdalla Mubarak wanted limitations on the oil company's private police force, to which Britain conceded.

Abdalla Mubarak and Fahad were hardly close, but they did share a common hostility to the Committee. The Committee's inability to control them ended British hopes that an advisor system would allow them more influence. In 1954 Hasted, the British engineer, quit in frustration after clashes with Fahad. Hasted, a defender of the five British contractors, had now incurred the merchants' enmity by refusing to open bidding. His departure left the five unprotected and hastened their decline. With Hasted gone, Jabri, Fahad's Syrian engineer, now found that he had served his purpose. His troubles with Fahad increased and in 1955 Jabri too quit. Crichton, the financial advisor hung on a little longer, resigning in mid-1957 over Fahad's refusal to allow him any say in his own budget. Finally, the Committee itself threatened to resign unless it received the Shaikh's clear support. When unambiguous support was not forthcoming, the Committee's shaikhs stopped attending meetings and the Committee slowly faded.

In 1956 Shaikh Abdalla created a new advisory body, a Supreme Council, to replace the High Executive Committee. This body marked the last phase of the Shaikh's efforts to bring the family into politics. The Council of ten consisted only of shaikhs. This Council functioned as a protocabinet, handling most state affairs. It also took some steps to limit Abdalla Mubarak and Fahad Salim. In 1955 at a family meeting Fahad had reportedly led a movement to defeat Abdalla Mubarak's succession claim, putting forwad Jabir Ahmad (now, amir) as his candidate.[30] In 1957 the Council tried again to limit Abdalla Mubarak's power by consolidating some of his forces into Sabah Salim's police and placing a grandson of Shaikh Ahmad to watch over him. Abdalla Mubarak was not fully ousted until 1961, but the process had begun. In 1961 a final disagreement between the ruler and Abdalla Mubarak led to Abdalla Mubarak's forced exile. In April Abdalla Mubarak resigned his position as commander-in-chief and deputy ruler and left for exile in Beirut, Paris, and Cairo. Abdalla's shaikhs also tried to restrain Fahad, but with less enthusiasm. Fahad was immediate family, in the line Abdalla was trying to strengthen. In the end, fate settled the matter with Fahad's death in 1959. By the late 1950s, Abdalla was feeling confident enough about the relatives around him, especially his closest kin, to delegate more responsibility. In 1959 he reorganized the administration. His brother Sabah, who would eventually succeed him, took over the health department. His son Saad assumed more duties in the police force. On the Jabir side, Jabir al-Ahmad who ran security at Ahmadi assumed control of finance and oil. This reorganization was an important delegation of authority, for Abdalla had alone controlled finance since the 1938 uprising. By the end of the 1950s then, Abdalla was well on his way toward employing, streamlining, and controlling his family.

The judicial system was also reorganized in the 1950s both to bring in the ruling family and organize their power. The court system was among the first touched, in part because it was an area where Britain exercised some direct control, in part because it offered shaikhs too much opportunity for developing independent bases. In the 1950s the British court Registrar later wrote:

There was then what was known as the Courts Department but at the same time the various other departments had their own separate little "Courts." The Police Department for example tried all persons arrested by members of its force and hardly ever bothered to refer them to the courts. The Public Security Department did the same with persons arrested by members of its force. The same was true of the Customs Department and the Municipality Department. (Hijazi 1964: 429)

In the early 1950s Britain considered pressing the Shaikh to centralize the courts but backed down when it felt he might not withstand simultaneous pressure from both Sabah Salim, in the police, and Abdalla Mubarak.[31] Now Kuwait's development was bringing new legal needs – an increase in real estate litigation stemming from the land purchase program, personal injury cases from increasingly common car accidents (Liebesny 1956: 42). Britain was anxious to rid itself of a system that, with Kuwait's growth, was becoming an administrative burden. In 1953 the British court heard 4 cases, in 1955 over 200, the increase due largely to the influx of expatriates (Hijazi 1964: 432). The Kuwaitis were anxious to establish more control. The presence of the British court united the opposition: the younger nationalists who opposed the British, the ruler, who felt it infringed on national sovereignty, and "the merchant class whose members were quite contented with the national system, under which they occupied a rather privileved position. This class resented the British Jurisdiction because they felt that it was too weak and rather ineffective as against the sharp adventurous foreigner" (Hijazi 1964: 432–3). In the Nasserist 1950s, this was unnecessary grief. A new system was established with Arab judges and in 1960 Kuwait assumed jurisdiction over the 100,000 foreigners.

By the mid-1950s Britain was forced to abandon its goal of increasing internal control. In the early 1950s, Britain tried to devise a new policy for dealing with the Shaikh, by opening a new channel of advisors. In this it was successful. It was unable to get Abdalla to take on a Senior Advisor. The advisors it did manage to push on Abdalla were unable to resist his family rivals, notably Fahad. British efforts to oust Fahad were likewise unsuccessful. When they pushed too hard, Abdalla threatened to resign and they backed down. The threatened resignation prompted the first serious review of British policy.[32] As the Political Resident wrote during the abdication crisis of 1953, "it is tempting in some respects to think that if our support is asked by [Abdalla] Mubarak we can attach conditions, such as appointment of an advisor. This was considered on the death of the previous Ruler . . . but rejected on the grounds that if the new Ruler succeeded by universal consent we could not withhold our recognition . . . and we should therefore look silly."[33] Britain wrote off the effort to push advisors as fruitless and reverted to the Political Agency as the primary channel of influence. The Foreign Office now wrote:

Advice to the Ruler must . . . not be pressed beyond the point at which it defeats its own ends and arouses feelings which might weaken the position of the Agency. The Ruler has been left in no doubt about the reforms which Her Majesty's Government would like to see accomplished in his administration. Our persistent representations, it would appear, have made him uneasy and lowered his confidence. There may therefore now be reason to abate the pressure somewhat and to give the Ruler breathing space.[34]

The Foreign Office concluded, "relations with Shaikh Fahad should be carefully cultivated." In 1955 the Political Agent conceded defeat:

While it has been our *declared* policy over the past two years to increase our influence in the internal affairs of Kuwait, in order to achieve a close hold over our moral and material interests, it has been equally the firm determination of the Ruler and his family to resist us in doing so; and the Ruler has in great part succeeded . . .

I do not believe that we can afford to go any further than we have already gone without a revolutionary change of policy and without being prepared to take over, by force if necessary, a large measure of internal control.[35]

They were not prepared to use force. The decade started with British efforts to increase influence; it ended with Britain preparing to leave Kuwait.

The merchants

As Abdalla reorganized the ruling family he also moved to limit the political power of the merchants. New revenues not only allowed him to placate the family, but also to dispense with the traders – their loans, their customs dues, their demands, his concessions. In 1952 the Political Resident noted the trend: "as the shaikhs got richer through oil royalties their actual dependence on the merchants for money, if not their voracious appetites for it, grew less."[36] His successor agreed: "the checks and balances of mediaeval society have been upset. The Shaikhs with, comparatively speaking, unlimited wealth have become independent of the merchants."[37] Oil quickly allowed the ruler to reverse his historical relationship with the merchants. In 1950 Abdalla arranged to pay the family's merchant debts; in 1951 he lowered customs tariffs.[38] No longer would the family or the state need to rely on port dues paid by traders.

Financial independence in turn allowed Abdalla to limit the merchants' political participation. In the 1950s he moved to curtail their role in government. With the establishment of the Development Board, the merchant-dominated municipality declined (al-Jasim 1980: 54–8). In 1954 the Shaikh replaced the elected municipality merchant board with an appointed board which included shaikhs. A new law redefined and restricted the municipality's tasks. In the early 1950s elected merchant committees attached to government departments had had some say over department policies. They were now eliminated. When the leading merchants responded with a petition for a consultative council with merchant input, the ruler instead produced the High Executive Committee with only three non-shaikhs, all of whom (including his state secretary, Izzat Jaafar) were considered beholden to the Sabah family. At this the department committee members resigned. A British observer caught this change:

It is indeed unfortunate that the Ruler has not permitted a number of leading citizens to become members of the Higher Committee. Three or four years ago, when there were in existence several committees, the Health, Education and Municipal Committees, the citizens had far more say in the affairs of the State. The citizens are wealthy and naturally wish to conserve and enjoy their wealth. Under the present system the extent to which they can press their claims without some danger is limited.[39]

Merchant requests for participation in an advisory council, repeated through the 1950s, went unheeded.[40] By the end of the decade Abdalla was relying on a Supreme Council completely devoid of merchants. Rapidly the old dependency relationship between the Sabahs and the trading families withered.

If the merchants were concerned about their political position, their first priority remained their economic position. Here there was also cause for concern. World War II had created sharp income inequalities in Kuwait. With the outbreak of war, prices rose quickly and shortages appeared. For the merchants who smuggled the desperately needed goods, it was a profitable decade. In 1943 the Political Agent wrote that the large profits in recent years, the price controls, and the absence of consumer goods had led to "accumulations of capital feverishly seeking for outlets."[41] In 1944 Ahmad had made peace with his 1938 opponents, proclaiming an amnesty for those involved in the *Majlis* Movement. Those still in prison he freed; those who had fled to Iraq were allowed back. The exiles returned to trade. After the war, oil brought new economic opportunities. In the 1940s, the merchants were just beginning to prosper. In the 1950s, oil-based development offered more opportunities. By 1956, KOC was spending over $8,000,000 locally on supplies and services (Finnie 1958: 173). In 1951 an ambitious development plan was drawn up and work begun. Haltingly in the early 1950s the *ad hoc* development policies of the 1940s were organized and routinized. Construction boomed as the government began to spend on social services, education, health care.

The first plan faced many problems. It was written quickly on little information and virtually no research and the city's phenomenal growth soon outdated it. There were the usual bottlenecks and congestion as everything was begun at once. Even so, development was generating income. The merchants, however, were becoming increasingly concerned that much of the plan's funding was being siphoned off by the ruling family and foreign contractors. A contemporary critic observed,

the entire 15-year development plan was apportioned out among five British firms. The government did not carry out preliminary cost survey, did not call for tender and simply awarded contracts on a cost-plus basis . . . no anti-inflationary precautions were taken, labour and materials costs rocketed, much of the finished work was of inferior quality, and the Ruler's rage overflowed when the time came to pay the price.   (Johnson 1957: 54)

Cost overruns, corruption, and the government's limited administrative absorptive capacity, its inability to monitor expenses, turned the plan into an undertaking far costlier than expected. Local development expenditure, the bulk going to the five firms, was running at £30,000,000 a year by the mid-1950s.[42]

By 1953 a crisis had emerged. The ruler's development plans were casting money widely, but not widely enough for the merchants. The contracting arrangements favoring the ruling family met with particular opposition. The firms not included as local partners pressured for open bidding. Now even that development was slowing down. The merchants were unhappy about this slow-down, so unhappy they petitioned the Shaikh, drawing his attention to the costly corruption of his administration. Abdalla was unhappier. To finish the year, he had to turn to the traders for loans (Smith 1957: 166). Short of cash, caught between Britain and the shaikhs, borrowing again from the merchants, the richest man in the world wanted to resign. In early 1954 Abdalla called a halt to development and issued a stop spending order. Projects underway were cur-tailed, postponed, or eliminated. Only a few – the distillation plant, the power plant – continued unharmed. The ships in the bay, backed up and holding, now left as development ground to a halt.

Abdalla's response to this crisis was to strike a tacit deal with the merchants. They had lent him money; they wanted something in return. He offered to guarantee their wealth and see that they received a sizable portion of the new oil revenues. Abdalla's personal popularity with the merchants, stemming from his support of the 1938 *Majlis* Movement helped. This was their chance and they took it. Two mechanisms were crucial in preserving and augmenting the merchants' wealth in this period. The first was direct support. Initially aid was *ad hoc*: the ruler helped individual merchants through preferential monopolies and dealerships and, in an historic reversal, personal loans.[43] The second mechanism was the preservation of the private sector, or an important sliver of it. Abdalla agreed to distribute significant revenues through the local market and to legitimate the merchants' position through a free enterprise ideology. Now Abdalla abandoned the cost-plus system. He canceled most of the original con-tracts. He prohibited the five British firms from submitting tenders. When the new port, the first big state project, was put to tender they were not allowed to bid on it. Development was resumed using open bidding and fixed price tenders, with much of the work now going to local firms. The Development Board kept a list of approved contractors. Where merchants were happy to invest – trade, construction, services – the government not only stayed out, it offered encouragement. It privatized some newly governmental functions, ranging from the KOC tanker agency work, turned over to a select group of rich merchants in 1956, to the school lunch program.[44] The ruler also made a quiet promise to keep Sabahs out of Kuwaiti business. This was a standing grievance. It is notable that in 1938 the Council did not attack the ruling family's state allowances (which for a time it distributed), nor its income from date gardens in Iraq. It did, however, crack down on Sabah privilege and involvement in local business and trade.[45] Now the Sabahs invested their money abroad or, if at home, discreetly, preserving the merchants' monopoly. Sabah names were conspicuously absent from the historically merchant dominated Chamber of Commerce and from the corporate boards that emerged.

For the merchants, construction and imports were the first areas to develop. Importers received exclusive agencies from manufacturers to bring in products demanded by Kuwait's newly wealthy consumers. Foreign companies wanting access to state or private business had to go through Kuwaitis. If they wanted special access to the shaikh awarding the contract, they went through the merchant partners, largely the old notable families of the 1938 rebellion. By the late 1950s Kuwait was flourishing. Fahad al-Salim Street, center of the new downtown district, was a boom of offices, shops and apartments. The *New York Times* (11 March 1961) reported six Kuwaiti merchants there with fortunes over $50 million. Important merchant ventures of the 1950s included the National Bank of Kuwait, Kuwait Airways, Kuwait Cinema, Gulf Fisheries, and the Kuwait Oil Tankers Company. The overlap between the pre-oil elite and the board members of these modern firms was striking as is readily apparent in a comparison of the names of trading families and board members (Dickson 1956; al-Qinai 1982; US, US Embassy, Kuwait 1982; Baz 1982; Ismael 1982: 84).

The second mechanism crucial in augmenting the merchants' wealth was the land acquisition program. Urban private property predated oil, but only in the 1950s was formal title extended to the desert outside when the state zoned regions and divided them into numbered plots. At first this land was grabbed by ruling family members. Now Abdalla instituted a formal redistribution of land under a municipality appraisal committee of notables. Downtown land, generally owned by merchants was purchased by the state at high prices and resold at low prices largely to wealthy merchants. The net effect was a significant transfer of revenues from the state to this group. By the early 1960s, the government had recovered only 5 per cent of its outlays on land in resale (International Bank for Reconstruction and Development, IBRD 1965: 89). Land purchases soon became the largest item in the state budget. Land prices rose rapidly – an average square meter cost 4 Kuwaiti dinars in 1952, 129 in 1960 (Ffrench and Hill 1971: 36). The IBRD concluded:

The Government buys land at highly inflated prices for development projects and for resale to private buyers. Land purchases amounted to between KD 40 million and KD 60 million in most recent years. Whatever the political or developmental justifications for this practice, the prices fixed by the Government for these transactions and the small amount thus far collected on the resale of the land make the public land transactions a rather indiscriminate and inequitable way of distributing the oil revenues.

(IBRD 1965: 4)

Were it truly indiscriminate, however, it would have been far more equitable. The ones to benefit were those already owning prime downtown land, the notables who assessed it, and those with access to (if not control over) information on future areas of development and state purchase.

As a result of these state policies, old families rose as modern contractors. While they rose, they also maintained a strong corporate sense of themselves. The Chamber of Commerce and the official stock market were the forums that reinforced this corporate sense. Social mechanisms also maintained the group's cohesion: outmarriage taboos and, especially, the *diwaniyya*, a men's social institution adapted from the pre-oil era, a regular forum for discussing social and political issues. With the development of oil and a more hierarchical class structure, the *diwaniyya* developed into an institution that reflected and preserved these new stratifications. Increasingly it came to include only those of the same social class and status, members who would use the *diwaniyya* to further the interests of those like them (Farah 1979: 61; al-Amiri 1986). The merchants' *diwaniyya* served one other function: it was also the ruler's listening post. Through it he monitored the merchants' economic grievances.

The rise of the trading families to economic prominence through these mechanisms can be seen in the history of the al-Ghanims.[46] Part of the original Bani Utub migration to Kuwait, they were already prominent as large ship-owners and traders by the eighteenth century.[47] In the twentieth century Ahmad al-Ghanim, a successful pearl merchant and shipyard owner, served at the suggestion of the ruler (who married an al-Ghanim) as the oil company's local agent. Around 1930 he turned the post over to his son Yusif. Yusif built on these ties to, and knowledge of, the oil industry. In the 1920s he bought a quarry and supplied gravel for construction of the Abadan refinery. In the 1930s, by one account, royalties from the family were providing the government with two-thirds of its revenue (*Middle East Economic Digest, MEED*, February 1980: 35). Yusif, like others in his family, joined the 1938 *Majlis* Movement and when it failed left the country with relatives. Returning in the general amnesty in 1944 he expanded the trading company. By the end of the war he was employing 7000 men, by one account half the Kuwaiti workforce (*MEED*, February 1980: 35). In 1948 the Political Agent listed him as one of Kuwait's top three merchants.[48] With the arrival of KOC he became its top supply and labor contractor, taking 15 per cent of the wages plus a per/man commission. In 1948 al-Ghanim had 790 men under him in the oil company.[49] Yusif was also a leading lender to the ruling family; in 1950 when Abdalla settled ruling family debts to merchants, Yusif was one of the leading beneficiaries.[50] With oil Yusif began to diversify. He formed a company with Khalid al-Zaid, a prominent royalist in the 1938 movement, to bring water from Iraq. He got the local monopoly on ice, he imported air-conditioners, and acquired agencies, sometimes with the ruler's intercession, for General Motors, Frigidaire, Phillips TV, BP lubricants, Link Belt Cranes, British Airways, Air India, Gulf Air, and Learjet, among many others. From this base he expanded. By the early 1980s the family, in the hands of his children, had added several new branches, notably the Kirby Building Systems. In 1982 the firm had an income of about $400,000,000 and by Field's (1985: 9) estimate was the fifth largest Arab merchant house. The al-Ghanims, like other merchant families, had profited from the new arrangement with the ruler.

Distributive policies

The arrangement with the merchants was a temporary solution, an armistice imposed by the Shaikh while he tried to develop other allies and broaden his support base. Abdalla first tried to buy the support or at least acquiescence of the poorer Kuwaitis through mass-based distributive policies. In this Abdalla inherited little from Ahmad: a hospital, a few schools. Now, in the early 1950s development focused on infrastructure and basic services: roads, water, electricity, hospitals, schools. The 1951 plan, for all its faults, guided the city's growth for a decade. Under it the first distillation and power plants were built, as well as many roads, schools, mosques, and other projects begun. These benefits were directed at and indeed reached the poorest Kuwaitis. Health care and education, provided without charge, became accessible to all families.

Education grew rapidly. New schools were built. A new educational system and teachers' colleges were introduced. By the end of the 1950s 27,698 boys and 17,859 girls were in school (IBRD 1965: 146). Where higher education had once been the preserve of the merchant families who, often with state support, sent their sons for education abroad, now even the poorest Kuwaiti could attend school. Health care also developed. Until 1949 the American Mission ran Kuwait's only hospital, with the municipality providing a few doctors. Kuwait's first major health investment was a state hospital which opened in 1949. In 1951 the Political Agent observed, "the Kuwaitis seem bent on creating a health service that will be a model for the Gulf."[51] In the 1950s other health institutions opened – TB facilities, mother-baby centers, a mental hospital, an infectious disease hospital, and the large Sabah hospital, completed in 1962. Other social services were also introduced. In 1951 the state nationalized the electric company and lowered prices. By the mid-1950s most of Kuwait was electrified. In 1954 a social affairs department was established, providing low income housing and job programs for the unemployed. By 1959 almost 4000 Kuwaiti families were receiving state aid (US, American consulate, Kuwait 1960: 35).

State employment, however, was the most important distributive mechanism. The idea that Kuwaitis should have precedence in state jobs had been in the air since the 1938 rebellion, when Ahmad had included such a provision in his draft constitution.[52] To provide employment, unnecessary jobs were now rapidly created and filled with unqualified personnel. By 1962 there were (excluding military and police) 36,300 state employees, 46 per cent of whom were Kuwaitis, one for every 10 residents (IBRD 1965: 40). Of the Kuwaitis, less than 5 per cent were high school graduates and 30 per cent, some 3000, were illiterate. To give one example, an expatriate doctor wrote in the early 1960s:

> For Kuwaitis who come from the poorer classes, jobs are invented or overstaffed. For instance, there are ten guards for the grounds at the mental hospital who are paid $150 to $175 per month when in point of fact no guards are needed. Similar occupations, such as the municipal policemen . . . are quite frequent, and the town is liberally sprinkled with such individuals who really do nothing but walk around in their uniforms and lean against the buildings.   (Kline 1963: 766–7)

Beduins often received such pseudomilitary jobs.

For these services, the Kuwaitis were grateful, but it was unclear how long they would remain so. Already in 1955 the Political Resident observed, "amongst all classes of Kuwaitis the idea is growing that while paying no taxes they are entitled to free or State-subsidised education, health, water, electricity, telephones and other services."[53] To maintain an aura of privilege around these new entitlements, in the 1950s the government institutionalized preferential treatment based on nationality through a series of nationality laws. State benefits and services were available exclusively or preferentially to Kuwaitis. Other policies reinforced this national awareness. At the government's insistence the 1951 plan, through the new residential areas, segregated Kuwaitis and non-Kuwaitis. Public housing segregated non-nationals. Given the number of foreigners, preferential treatment based on nationality was becoming a privilege. By 1957 there were, according to Kuwait's first census that year, 92,851 non-nationals, about 45 per cent of the population (Kuwait, Ministry of social affairs 1958: 57, tables 25, 34). They did the work. Only a third of the workforce of 83,478 were Kuwaiti, concentrated largely in such traditional categories as police and guards, or in trade. In the modern sector they were well represented in only a few categories, for example, drivers. In 1957 there were two Kuwaiti doctors and four nurses to 144 foreign doctors and 388 nurses, 128 Kuwaiti teachers to 1136 expatriates.

As the expatriates grew, the government enacted stricter nationality laws to regulate the special treatment of Kuwaitis. In 1948 two decrees established the first legal basis for nationality.[54] In 1959 a stiffer nationality decree was issued which broadened the definition of "originally" Kuwaiti, to descendants of those in Kuwait since 1920 (previously 1898), but tightened naturalization. A 1960 amendment allowed some naturalization after long residence, but the clock started at 1960 and the limit was fifty per year. The Civil Service Law of 1960 held higher posts and pensions exclusively for Kuwaitis. The benefits available to Kuwaitis had grown significantly. Nationality now had real economic worth.

By the late 1950s there were nearly 100,000 expatriates. Arab nationalism was growing, and a more explicit policy was needed. The government developed three policies. First, it tried to separate Kuwaitis and expatriates through the preferential treatment accorded by nationality laws. It also required firms to give preferential treatment to Kuwaitis. This was a longstanding grievance, especially in the oil sector, the first to bring in expatriates on a large scale. By 1949 the KOC staff had grown to 10,000, 40 per cent Kuwaiti, but mainly unskilled laborers.[55] In 1955 there were no Kuwaitis among the senior staff, who were overwhelmingly British.[56] The 1934 concession had obliged KOC to give preference to local subjects, then to Arabs. In the mid-1950s Kuwaitis even formed a government employees union, initially at KOC, with the aim of replacing all foreigners in important positions.[57] The 1959 Labor Law now specified national hiring priorities.

Second, having separated the expatriates, the government introduced policies to control them. When there was trouble, the government had a standard response: immediate expulsion. The US consul observed in 1959, "whenever a temporary labor surplus develops or whenever Kuwait authorities become disturbed at the size of the foreign community, the illegal workers are rounded up and shipped back to Iran or Iraq." (US, American consulate, Kuwait 1960: 35). Third, it introduced a series of labor laws to differentiate and differentially control Kuwaiti and expatriate labor. For a while there was less need. There were a few labor disputes in this period: a small Baluchi riot at KOC in 1949, a Pakistani distillation plant strike in 1952, an Indian and Pakistani artisan strike in 1953 – but nothing on the scale that Qatar saw. Because the oil industry itself was an enclave, an autonomous oil town in Ahmadi, miles outside the capital, labor troubles there were easily contained. In 1955 the ruler passed the first public sector labor law, followed in 1959 by the first private sector law and in 1960 by another public sector labor law. Unions could form only under strict state control. The private sector labor law of 1964 was the most important piece of legislation. It limited contracts to five years and required workers to register with the state, with job priority to go to Kuwaitis, then other Arabs. The law allowed workers to form subsidized unions under certain conditions. Foreigners could become non-voting members after five years residence. Political, religious, and ideological activities were forbidden. The law called for compulsory arbitration, but forbade strikes. In 1965 two union federations (later united into the General Confederation of Kuwaiti Workers) were formed in the oil sector and the government. These policies encouraged Kuwaitis, including potential dissidents, to set themselves apart from expatriates. Once set apart they could then be coopted. In the 1950s and 1960s, as Nasserism grew around the Arab world, this policy was a very important containment mechanism.

Opposition

Opposition to the regime did begin to appear with increasing frequency in the 1950s. It focused on the barely restrained extravagance of the shaikhs and it developed in the shadow of Nasserism, carried to Kuwait by the many expatriate Arabs, especially Iraqis and Egyptians. At first the dissent focused on domestic issues. In 1954 a group called the Kuwait Democratic League began issuing pamphlets criticizing the ruler and the shaikhs.[58] One such pamphlet read:

The nation is very disappointed by the strange situation in which the country has fallen ... For example, there are the Shaikhs, each of them thinks of himself as an independent ruler and demands absolute obedience to his wishes and insists that his particular schemes must be carried out. There are thus many clashes and disagreements ... In these circumstances the nation has no alternative but to offer you the choice of either using your authority to strike down those who are creating disorder and confusion and to allow the people some share in governing themselves, and so fulfill what the nation expected of you, or that you should recognise your disability and resign.[59]

Throughout the early 1950s, opposition to Abdalla and, especially, to the shaikhly corruption around him grew. Arab nationalism was attached to this political awakening, but it was not in the forefront, and then only briefly, until the Suez crisis of 1956. Now, despite all the ruler's efforts, cooperation between Kuwaiti and expatriate Arab opposition grew. In August 1956, in response to Nasser's call for a strike, 4000 demonstrators met at the National Culture Club, the new center of radical opposition, to hear pro-Nasser speeches.[60] In September more disturbances followed. In October a strike protesting the French arrest of Algerian leaders closed government offices and shops. After 1956 anti-British and anti-French sentiments were grafted onto the anti-government statements.

Abdalla responded to the opposition at first with tactics designed to divide Kuwaitis and expatriates and then coopt the Kuwaitis. One catalyst to the government's mass distributive policies was its fear of Arab nationalist opposition and its potential to galvanize the street. The expatriate population had not only risen in number, but in political volatility. Because this volatility could easily spread to Kuwaitis, the government was anxious to use social policy and nationality laws to create as much of a rift as possible between expatriate Arabs and Kuwaitis. In this it was largely successful. It could not halt the importation of Arab nationalism, but it could contain it. Abdalla's second tactic was to tolerate a relatively high level of Kuwaiti opposition activity in the forms of clubs and papers, in the hope that it would simply run its course. In the mid-1950s Abdalla finally began introducing more repressive policies – censorship, bannings, large-scale arrests. In this he relied on Abdalla Mubarak, who had opposed his earlier, more tolerant policy toward the opposition. In the demonstrations of the mid-1950s, when Abdalla Mubarak's forces were let loose, they were swift and severe. This reaction in turn prompted still more severe opposition. By the late 1950s the opposition had taken to setting off bombs in the Ahmadi oilfield.

As elsewhere in the Gulf, the opposition was organized around social clubs: the Graduate Club, the Teachers Club, and especially the National Culture Club which had candidates on local councils in 1954, pressed demands for an assembly in 1955, and was active in the 1956 demonstrations. Together the clubs formed the Committee of Clubs and organized joint protests, often in cooperation with the education department, under a sympathetic director, Abdalaziz Hussain. The leader of the opposition was the National Culture Club's Ahmad al-Khatib. The son of a receptionist in the house of Abdalla Mubarak, al-Khatib had been one of the first poor Kuwaitis to benefit from the distributive policies of the 1950s. Like others of his day, al-Khatib was educated abroad, at the American University in Beirut, and in England. In Beirut, al-Khatib took up with George Habash's Arab Nationalist Movement. On returning home he founded Kuwait's opposition. In the early 1950s, he was active in the many clubs and publications that sprang up. By the mid-1950s he was a popular public speaker at demonstrations. In this period, the relationship between the state and the opposition was still polite and al-Khatib also maintained ties at the top. He enjoyed a special status as Kuwait's first and Abdalla Salim's personal physician (although he also worked in the state hospital). Al-Khatib also developed a friendship with Abdalla's son Saad while studying in England. His marriage to Sharifa, daughter of Abdalla Salih, from the family that had advised Kuwait's rulers for decades, kept him in interesting political circles.

Al-Khatib and the other organizers drew their support from a variety of sources. There were, of course, the expatriates and their Kuwaiti supporters, concerned with issues of foreign policy – the Arab-Israeli conflict, imperialism. They drew on discontent in different segments of Kuwaiti society. There were the poorer Kuwaitis who, like al-Khatib, were benefiting from the state social policies, and beginning to demand more. They criticized the great wealth that was being wasted by shaikhly corruption and invested abroad. Some merchants, too, played a role in the opposition. For the merchants, this period was a critical time of change, as they were being asked to relinquish political rights in favor of economic privilege. Some younger merchants, who also comprised much of the educated population, sided with the opposition and participated in club life. Some merchants even participated actively in organizing the boycott of British and French goods. Others simply took advantage of the boycott to raise prices on foreign goods such as typewriters.[61] But most stayed with the government. In 1956 the KOC tanker privatization produced protests from reformers who, correctly, saw a tension between the merchants' retreat to economic life and their own hopes for representative government.[62]

The opposition even had some support within the government. The clubs had the quiet support of senior civil servants, many from leading families.[63] The education director, Abdalaziz Hussain, was openly sympathetic to the opposition. In 1956 when police were sent to disperse the crowds, this intervention provoked protests from many government officials and several, including the police director, Jasim al-Qitami, resigned in protest. His protest did not stop there. In 1959 when al-Qitami made a pro-Nasser speech at a UAR anniversary rally he was put under house arrest along with other officials.

In general though, especially by regional standards, the opposition was contained. By the end of the 1950s Kuwait had turned a critical corner. The basic infrastructure of roads and buildings was in place; basic services were now available. The ruler was rid of his two strongest family opponents. He had bought the merchants' support and the general acquiescence of the population through distributive policies, although there was some tough going for a few years in the mid-1950s. He was also well on his way to creating a new administrative state. The state's functions had expanded greatly in personnel, scope, and impact on the population. The administrative machinery to run it had been created. Abdalla doubtless felt Kuwait was quite ready for independence.

Independence, state formation and coalition building

In June 1961 Kuwait and Britain signed an agreement ending the 1899 treaty and formal British control. In the following years the amir (the title he now assumed) and his successors institutionalized the tacit agreement with the merchants. At the same time, they also began a search for allies outside the old merchant elite. One forum for this search was the National Assembly. There the amirs balanced the merchants with beduins, Shias, and progressives, in turn politicizing each community. Once politicized, however, these communities became harder to control. This was particularly the case with the Shias who, under the further influence of the Iranian revolution in the 1980s, came increasingly to exercise their new political power in opposition to the state. As this politicization occurred, the rulers, disillusioned with the effectiveness of their quasi-representative institutions, turned increasingly to repression to deal with the Shias. This heavy-handed response politicized the community further. As Shia opposition grew, the rulers retreated. They began to renew the arrangements of the 1950s, turning again to the ruling family. As the ruling family's role grew, the Assembly, an exclusively commoner institution, declined in power until it was finally closed. As the Assembly weakened, and with it the amir's allies there, the amir turned again to the merchants, renewing the post-oil arrangement with them, using the occasion of the Suq al-Manakh stock market crash to grant them new economic support. Finally, having exhausted the range of allies at home, the amir turned outward, to allies outside the state. In the 1980s as the government felt itself challenged internally from the Shias, and externally from Iran, Shaikh Jabir turned to the US for support. The search for allies abroad left the amir at risk of a new kind of political dependence. In the early days of oil the rulers had used their revenues to weaken their dependence on the merchants. For that they had paid a price. The independence from the merchants, from domestic allies, was exchanged for a new dependence on external forces, on those who purchased oil. Independence from the merchants was bought on credit; in the 1980s the bill arrived. Kuwait, like the other oil-producing states, was by now too important an oil source and too wealthy and weak to be ignored by other states.

The National Assembly and the merchants' decline

Britain had hardly announced its intent to grant Kuwait independence before Iraq laid its claim to the new state, threatening it with annexation. Amidst rumors of invasion, Britain returned, followed by Arab League forces. British action not only preserved Kuwait's independence, but allowed Abdalla an unprecedented measure of popularity. The pressing need to present a united domestic front against the Iraqi threat in turn allowed the amir to set firmly in place the political changes he had engineered in the 1950s. In the decades that followed, the patterns established in those preindependence years were routinized and reworked. In domestic politics, the amir now devised a new set of institutions to incorporate and adapt the political realignments of the 1950s.

Abdalla began with his cornerstone institution, the ruling family. He separated the family politically from other groups by providing them with more, and more powerful, executive positions. With Fahad's death in 1959 and Abdalla Mubarak's departure in 1961, Abdalla was finally free of important family opposition. Now he used his popularity and the national unity from the Iraq crisis as an opportunity to routinize succession and accelerate the centralization and formalization of family rule. In 1962 the first cabinet was formed, small and dominated by shaikhs. In an unprecedented move, Abdalla now named his brother Sabah heir apparent. Sabah, always in the shadow of Fahad and Abdalla Mubarak, was a compromise choice, a surprise to many. His nomination broke a pattern set by the previous three amirs of alternation between the Jabir and Salim lines. Notably, the amir passed over Jabir Ahmad, finance director and, eventually, Sabah's successor. Jabir, younger and more progressive, enjoyed support from the younger and more educated segments of the population, a group whose pro-Nasserist bent worried the family. Sabah was the least controversial candidate. He allowed Abdalla to finish the project, now largely completed, of reining in the most controversial and ambitious shaikhs. Sabah's designation marked an end to the era of personality politics.

Although low key, Sabah was experienced, having served as head of police, health, and public works (deputy director) and, with independence, as deputy prime minister and foreign affairs minister. Sabah's interest in the post had been known to close observers for some time. In the late 1950s the Beirut Chancery (Sabah, like many shaikhs, summered in Lebanon) wrote that Sabah was on a goodwill offensive and "making a determined effort to supplant Abdalla Moubarak as heir presumptive."[64] He succeeded. Having consolidated the ruling family, the amir now turned to the rest of the population, connecting them to the state through the National Assembly.

In the following years the Assembly would fulfil many functions for the amir by drawing a variety of politically important distinctions. Its first function was to reinforce the division in Kuwaiti politics between the ruling family and the rest of the population. If the highest posts were retained for the amir's kin, the Assembly was the one body that was reserved for everyone else. Abdalla carefully separated the ruling family from this new institution. No Sabahs ever ran for office or served in that body. The Assembly's second function was to draw a distinction between the merchants and other politically important groups and to serve as a vehicle for balancing and, in part, replacing them with new, more controllable allies. At first these allies were simply regular citizens, outside the ruling family, outside the merchant elite, outside elite politics – those who had benefited from the distributive policies of the 1950s and had a predisposition to support the amir. With successive Assemblies, the amirs became more focused in their search for allies, targeting different groups for Assembly seats, depending on which opposition groups needed balance. In the following years beduins, Shias, religious conservatives, progressives, were all brought in. The third distinction drawn by the Assembly was between Kuwaitis and non-nationals. Because the Assembly was purely Kuwaiti, it served as an important institution for encouraging Kuwaiti identification and discouraging Arab nationalism, in its Nasserist and other forms, by separating Kuwaitis from their expatriate Arab allies. As a national institution, the Assembly was also a forum for containing opposition, a way of letting off steam. It gave the ruler an opportunity to take the country's pulse. Only when the Assembly went too far for the ruler were other institutions, such as the *diwaniyya*, adapted to play this role. Finally, as a national institution the Assembly also served at times as a foil for the amir when faced with difficult external problems – in the 1970s with the oil companies, in the 1980s with the Gulf Cooperation Council (GCC).

The Assembly had solid – and popular – historical roots in the *majlis* of 1938. In the 1950s the idea of representative institutions was revived by the merchants and the progressive opposition. In 1951 and again in 1954, the ruler held elections for the committees which administered the health, education, religious endowments departments and the municipality – with an electorate of 5000.[65] In 1955 Ahmad al-Khatib's National Culture Club proposed holding public elections for representatives of a committee to work towards an elected national assembly. Although the group was not allowed to meet publicly al-Khatib was allowed to present the ruler with petitions calling for elections.[66] The call for an elected council continued through the 1950s in opposition pamphlets and declarations.

In June 1961, with the Iraqi threat on his border, the amir announced he would establish a constitution and a new system of public institutions, harnessing and building on the popular support produced by the Iraqi crisis, which had sent crowds of demonstrators to the streets. Some ruling family factions objected, but with the two leading opponents, Fahad and Abdalla Mubarak, gone and a crisis at hand, the amir was able to push through the proposals. In August he appointed an Organizing Body to oversee the transition. In December a Constituent Assembly was elected to draw up a constitution. In January 1963 Kuwait held its first Assembly elections, returning five members from each of ten districts. Despite a party ban, a clear opposition soon developed. At the core was a progressive Nasserist faction, the National Bloc, led by Ahmad al-Khatib. Although progressive, al-Khatib's support base drew heavily on traders. Al-Khatib won his own seat in a largely Najdi district. His political ties were to traders' sons, returned from study abroad. Although the merchants kept a low political profile, they had their grievances and some of these were now expressed through the student-dominated nationalist opposition. Perhaps one reason that Abdalla tolerated al-Khatib's early radical opposition was in order to gauge the merchants' response to the new political arrangements. Later, as the nationalist opposition radicalized and as the merchants distanced themselves from it, al-Khatib broadened his support base. But in the early days the Assembly was a convenient and disguised vehicle for expressing merchant grievances.

The Assembly opposition made its debut in 1963 when it seemed briefly that Egypt, Iraq, and Syria might form a union. Twelve Arab nationalist deputies introduced a popular but unsuccessful motion to end the 1961 treaty with Britain and begin unity negotiations. The National Bloc faced a basic problem, however, in pursuing pan-Arab goals. Electoral success required Kuwaiti support. Arabs, from outside Kuwait, no matter how enthusiastic, could not vote. Because of the large number and placement of non-nationals, foreigners, even Arabs, were seen by many Kuwaitis as potential enemies, not allies. It was easier to galvanize a crowd with xenophobia, offering the expatriates as scapegoats, than as Arab allies. In 1963 when al-Khatib made an Assembly speech calling for the extension of Kuwaiti privileges to Arab workers, public reaction against him was so strong that he was forced to back off (Stoakes 1972: 203). This contradiction is basic to Kuwaiti politics. Al-Khatib apparently did not learn this lesson and repeated his mistake during the early years of the Iranian revolution, by briefly publicly backing Shias, then seen by many Sunnis as a fifth column (*The Middle East*, April 1981: 14).

Al-Khatib's inability to develop national support for expatriate issues helped the government turn the Assembly into a forum for national, not pan-Arab issues. Consequently the Assembly's first crisis focused, not on pan-Arabism, but on divisions within the domestic body politic. It erupted over the December 1964 cabinet which included six prominent merchants. In the crisis surrounding independence the amir had briefly reversed his own policy of the 1950s and turned again to the merchants, including three in his first cabinet, several on the Organizing Body, and now six in the new cabinet. The commoners in the 1962 cabinet were merchants from well-known Sunni families who had served in both the Organizing Body and the Constituent Assembly. The health minister, Abdalaziz al-Saqr, was the youngest son of the chairman of the 1921 Council and a wealthy trader and shipyard owner in his own right. Hamud al-Khalid, justice minister, and Muhammad al-Nisf, social affairs and labor minister, were the sons of traders and traders themselves, members of several corporate boards, and both honorary vice treasurers of the Chamber of Commerce. The cabinet was thus in part an attempt to placate the merchant community. It followed a year of recession felt most acutely in the trade sector.

The Assembly objected to the cabinet. It called the merchants' inclusion a constitutional violation of provisions regulating conflicts of interest.[67] After angry debate, ten deputies resigned in protest and twenty-seven withdrew, preventing the cabinet from taking its oath of office. The ruling family added its objections to the cabinet. The Jabir faction, under Jabir Ahmad, objected because they had lost more posts, in particular the key defense ministry which had gone to interior minister Saad. The Salim faction, led by Saad, likewise objected to the omission of their cabinet favorites. The amir, interrupting a vacation in India, returned home to accept the cabinet's resignation. In January he formed a new cabinet, replacing the six merchants with technocrats.

This exceptional crisis – the only successful Assembly removal of a cabinet – was possible because the cabinet itself defied the tacit rules of Kuwaiti politics: merchants were to stay out of formal politics. When the amir tested this rule, the ruling family and its non-merchant allies objected and he was forced to back down. The attempt was not repeated. Clearly the Assembly was not simply a merchants' forum as its predecessors had been. Despite their economic growth, the old families had deteriorated as political powers. Their informal access to the top declined as the amir turned more to family councils and as the family itself turned inward. Formal access declined as new institutions such as the Assembly emerged, dominated by the Sabahs and their new allies.

In November 1965, following a heart attack, amir Abdalla died. He was succeeded by his brother, prime minister Sabah Salim. The new amir announced that Jabir Ahmad, passed over for succession before, would now become prime minister and crown prince, returning the alternation to the Jabir line. Sabah and Jabir (who would increasingly run things during the amir's extended absences abroad) reacted to what was now gathering opposition by introducing stricter security measures. Encouraged by their successful ouster of the cabinet, the Assembly opposition had become increasingly vocal, directing their criticisms at ministers from the ruling family. This was edging beyond the bounds of tolerated dissent. In 1965 the amir had already introduced laws giving the information minister more leeway in closing publications and tightening club registration. These moves prompted the resignation of eight progressive deputies who were replaced by conservatives. Now the crackdown had two targets: local press and foreign workers. In May the government suspended a range of papers, from the progressive *al-Tal`ia* to the conservative *al-Ra'i al-Amm*. Large-scale deportations followed.

In this tense atmosphere elections for the second Assembly took place in January 1967. When the ballots were in, the government's count showed an overwhelming defeat for the progressive opposition – only four of their thirty-seven deputies were reelected. Ahmad al-Khatib lost to the conservative editor of *al-Ra'i al-Amm*, Abdalaziz al-Musaid. The opposition, however, accused the government of fraud. A series of election irregularities turned up – ballot stuffing, miscounts, gerrymandering (Al-Nafisi 1978: 99–114). When the new Assembly opened, seven members boycotted. The loyal opposition called for the Assembly's dissolution, reapportionment and new elections. Others took their opposition beyond the official lines of debate. In January 1969, on the anniversary of the disputed elections and following an oil workers' strike, bombs exploded at three government centers. The prime minister reacted swiftly, detaining, then deporting, hundreds and erecting gallows in the Palace grounds, in view of the troublesome Assembly, the better to concentrate the deputies' minds. The rise in opposition convinced the government that it had to develop new allies. It now turned to groups outside the old trading elite: beduins, Shias, lesser-known Sunni families.

The beduins were the first. The process of incorporating tribes as political allies was already underway. In 1961, with the Iraqi threat looming, the government granted beduins citizenship in large numbers, offering social services, housing and all the advantages of citizenship and more in exchange for joining the army (historically a beduin occupation), paying tribal shaikhs to encourage members to join. The response was so overwhelming the state was unable to meet the housing demand and beduin shanty towns sprang up. By 1975 Kuwait had a shanty population of 131,275, 80 per cent beduin (al-Haddad 1981: 110). The government took the housing crisis as an opportunity to insti-tute policies to strengthen tribal identification for political purposes while simultaneously weakening the tribes' historical internal social and political cohesion. It settled beduin away from grazing land. To weaken clan ties, it mixed tribal and clan affiliations in housing. It distributed land titles individually, not collectively (as was done in Saudi Arabia), with no relation to tribal patterns. It encouraged nuclear families to leave their clans by offering marriage and housing loans on condition of resettling in small nuclear family public housing. New marriage laws encouraged the formation of nuclear families. Because the government insisted on direct contact between individual beduins and state offices (courts, municipality, clinics) for services, the tribal shaikhs' role declined.

The amir demanded one favor – electoral loyalty. As a result, a process of political retribalization occurred. The state encouraged tribes to run Assembly candidates, whom they selected through tribal primaries. This electoral tribal politicization reinforced the government's attempts to break down clan loyalties by replacing them with both smaller family loyalties and larger tribal loyalties. Al-Haddad (1981: 143–5, 163, 169) illustrates this process with the Ajman. The government restricted the number of names they could use and many changed their name from smaller units such as the family or clan to the tribe (e.g., al-Ajmi) so they would be recognized on a ballot. This was an effective policy. The same tribes, settled simultaneously in Saudi Arabia, rarely use tribal names. In Kuwait, clan names disappeared. To increase their electoral strength the Ajman in turn appealed to more of their relatives outside Kuwait to register.

In the 1967 election the government undertook a mass naturalization program, enfranchising tens of thousands of beduin. In exchange for voting loyalty, they again received low income housing and jobs in the police and army. The electoral power of the beduin rose, from 21 per cent of the electorate in 1963 to 45 per cent in 1975, their seats from fourteen in 1963 to twenty in 1967 to twenty-three in 1975 (al-Haddad 1981: 143). In exchange for these economic benefits, the beduins voted loyally and conservatively. The government had acquired a new set of allies.

The merchants and the state

By the 1960s the arrangement between the government and the merchants had to be reevaluated. It had been established during a time when the government had few allies and, more importantly, in a period when the government's role in the economy was quite limited. The recession of the early 1960s, following the boom of the 1950s, and now the growing awareness that oil would someday run out contributed to the government's awareness in developing new income sources.

The oil industry was the first area the government developed. Because oil, from the start, had never involved the merchants – or any other significant domestic grouping – the state did not have to move with the same care it had exercised in trade and construction. In 1960 the state began with the Kuwait

National Petroleum Corporation. KNPC took over local distribution, transport, refining and petrochemicals. Subsidiaries and new organizations followed: the Petrochemicals Industries Company (1963), the Kuwait Chemical Fertilizer Company (1964). In 1966 KNPC bought a Danish subsidiary, becoming the first Middle Eastern oil company to retail oil in Europe.

The government also reversed its earlier position and began backing diversification. In the 1950s, the state did not have an industrial investment policy. Now it developed an active policy of intervention in the economy. At first it involved itself deeply in areas considered crucial but of little interest to merchants, notably industry. Kuwaiti private investment was heavily trade oriented and the few Kuwaitis to venture into industry stayed with light industry. Now, to encourage industry, the state established a credit bank, an industries department, and a national industries company. In 1964 it created the Shuaiba Industrial Development Board, which offered central planning and integrated facilities and infrastructure at one location. New laws regulated and encouraged domestic industry through tariff protection, loans, and subsidized facilities.

Rather than competing with the merchants, the government offered a variety of incentives to encourage their participation. In the 1960s several industrial joint stock companies were established. These companies (whose shareholders had to be Kuwaiti) enjoyed preferential treatment in government sales. They also enjoyed an implicit promise of state support in the case of losses, as occurred in 1970 when shareholder criticism of the Petrochemicals Industries Company's financial records prompted the state to buy most of the private sector shares.

As the state expanded its role in the economy, it was careful not to intrude too far on the merchants' turf. In trade and services, the merchants were not only allowed to keep their monopoly, but received new legal sanction. The informal aid to the merchants of the 1950s was now routinized through law. The Chamber of Commerce received new powers to regulate permits for foreigners, their main competitors. The 1960 Commercial Companies Law required that 51 per cent of all companies belong to Kuwaitis. Only Kuwaitis could own businesses or property outright. Expatriates were banned entirely from finance and banking. In 1964 the government restricted the import business and commercial agencies to Kuwaitis. The Central Tenders Committee, established in 1964, was authorized to give preference to local products. The Industries Law of 1965 limited the right to establish businesses to Kuwaitis. Other laws gave Kuwaiti companies preferential treatment in state contracts. This economic nationalism largely benefited the established merchants. Government contracts went to a few old, established domestic firms. In practice, the nationals in these firms often contributed neither capital nor management. Purely paper participation proliferated. In this way, the government was able to reconcile what it saw as a national need for diversification with its earlier promise to protect the special needs of the merchants.

The one economic arena that the government would not relinquish to the private sector was oil. Here it wanted to obtain, then maintain, sole control. To do this, it needed to come to new terms with the oil companies. In this the Assembly played a decisive role. Oil became the leading issue in the third Assembly, elected in 1971. In the 1940s and 1950s Kuwait had been the fortuitous but passive beneficiary of oil wealth. In the 1960s international factors and growing domestic interest – along with a forum for its expression – conspired to give it a more active role. In 1960 Kuwait became a founding member of OPEC. From then on the government focused on renegotiating its relationship with KOC. In 1965 the government finally reached an agreement with KOC on pricing, which it gave to the Assembly to ratify. When the Assembly refused to act by the deadline, sending the agreement to committee for hearings, the opposition picked up the issue. Twelve deputies who had opposed the agreement as insufficiently nationalist resigned in protest and took their dispute to the public. Through 1966 until its suspension in May the progressive *al-Tal`ia* ran a critical series of articles on oil policy. This coverage brought the oil issue to public prominence. The government responded in two ways. First, it took the Assembly and public opposition to the agreement as an opportunity to renegotiate. Second, through the rigged 1967 election, it assured itself a docile Assembly in future negotiations. In May 1967 this new Assembly ratified the renegotiated agreement with little trouble.

In the early 1970s the oil issue reappeared in the Assembly, this time over production levels. In 1973 when the government signed a participation agreement the finance committee, again with much public support, rejected the agreement, calling instead for nationalization. The government again took this as an opportunity to renegotiate. It was at this juncture that the 1973 war and subsequent price increases intervened. Within three months prices tripled. The government's support for the OPEC price hikes, the OAPEC boycott, and the 1973 war, with its residue of nationalism (the war had seen a few Kuwaiti casualties) and sense of efficacy all left the government in a stronger domestic position. In 1974 the government signed an agreement giving Kuwait 60 per cent ownership, which the Assembly ratified. The next year the government announced it would nationalize the remaining 40 per cent. Through a combination of international forces and domestic Assembly pressure the government had rapidly assumed ownership of oil. This transformation had long-range consequences. Ultimately it would change the government's position in the oil industry, moving it from a peripheral country dependent on the moves of distant multinationals to an important player in the international oil industry in its own right.

The government had used Assembly opposition to secure new agreements from the oil companies, but in doing so it had also contributed to the politicization of an Assembly opposition that it now considered increasingly dangerous. In the 1975 elections, the freest yet, a record number of candidates stood. Half the elected deputies were new. A vocal opposition soon formed over a variety of domestic and foreign policy issues. This opposition led the government to dissolve the Assembly in 1976. Four factors were instrumental in the dissolution. The first was that the Assembly had crossed the government on too many issues, ranging from press laws and oil agreements to pointed attacks on the amir and his family. The party ban may have encouraged this by polarizing politics, leading the small factions to vie for public support through extreme positions. Second, the Assembly had alienated domestic supporters. The opposition lost merchant support when it tackled stock market regulation, finance, planning, price controls, and state corruption. It lost mass support through narrowly partisan measures, such as quintupling the pension value of Assembly service. Third, the Assembly had become increasingly linked to opposition groups outside the state. Inter-Arab politics also played an increasingly important role. Students regularly protested not only in solidarity with Palestinians (the largest expatriate group in Kuwait), but also with regional opposition groups in Bahrain, Oman, and elsewhere in the Gulf. The government was particularly sensitive to internal events that affected its relations with other states (this was the usual reason for press suspensions). Shortly before the dissolution the Assembly passed a resolution condemning Syrian intervention in Lebanon and calling for a cutoff of aid to Syria. The new press law emphasized this concern with foreign powers. It permitted two-year suspensions for papers serving foreign interests and it banned papers from accepting unapproved foreign ads. Finally, Saudi disapproval and suspicion of parliaments may also have played a role.

When the usual opposition groups condemned the dissolution, reprisals followed. The trade union federation president was arrested with other union members for leafleting against press curbs and the dissolution. The teachers association board was replaced, the student union paper banned. The government also dissolved the boards of the writers', lawyers', and journalists' associations and suspended some newspaper editors. In September a new cabinet was formed which included more Sabahs. The dissolution cabinet in turn introduced several administrative changes. It created a new minister of state post, in part to replace the Assembly's functions, and a new planning ministry. In October administrative committees replaced the Assembly committees. The cabinet also tipped the balance back away from the progressives in favor of the religious forces. In the years before the dissolution the religious and progressive factions had often been at odds, in particular over women's rights. The dissolution was preceded by an Islamic law campaign, including several arrests on public morals charges. Now the new cabinet included Yusif Jasim al-Hajj, Islamist president of the Social Reform Society, in the Islamic affairs post, which only a few years before had been absorbed by the justice ministry.

Once again, the government was trying to juggle allies. This time it hoped both to undercut domestic opposition from the progressives and perhaps to coopt the nascent religious opposition. It was a good short run calculation. Despite opposition, Kuwaitis did not revolt. The bulk of the population acquiesced without protest, many with enthusiasm, to the dissolution. Sabah rule was secure. Nonetheless, the dissolution proved to be only an interim solution. The same forces, domestic and regional, which had led to the Assembly's original creation also prompted its restoration.

Jabir's accession and the ruling family

In December 1977 Shaikh Sabah died of a heart attack. He was succeeded by his cousin's son, the crown prince and prime minister Jabir Ahmad. The new amir was well-prepared for the job, to which he had aspired for years. The British had spotted him as a likely ruler as far back as the early 1950s.[68] He had been handling financial affairs since the late 1950s. As an active prime minister he had been involved closely in state affairs. He had a reputation for hard work, detail, and punctuality. He even summered in Kuwait. Because Sabah in his recent years of illness had gradually relinquished all but the ceremonial functions of state, the transition was easy. But as the days of mourning passed the court wondered anxiously who Jabir would name as his own successor.

Three contenders appeared. On the Salim side, a strong candidate was defense and interior minister Saad Abdalla. Saad had been with the police since the 1930s. He had studied police work in England in the 1950s, then served as deputy police chief. At independence Saad became minister of interior and, shortly after, defense. The second candidate was also a Salim, the powerful but controversial Jabir Ali, acting prime minister during the transition. In the 1960s Jabir Ali had served as information minister and deputy prime minister. He had beduin ties (his mother was Ajman) and enjoyed beduin support. As their political importance had risen, so had his. He played a key role in settling, naturalizing, arming, and electing beduin royalists to the Assembly. But this same policy had been at the price of antagonizing the Saudis who would have preferred the Ajman to settle on Saudi territory. Jabir Ali was ambitious and contentious. From 1971–5 he stayed out of the cabinet after being offered only the information post, returning as information minister and deputy prime minister. Since the Assembly dissolution in 1976 he had pressed for the separation of the prime minister and crown prince posts. Some now speculated that the amir would separate the two, perhaps giving one to Jabir Ali. Like Saad, Jabir Ali was older than the amir; there was no reason to think either would succeed him. The appointment would clearly leave to the future a generational succession crisis. The third possibility was that Jabir would dispense with the alternation. He himself had been passed over in 1962 for another Salim. Perhaps he would take that as precedent and appoint as crown prince another Jabir. If so, the clear candidate was his brother and close advisor, foreign minister Sabah Ahmad. Or, perhaps if the posts were separated, Sabah Ahmad would become prime minister.

Jabir Ahmad made his decision with unexpected speed. After a heated family council in which Jabir Ali's supporters walked out in anger, the amir named Saad crown prince and prime minister. He then named a cabinet. Jabir's decision indicates how far the ruling family as an institution had evolved. The Jabir–Salim division, which in the 1930s and 1940s threatened to tear the regime apart, had evolved into a succession mechanism. Centralization of political and administrative power at the apex of the family was now also routine. Jabir exercised control of the state through his immediate family. Several brothers were now well placed: Sabah Ahmad, foreign minister and deputy prime minister; Khalid, minister of palace affairs; and Nawaf, interior minister. Another brother, Mishaal, headed police security, and the youngst brother, Fahad, became head of Kuwait's Soccer Association, taking the team to the World Cup Finals. On the Salim side were the prime minister and crown prince Saad, the reluctant information minister Jabir Ali, and defense minister Salim Sabah. Jabir Ali's brother Salim was also head of the National Guard. Central control was now exercised with discretion. Only the most powerful ministries were placed under Sabahs, and that sufficed.

Administrative reform

The amir also moved quickly on civil service reform. In the 1960s, independence had catalyzed a series of institutional changes. Independence naturally necessitated the creation of new foreign policy institutions, starting with the transformation of the Political Residency into a diplomatic mission. A foreign affairs ministry was now established and Kuwait entered into formal relations with countries around the world and joined a series of international organizations. Kuwait, militarily weak, also set about developing foreign aid as a pillar of foreign policy, beginning with the Kuwait fund for Arab Economic Development. Defense was likewise affected both by independence and the Iraq crisis. On independence, Kuwait had no navy, an armed force of 2500 (including 900 beduin) with no combat experience, equipped with four planes and four helicopters (*New York Times*, 27 June 1961). During the crisis the amir quickly armed several thousand beduin, formed a National Guard and established a Supreme Defense Council. The crisis, however, illustrated Kuwait's military dependence. In the following decades, the amir spent heavily on developing a defense force and especially an air defense system. By the early 1980s, Kuwait's forces numbered over 12,000 (*al-Majalla*, 7 July 1984: 11).

The growth of the state's role in the economy coupled with the rulers' use of bureaucratic posts as a form of income distribution had catalyzed tremendous but essentially disorganized administrative growth. Despite several starts, Kuwait had little formal planning and a weak institutional framework. The first reforms began in 1960 under Saba Shiber, a Palestinian advisor in the public works ministry. He was instrumental in controlling the damage of the 1950s. The next step came in 1961 when then finance minister Jabir Ahmad asked the International Bank for Reconstruction and Development (IBRD) to visit Kuwait. Their criticism of the public sector included inappropriate hierarchies, a proliferation of separate agencies answering directly to the Supreme Council, a lack of coordination, little delegation of authority and large numbers of unqualified personnel. No distinction existed between public and private interests. The IBRD report said:

> no clear-cut separation has yet been made between the public duty and the private interest of the civil servant. Many officials in the higher ranks . . . are also still actively participating in commercial and other private activities. This has its counterpart lower down the scale in the employment of civil servants out of office hours in private jobs such as taxi driving, small trades and the like. This is openly recognized and is considered not at all incompatible with the position of civil servant. (IBRD 1965: 39)

Conflict of interest was as much an issue in the bureaucracy as in the Assembly. The IBRD visit was followed by a new development plan for 1967–71, in turn followed in 1970 by a comprehensive plan which faded after a splash of publicity. This was followed by a new Planning Board in 1975, a new set of civil service requirements, and a new five-year plan in 1976. This tinkering, however, while it did allow the state to continue its distributive functions, did not solve the new problems of rapid, disorganized bureaucratic growth.

In the 1970s, growing oil revenues prompted an increase in state growth. The recession of 1977, combined with Jabir's accession, provided the occasion for a new set of administrative reforms. The first wave culminated in a new civil service law, the second in an oil sector reorganization. In the oil sector, ownership of KOC was assumed in 1977 and expansion begun. The success of Kuwaiti policy in this area owes something to the attention given it by the amir, who began his training in the field as liaison with Gulf and British Petroleum in the 1950s. Kuwait began with the foreign-owned portions of the oil industry, Gulf and British Petroleum, and from there moved to buy up the locally owned private shares of groups connected directly to the industry (e.g., the Kuwait Oil Tankers Company). As the state assumed control not only of production, but of up and downstream operations as well, new administrative structures emerged. Through the 1970s a debate developed over whether the oil industry should be centrally controlled or its component parts run autonomously. The state, unsure what policy to follow, rapidly established several overlapping organizations.

This expansion in government functions quietly but radically changed the nature and goals of administrative reform. As the government became more complex, policy became aimed at improving efficiency. Manpower planning moved in a few decades from the realm of opportunity (to go to new schools) to sanctions (or else forgo promotion). Policies also emerged aimed at limiting corruption. Fiefdoms at the top existed, to be sure, but not the unchecked empires of the 1950s. Gone were the machines of Abdalla Mubarak and Fahad Salim. In the 1970s when a scandal rocked the oil industry (involving kickbacks between ministry officials, local agents, and oil clients, mainly smaller independents, who reportedly paid bribes of up to 10 cents a barrel), investigations resulted in the eventual ouster of the oil minister, Abdalmuttalib al-Kazimi, in 1978. Corruption of the highest order still occurred but it was no longer allowed to expand unchecked.

In the end the government would not tolerate uncontrolled bureaucratic proliferation in matters it considered vital. Bureaucratic control in general was a problem, but in the oil sector it was critical. Here the ruler devoted greater efforts to assure control. In 1980 he finally unified the oil industry into the Kuwait Petroleum Corporation, under the oil minister. KPC restructured the industry, expanded exploration, drilling, production, tanker capacity, and refinery modernization. In 1981 it bought a US corporation, Sante Fe International, whose subsidiaries included Braun, a high-tech engineering firm. By 1982 Braun had received several large state contracts, confirming western fears of shrinking Kuwaiti markets. In 1982 KPC bought into Gulf's European distribution system, giving it a refinery and hundreds of gas stations, through which it now marketed Kuwaiti oil directly, under the logo Q8. It also expanded petrochemical holdings. In 1987 it even tried to buy 22 per cent of British Petroleum, but was blocked by British courts. By 1987 Kuwait had an expanding marketing network which included refineries and 5000 gas stations in seven European and a few South Asian countries. By 1987 only 10 per cent of Kuwait's oil was sold as crude, formally regulated by OPEC pricing (*Wall Street Journal*, 25 June 1987: 13). In 1986, when oil prices collapsed, Kuwait's diversification had left it somewhat insulated from the market forces which shook other oil producers. It was clearly Kuwait's objective to become competitive in upstream and downstream facilities with the oil majors. By the late 1980s Kuwait seemed well on its way to becoming a major player in the international oil market. Kuwait also developed a small bureaucracy to handle its increasingly large and diverse foreign investments which now ranged from Spanish industry and German pharmaceuticals to British and US property. By the 1980s Kuwait was earning more from these investments than it was from direct sales of oil: in 1987 Kuwait's foreign investments generated $6.3 billion, oil $5.4 (*The Economist*, 26 March 1988: 59). By choosing to invest in oil diversification and foreign markets rather than in local development, the rulers had decided to reproduce the *rentier* nature of the oil economy through investment abroad rather than face the risks, political as well as economic, of local development. This choice has generated a substantial non-oil income, but one which, like oil, continues to flow directly to the state, reinforcing the rulers' oil-generated independence from other elites, but at the cost of dependence on distant financial markets.

Suq al-Manakh and the merchants

As Kuwait's dependence on foreign markets increased, the ruler moved to reassure the established merchants that he would continue to protect their economic interests at home. The Suq al-Manakh stock market crash in the early 1980s gave Jabir the opportunity for this reassurance. It allowed him not only to formally reacknowledge merchant economic institutions, such as the Chamber of Commerce, but also to remove the old merchants' new economic competitors from a niche that they were trying to build for themselves in the new economy.

The Suq al-Manakh crisis had its roots in the financial developments of the 1970s. As Kuwait's income grew, a large financial sector had developed, with new companies in banking, investment, insurance and real estate. In the 1960s, government regulation followed the growing financial market. The first laws on the securities market were introduced in 1962. In the 1970s Kuwait's financial sector changed radically. Lebanon's decline as the Arab banking center, which accelerated with the civil war and the parallel development by Gulf Arabs of their own banking capacity, brought business to the Gulf. By the mid-1970s an informal division of labor had emerged in the region. Bahrain became the money market center, Dubai the center for merchant banking. Kuwait, with a bond market, a stock exchange, and more highly developed financial institutions became the investment center (Wilson 1983: 100).

The influx of money and the relative lack of local investment opportunities led to a rise in stock trade. Both the number of transactions and the price of stocks rose steadily. Transactions were large, usually with a minimum of 1000 shares, excluding the small investor (Sabah 1978: 85). In 1973 speculation prompted the central bank to ask banks to observe a credit ceiling. In 1974 the state introduced a 25 per cent liquidity requirement, suspended forward market transactions, and formed a committee to study shareholding companies. But trading and speculation continued.

In 1977 the boom crashed. Prices plummeted, trading fell off, and hundreds of merchants faced bankruptcy. The state responded by bailing them out. After consulting the Chamber of Commerce it introduced a stock market, lifted some of its earlier restrictions, and ordered local banks to extend loans, with the government paying the interest. It also bought shares at low prices to shore up the market. Having revived the market, it then introduced stricter regulations, including the exclusion of companies registered outside Kuwait. Ironically these measures were only too effective. They contributed to the development of an alternative market, known as the Suq al-Manakh after the building where the trading occurred. The nature of the trading in the official market and the old family domination through large blocs of privately traded shares also encouraged Suq al-Manakh. The Suq appealed to the small investor, since its minimum investment was less than half that of the official market. It dealt primarily in the shares of companies banned in the official market, companies often lacking both records and assets, owned by Kuwaitis but registered elsewhere in the Gulf, usually the UAE or Bahrain.

From the beginning the government had an ambiguous attitude toward Suq al-Manakh. It did not officially sanction the market, but neither did it close it. Among the market's highrollers were ruling family members, a few of whom (Khalifa Abdalla, Duaij Jabir Ali, and Muhammad Khalifa, the oil minister's brother) were later badly caught when the market collapsed. Then, too, some in the government saw the market as a harmless, distracting entertainment, even as a beneficial way to redistribute wealth among the Kuwaiti population. It was a national sport, so the government tolerated the market.

The weakness of the market was not just that companies often existed only on paper, but also that speculation increasingly involved the widespread use of forward dealings – postdated checks carrying premiums of 25 to 500 per cent. Stocks were transferred immediately against checks written two or three years in advance. The arrangement was based on trust; postdated checks had no legal status and could be cashed immediately. The first wave of expansion came in 1981, fueled by land purchases, easy bank credit, and unstable international markets. Share prices quickly doubled and quintupled as billions of dinars changed hands. By the end, tens of thousands of Kuwaitis were involved, from ruling family members, through at least four ministers, down to newly settled beduin cab drivers and Kuwait University students.

In 1982 the market began to sag. The Gulf war, the end of Ramadan, a tightening of local credit, all contributed. In August the unthinkable happened: someone cashed a postdated check and it bounced. The crash started. Within weeks the system was swamped with billions of dinars in claims and counterclaims.

The government was slow to develop a policy on the crisis. The cabinet was split between the hardliners, represented by Abdallatif al-Hamad, finance minister, and those who wanted to bail the investors out, represented by Yusif al-Marzuq, head of the Chamber of Commerce. Al-Hamad pressed for prison sentences from the start. He told the press he expected a hundred people to go to jail (*The Economist*, 4 December 1982: 86). He had the support of the press and the Assembly which criticized the government for favoring the big dealers, calling for criminal proceedings, not arbitration committees.

The government's first step was to create the Kuwait Clearing and Financial Settlements Company, following Chamber of Commerce proposals, to register and net out postdated checks. Voluntary groups also carried out other clearing operations. The government then ordered the central bank to extend some credit. It moved to help the small investor by buying shares. It required registration of all postdated checks and created government arbitration boards empowered to freeze accounts and passports.

The real problem lay with the large investors. Eight dealers alone accounted for two-thirds of the claims. Jasim al-Mutawwa, whose bounced check had triggered the crash, accounted for nearly half. These eight received special attention. The board froze their assets and passports. In December the Chamber of Commerce announced a plan for the larger dealers. The Chamber had a history of settling small commercial disputes. Its rulings had often been used as the basis for legal judgments by Kuwaiti courts. It now invited dealers to give it a mandate and many signed on. The Chamber worked alongside the state board, handling the cases more amenable to voluntary settlement. Its plan involved the writing down of premiums 25–50 per cent, in keeping with a growing consensus among dealers that some writing down of premiums was needed. But talks stalled. By January the government's patience had run out. It ordered dealers who had moved assets abroad to liquidate and repatriate. It announced that a dozen dealers would go to court. It placed under house arrest sixty dealers who accounted for the bulk of the postdated checks. It started confiscating luxury cars. It also set up a fund to settle debts and assume the large dealers' assets. With this warning, others were again encouraged to work out voluntary settlements. Many did.

In July the amir called an extraordinary Assembly session on the crash, extraordinary indeed in July – only sixteen deputies were in Kuwait: the government had to call around Europe for a quorum. Optimism set off by the Assembly recall revived the Suq al-Manakh trading, right down to postdated checks, leading to a stern government warning. In August the Assembly passed a bill settling debts at the market prices at transaction plus a premium of no more than 25 per cent. The cabinet also approved a new bill regulating the stock market. These bills, effectively lowering the debts, precipitated al-Hamad's resignation. Even under the new law, over 100 dealers were unable to pay. In September the first dealer was jailed for a Suq al-Manakh default.

The Manakh crash sent shock waves through the economy. Finance and insurance companies, which played a prominent role in both markets, were deeply affected. Among the few untouched were Kuwait's Islamic Finance House. Kuwait's neighbors who had dabbled in the market were also hurt. The crash badly damaged Kuwait's investment climate and international reputation. Some American banks stopped granting Kuwaiti companies credit. The crisis also increased the state's role in the economy, reversing two years' effort by al-Hamad and others to introduce austerity measures.

The Manakh crash was a crisis for many, but for a few, an opportunity. For the government it was an opportunity to reestablish its link with the older merchants. This group played an important role in the resolution of the crisis. Their Chamber of Commerce negotiated many settlements and they provided many of the members for the government arbitration boards. For many established merchants, it was a chance to grow still wealthier. Many of the older merchants who dominated the official market adopted a hardline position. As one US embassy cable noted, "established merchant families are eager for the stock market nouveau riche to be nailed to the wall" (Epstein 1983: 18). As dealers were forced to liquidate assets a significant transfer of wealth occurred. Many felt the largest merchants profited most, the ones who dealt on the official exchange, with the least exposure on the Manakh. In the following years, the merchants consolidated their position. They were able to use the recession prompted by the crash and then the falling oil prices to promote protectionist policies in the government. As the recession deepened, the Chamber of Commerce promoted and obtained tariff protections and other economic support. Government advisory committees relied increasingly on the reports and staff of the Chamber of Commerce (*al-Majalla*, 10–16 November 1984: 36). At the end of 1986 the government dusted off an old policy, announcing that it would resume high levels of expenditures on land purchases, earmarking an additional $340 million a year, in an effort to stimulate the economy (*MEED*, 20 December 1986: 17). The older merchants had thus benefited from the crisis. For Kuwait as a whole, however, the Suq al-Manakh crisis was increasingly overshadowed by the Iranian revolution and Gulf war.

The Iranian revolution and domestic alliances

In late 1978 UFOs were sighted up and down the Gulf. In Kuwait one landed briefly at an oil-pumping station near Umm al-Aish. A special ministerial committee was formed to investigate the sighting (*Arab Report and Record*, November 1978). Amid such excitement it was hardly noticed that Kuwait had refused asylum to an exiled Iranian dissident, the Ayatolla Khomeini. Three years later his planes were bombing Umm al-Aish.

The Iranian revolution had an inevitable impact on Kuwait. Kuwait's development policies and small domestic manpower base necessitated foreign workers. When the revolution erupted, Kuwait's 30,000 Iranians received it with joy. In February 1979 the Iranian embassy in Kuwait was the first to recognize the regime. That month Iranian merchants in Kuwait closed their businesses in sympathy with the Ayatolla's call for a general strike. In March when 10,000 Iranians voted at their embassy on a referendum on the new republic, clashes left a handful dead and dozens wounded. As long as the revolution was in Iran it could still be treated as a foreign policy issue. Kuwait tried to treat it as such; in July, Kuwait's foreign minister paid his first visit to the

Islamic Republic. But the revolution was not just a foreign policy issue. Kuwait's Shias formed a structural area of permeability. The revolution became an organized domestic issue as a result of previous political decisions. When the amir had sought allies outside the merchants, one of the groups he had turned to was the Shia population. He had relied on them to balance both the merchants and the progressives. But by developing new allies he had inadvertently politicized them.

This was not the first politicization of the Shia community, but it was the first in some time and the first on such a scale. Shias had demonstrated in force in 1938 during the *Majlis* Movement. Tension had reemerged in the early 1950s when the decline in work at Abadan had led to an influx of Iranian Shias, to the alarm of Kuwait's Sunnis. Kuwait's Shias, in turn, were concerned over their virtual disenfranchisement from the electorate that voted for government department committees in the early 1950s.[69] But when Shias demonstrated in 1938 and at other times, they were under the control of established Shia leaders, large merchant families like al-Kazimi, Marifi, Bahbahani, Qabazard. In recent years the state had felt sure enough of its control to encourage sectarianism as a counterbalance to radicalism. With the government's support, including redistricting, Shias won ten seats in the 1975 Assembly. The government, apparently confident that the Shias would be controlled by their established leading families, failed to anticipate and later assess the mass appeal of revolutionary Iran and the domestic consequence of encouraging sectarianism. When the government did realize the danger, it overreacted.

With the revolution, the Shia community became much more of a mass political movement. In January 1979 the US Embassy in Kuwait noted the amir's concern "about the spread of shi'ite troubles to Iraq, and perhaps beyond" (Muslim students: 75–6). In September 1979 large Shia demonstrations in Kuwait followed similar protests in largely Shia Bahrain. Now the Shias, comprising the poorest of admittedly wealthy Kuwaitis – drivers and small merchants – met spontaneously in mosques, giving a mandate to a new set of leaders. At first their grievances were religious: they had only a few mosques, their only mosque in one town had been damaged by an angry crowd, they were forced to submit to Sunni law. Then their mosque sermons became more political. In 1979 after several confrontations, the ministry of religious affairs ordered prayer leaders to restrict themselves to religious topics and avoid politics (a distinction that was becoming increasingly hard to draw), inter-Arab disputes, and criticism of people or factions.

The official position was that Kuwait's Shias were loyal: problems were caused by outside agitators (*al-Majalla*, 7 July 1984). But in September 1979 the government watched the Shia demonstrations and decided enough was enough. That month after the Ayatolla had called on Abbas al-Mahr (reportedly a maternal nephew of the Ayatolla) to lead the Shia Friday prayers in Kuwait, the government arrested him, charging him with seditious mosque speeches. It quickly deported him and his family to Iran (*Middle East Contemporary Survey*, *MECS*, 1979–80: 404; 1981–2: 451). In Kuwaiti style, they were allowed to put their business and financial affairs in order, appointing local overseers. The deportations were followed by a new public assembly law. In November, following the attack on the Grand Mosque in Mecca, which included four Kuwaitis among the rebels, the Kuwaiti government instituted a crackdown on undocumented workers, expelling thousands. When thousands rallied before the US embassy in support of the revolution, the police showed no hesitation in dispersing the crowd and arresting demonstrators. The revolution, the government feared, was coming to Kuwait.

If the revolution was to be kept at Kuwait's door, then Kuwaiti nationals would have to be separated from dissident expatriates. In order to divide Kuwaitis and expatriates (both Sunni and Shia), the government again turned to an institution from the past, the National Assembly. The revolution entered Kuwaiti politics not only through Shias, resident Iranians and, initially, some activist religious Sunnis who supported the general Islamic nature of the regime, but also as an example of a ruler overthrown by a disenfranchised people. Pressure for liberalization from progressives and intellectuals also played a small role.

Regional instability prompted the state's policy, but policy choices of earlier decades shaped the nature of the response. Among the institutional legacies of earlier choices was the Assembly. In a moment of crisis, the government reacted in an historically reliable way. It broadened its support base and tried to encourage a rift between Kuwaiti nationals and expatriates. Just as the amir had created the Assembly in the early 1960s in part in response to the Nasserist opposition, so too the amir hoped to again contain the importation of regional ideologies, through this proven institution. It was a political risk. A more open system would make Kuwait still more permeable to foreign influences. The Assembly was an attempt to strike a deal with the public – to tolerate internal dissent in exchange for excluding discussion of foreign issues.

Saad, the force behind the restoration, began consulting local leaders in 1979. In 1980 he appointed a Constitutional Review Committee which included everyone: al-Khatib supporters from the first Assembly, eight Shias and five beduin. In August the committee announced that elections would be held in February. A month later the Gulf War began. The amir moved ahead with election plans. In an effort to reduce Shia and progressive electoral strength, new electoral constituencies were created. The elections produced a conservative victory. Institutional changes (redistricting, registration) sufficed. Few reports of election irregularities as in 1967 appeared. Tribal leaders took twenty-three seats. Arab nationalists, including al-Khatib, lost. Their weakness lay in the redistricting, in their support of Kuwait's Shias (opening themselves up to criticism of national loyalty or opportunism), and a government pay rise shortly before the election. The Sunni religious conservative candidates won, but redistricting had carefully split the Shia vote and only four Shias won, although they had put forward almost a third of the candidates. Soon all four were openly pro-Khomeini.

The opposition that emerged this time was nonetheless religious conservative, with five Sunni Islamists at its core. The religious Shias had not won, but they had helped catalyze a Sunni religious identification. The religious opposition, the Islamists, comprised two streams, the Muslim Brotherhood oriented Social Reform Society and the Salafiyyin of the Islamic Heritage Society. When the government responded by removing religious representation from the cabinet (removing the two Social Reform Society ministers, Yusif Jasim al-Hajj and Abdalla al-Mufarrij in religious affairs and justice) the religious opposition took their case to the Assembly. Their first issue was to have Islamic law recognized as "the" rather than "a" principal source of law. They also voted down women's suffrage and passed a bill restricting naturalization to Muslims. In 1982 they supported a ban on public Christmas celebrations and considered a proposal to veil Kuwaiti women. In 1983 they banned diplomatic alcohol. Outside the Assembly, Islamists took over the student union, teachers' union, half the elected cooperative council seats, three of ten municipality seats, and many of the four dozen clubs. The government responded to the Islamist wave by taking a more Islamist posture itself, tightening the ban on alcohol, increasing religious broadcasting, and supporting the Islamic Finance House. This first phase of cooptation lasted until 1983.

The turning point in both the public and the government view came in December 1983 when a series of six car bomb attacks occurred at the US and French embassies, the airport, a residential area, two ministries and the indus- trial area, killing five and wounding dozens. The attack was tied to al-Dawa, a Tehran based Iraqi Shia opposition group. The group's objective was to express opposition to Kuwait's support for Iraq in the war. The attack ended the govern- ment's efforts to coopt the Islamists. It now began a full-scale attack on the religious opposition. In 1984 a state security court convicted seventeen men in connection with the attack. Most were expatriates, Iraqis and Lebanese; almost all were Shia (although one was possibly a Maronite; Amin 1984: 16–17). Their presence in Kuwaiti jails prompted continuing political violence to obtain their release, including the 1985 hijacking of a TWA flight, and 1984 and 1988 hijack- ings of Kuwaiti airliners.

The 1985 election focused the recent concerns of Kuwaiti politics, turning them into campaign issues. The government for its part was particularly anxious to control the Islamists. The campaign began in the shadow of the 1984 trials. The government showed its concern with the religious movement by putting its tacit support behind the one group capable of deflecting it – the progressives. It is evidence of the state's concern with religious opposition that it was willing to court candidates who were virtually certain to cause it problems on winning. Al-Khatib was one of the first to be rehabilitated, appearing on public television, initially in the neutral role of Kuwait's first physician.

The election gave the Assembly twenty-eight new members, and a composition consistent with the government's aims. The progressive Democratic Rally under al-Khatib reasserted itself, taking thirteen seats (Gavrieliedes 1987: 179). Twenty-one tribal candidates won, solidifying their position. The religious candidates did not fare as well as they had hoped, returning six. Two prominent religious candidates, Khalid al-Sultan and Isa al-Shahin lost. Only four Shia were elected. However, the Assembly opposition proved much more vocal than its 1981 predecessor. Unexpectedly, an alliance emerged between the nationalists and the Islamists. This alliance gave the government new cause for concern.

The new Assembly did not end political opposition, and political violence was growing. In May 1985 the second turning point came with a dramatic and almost successful attack on the amir himself. The May attack was followed in July by the bombings of five popular cafes. With these two incidents, the state's concern with security became an obsession. After each incident the government deported several thousand non-nationals. Identity cards and fingerprints were now required of all adults. The government outlawed gatherings of over three people. Military reserve service was increased from one month to three. Security was so tight that a visiting American wild west show had to perform without its guns when airport security confiscated its props (*Washington Post*, 20 December 1985: 1). But the political violence continued.

At the same time growing economic problems both increased the level of opposition and decreased the government's ability to coopt it. At first the revolution's economic effects were positive. As in the early 1950s when upheavals in Iran were met with increases in Kuwaiti oil production, so too the government took advantage of the fall in Iranian production after the revolution. In 1979 Kuwait raised its production and that, along with the price increases, led to a 42 per cent increase in revenues for 1978–9 (*MECS*, 1978–9: 453). When the war closed Basra's port, the Kuwaiti trucking industry boomed.

The boom was shortlived. First the tanker war cut Kuwait's profits. In 1985 local insurance companies doubled their war risk rates. Then in 1986 came the decline in oil prices. Kuwait was in somewhat better shape than its neighbors to handle the falling revenues. Its infrastructure was largely complete. Its investment earnings had reached the point where they competed with, in some years exceeded, income from the direct sale of oil. Kuwait's downstream investments in retail outlets, some argued, also allowed it to circumvent OPEC quotas. Nonetheless, a decline of this dimension – oil prices fell from $30 to almost $10 in the space of a few months – came as a shock even to Kuwait, especially falling as they did, in the midst of the recession which the fall of the stock market triggered. Kuwait's support of Saudi policy – allowing prices to fall to recapture market shares – also placed it in direct opposition to Iran. The government formally attributed June 1986 attacks by Iran on Kuwaiti oil facilities to its oil policy, not its support of Iraq. By the summer of 1986, when the 1987 budget was being drawn up, the government conceded it would need to touch general reserves for the first time since the early 1970s (*MEED*, 30 August 1986: 18). The political strategy of restoring the Assembly was not curtailing opposition. Now economic problems were aggravating the political problems.

By the mid-1980s the government began to view the Assembly as a growing liability. To the government, the Assembly had one important drawback: an institutional inclination to represent. In the 1960s and 1970s the amir had encouraged several new groups to join the Assembly: Shias, beduins, Islamists, progressives. Each succeeding group, as it acquired an Assembly voice, eventually used that voice to express its own concerns, concerns that the amir did not necessarily share. The 1985 Assembly was, in the government's eyes, particularly obstructionist. It had blocked several government bills, including some designed to bail out companies caught in the stock market crash. Its worst fault, however, lay in directly attacking members of the ruling family. In 1985 the Assembly forced the resignation of justice minister Salman Duaij for using his position to financial advantage in the Manakh crisis. It then turned its attention to another shaikh, oil minister Ali Khalifa, questioning both his finances and the issue of security in the oilfields (the target of several bombing attacks). Shortly after, he too submitted his resignation, which was refused. Worse than attacks on the ruling family by commoners was the danger of a rift in the family itself as a result of those attacks. The 1985 Assembly had seen growing tension between the Salim and Jabir branches. Saad's supporters (education minister Hasan al-Ibrahim and communications minister Isa al-Mazidi) had been singled out for attack. In early 1986 Saad left Kuwait for three months, reflecting this tension in the ruling family. If Saad's family opponents were taking the strong step of almost openly encouraging allies in the Assembly, the amir felt strong measures were needed. Weeks before the dissolution, Assembly members called for the resignation of the ministers of interior and oil (both shaikhs), citing incompetence. The government did not want a repeat of Shaikh Salman's forced resignation as justice minister.

In July 1986 the government closed the Assembly, citing security concerns, excessive division, and the need for unity in the face of the Gulf War. The failure of the Assembly to coopt increasingly violent opposition, coupled with its recurring tendency to serve a genuinely representative function, its attacks on the ruling family, the likelihood of continuing dissension, given the growing economic crisis, and the opposition to the Assembly given the troubled regional environment, of other GCC members, all prompted the amir to close the body.

When the amir then formed a new cabinet, the ruling family was well represented – shaikhs held seven posts, all key.

There was little public opposition to the dissolution. The popular consensus seemed to be that the Assembly had gone too far. The public believed Kuwait faced a real security threat and seemed willing to accept the Assembly's dissolution as a way of containing it. The merchants expressed their approval of the dissolution of a body which had long ceased to represent them in a stock market rally which followed the announcement. The government was careful not to close off all lines of communication; indeed, others were encouraged. Following the dissolution Saad ordered all ministers to open their doors to public petitioners once a week. The government also began paying more attention to the *diwaniyya* (al-Amiri 1986: 12–15). These institutions, the amir now argued, were more genuinely representative than the Assembly had been, with fewer bars based on gender and nationality.

As the government shifted from representation to repression, it began relying more heavily on the police and the military, which had been developing in the last few decades. There had always been resistance to their use in national politics – in the 1960s the police chief and several officers resigned rather than use the force to rein in demonstrators. But opposition was not institutionalized and the forces continued to grow. By the 1980s a potentially powerful security apparatus had arisen. As the representative institutions weakened, it grew. It relied heavily on the amir's new allies, the beduin, who by one estimate comprised over half the military force as early as the mid-1950s (*Washington Post*, 20 December 1985: 19).

Increasingly, the Shias were the target of this force. Before the 1983 bombings the state's official position had been that political violence in Kuwait was largely, even exclusively, due to outside provocation. Unofficially, an informal policy of discrimination against Shias in key state positions had been in effect since the war. From the early 1980s on, high ranking Shias were eased out of key military and police posts. Other Shias were restricted to nonsensitive posts. In 1986, following the Assembly dissolution, Isa al-Mazidi, the only Shia minister, was demoted from communications minister to minister of state for social services. The government now also began deporting large numbers, perhaps thousands, of Kuwaiti Shias (*The Economist*, 23 June 1984: 46; *Christian Science Monitor*, 7 December 1987: 11). Shias complained of tight security surveillance in Shia neighborhoods, of tightening quotas at Kuwait University, of vanishing job opportunities in both the public and private sectors, and of growing restrictions on communal and religious life. These complaints increased the Shias' sense of political isolation. Soon even the established Shia families were beginning to identify with Shia opposition. In 1987 two Shias convicted in connection with an oil installation attack were from old, well-known Kuwaiti Shia families –

Bahbahani and Dashti. The government's policies toward the Shias was only exacerbating the problem. State discriminatory policies heightened sectarian identification even among those prone to support the regime. Deportations likewise strengthened ties between Kuwaiti and Iranian Shias – many exiled and deported Kuwaiti Shias resettled in Mashhad, the Iranian city to which a Kuwaiti airliner was hijacked in 1988 (*The Middle East*, May 1988: 6). The increased police surveillance troubled all Shias.

With the Assembly closed, with opposition rising, the government now began looking for allies outside the state. It reiterated its support for Iraq over Iran (which posed the imminent threat) financially – starting in 1984 Kuwait joined Saudi Arabia in earmarking the sales of Divided Zone oil for Iraq. Iraq, however, was not the basis for a lasting security policy; there had been too much trouble in the past. From 1938 on, Iraq had tried to nibble at Kuwait's sovereignty. In the 1950s Kuwait worried over Iraq's relentless interest in developing the Umm Qasr area, plans which always seemed to involve cession of Kuwaiti territory. In 1956 Shaikh Abdalla had even rejected an Iraqi plan to supply water from the Shatt al-Arab, because he felt it was leave Kuwait too dependent on Iraq.[70] With independence in 1961 the new Iraqi regime revived its claim with a new insistence. Iraq did not recognize Kuwait until the first republican Iraqi regime was in turn overthrown in 1963. Even then territorial claims and clashes continued into the seventies. Because Iraq could not be counted on, Kuwait also looked outside the Gulf. Economic considerations reinforced the policy. The alignment with Iraq had begun when oil revenues were high. By the mid-1980s the policy of supporting Iraq was simply proving too expensive.

Kuwait was reluctant to turn to the superpowers, from whom it had historically kept its distance. In the nineteenth century Kuwait had balanced between the Ottomans and the British. Even after it became a British protectorate, Kuwait had retained greater room for maneuver than the other small states. The war, however, made a new alignment necessary. Kuwait feared the effect of the Iranian revolution on its own sectarian political balance. Government policies to contain the perceived Shia threat had not only failed, but backfired, making it easier for Kuwaiti Shias to reach for and receive Iranian support. From the early 1980s on, Kuwait was increasingly shaken by political violence that it traced to Iran. In 1980 Kuwait's Iran Air offices, then the Iranian embassy were bombed. The summer saw attacks on the London KOC office, the hijacking of a Kuwait Airways jet, and an attack on the paper *al-Ra'i al-Amm* that left one dead. In November Iranian planes dropped bombs on Kuwait's border area. In 1983 the US and French embassies and government sites were bombed by an Iranian supported group. In 1984 another Kuwaiti plane was hijacked to Iran. In 1985 the amir was attacked and public cafes were bombed. In 1986 oil installations were attacked. In 1987, despite tight security, explosions occurred as leaders gathered for the Islamic Conference, a meeting Iran boycotted. Iran was posing a continuing domestic threat.

The war was also posing a direct threat. In 1984 Iran began attacking neutral ships, including Kuwaiti tankers. In 1985 these attacks escalated. On the war-front, Iran was taking more territory with each succeeding year, coming ever closer to Kuwait. In February 1986 Iran captured the Fao Peninsula, bringing the war to Kuwait's doorstep. In October a Kuwaiti tanker was hit. This was the last straw. In November Kuwait approached the GCC with a collective security proposal. In December Kuwait approached the Soviets and the Americans. Kuwait had a history of relations with the Soviets. In 1984 Kuwait had signed an arms deal with the Soviet Union. The recent revelation of US arms sales to Iran had prompted suspicion and displeasure from the Kuwaitis. Before, and again, Kuwait would communicate this displeasure by turning to the Soviets.

However, the real prize for Kuwait was US involvement. The US was well-positioned to assume a greater level of involvement. Having lost one of its two Gulf pillars in Iran (the other being Saudi Arabia), US policy was in a state of flux. At the same time the 1979 Soviet invasion of Afghanistan had prompted a renewed US presence in the Gulf. Perhaps the Kuwaitis assumed the US would reason along the same lines as Britain had in the 1950s, when in arranging to reflag Kuwaiti ships the Political Agent had written, "since we should no doubt be held responsible by the outside world for Kuwaiti-owned merchant ships we ought presumably to try to secure that they are registered as British ships."[71] But the Kuwaitis could not clinch that involvement without producing a Soviet threat. In late 1986 Kuwait approached both powers about reflagging. In January 1987 Kuwait presented a formal request. At first the US response was cool. The Soviets were more open. In February Kuwait announced a Soviet offer to protect its fleet. That was enough; in March the US agreed to reflag eleven Kuwaiti tankers. In July the first convoy went through the Gulf. Within days the first reflagged tanker hit a mine.

Outside support ran the risk of outside intervention. Under Britain, Kuwait had managed to limit that interference. Jakins, the Political Resident, wrote in 1950, "Kuwait is not Bahrain. It has always been more independent (as far as interior administration is concerned) and from its geographical position . . . it is much more exposed to outside influence."[72] That was the problem: reconciling the need for outside support which its greater exposure and weakness necessitated with a satisfactory level of internal autonomy. The Kuwaiti public was sensitive to this problem; the growing US involvement provoked much criticism in a Kuwaiti press long critical of general US Middle East policy. The government also had reservations; it initially opposed the growing US interest in military involvement in the Gulf. The Kuwaitis were also wary of US efforts to extract the release of those arrested in conjunction with the 1983 bombings in order to bargain for US hostages in Lebanon. The Assembly had been wary of any close US ties. Several deputies, including the Assembly Speaker, Ahmad al-Sadun, had called for ending diplomatic relations with the US and withdrawing investments (*MECS*, 1981–2: 505; *FBIS*, 4 April 1986). In August 1987 Saad held a highly publicized press conference to announce that he would not allow US bases and explain that the reflagging was simply a commercial operation (*Middle East International*, 8 August 1987: 5). Even when the government backed the policy, it was defensive. The Kuwaiti policy of obtaining support, reflagging from the US, for its threatened tankers was successful, remarkably successful. Even so, Kuwait's rulers remained wary of this foreign entanglement. As the war receded in 1988 Kuwait lost no time in distancing itself from this policy. For the Kuwaiti rulers, however, their room for maneuver is limited. Kuwait is a small power of some economic and strategic interest to much larger powers. It may not have the final word on the level of outside involvement, even if it has done well this time. The ruler is also one with substantial potential opposition at home. Jabir and his predecessors have been successful in manipulating those opponents. But where these strategies fail and the ruler is forced to turn for support to forces outside Kuwait, either regionally, to the Saudis or Iraqis, or globally, to the US, he may find he has less political space.

Conclusion

The historical transformation that has been most central to shaping Kuwaiti politics in the twentieth century has been the breakdown of the ruling coalition binding the ruler and the trading families and the relegation of the trading families to a bounded, primarily economic role in the private sector, leaving the political arena to the ruler, the ruling family, and shifting allies. On the eve of oil the merchants were at the height of their political power. Within decades however they had withdrawn almost completely from formal politics, in exchange for guarantees of their economic position and promises of still more wealth with oil, guarantees that took the form of direct aid, *de facto* redistribution of wealth through the land sale program, protective economic legislation, and preservation of the private sector, at least those parts of it of special importance to the merchants: the real estate market, construction, and services. In exchange for these guarantees, the merchants withdrew from formal politics into the economic realm.

A branch of the al-Humaidi family illustrates this process. Muhammad Salih al-Humaidi managed royal finances early in this century, collecting taxes and repaying royal debts. His position gave him political access and influence. His grandson Yusif, a municipality member, was active in the 1938 movement, serving on the 1938 Council. In the 1940s Yusif was rehabilitated and became a member of the new, weak Consultative Assembly of 1946 and, in 1947, of a government audit committee. In the 1940s and 1950s Yusif went into private business with his brother Hamad, starting with the Ford Agency. Social and family ties reinforced the political and economic bonds. Yusif also started a livestock company and the National Bottling Company with other old families, the al-Ghanims and al-Saqrs. With the ruler's private sector aid, business flourished. Yusif's son Yaqub became president of Kuwait Livestock and Ahli Insurance, and a board member of the Kuwait Dairy Company and the Kuwait Steamship Company. He also served as chairman of the Chamber of Commerce. In 1961 Yaqub, like his forefathers, went into politics, serving in the appointed Constituent Assembly. In 1963 he won an Assembly seat. Hoping for influence he was soon disappointed and in 1964 he resigned in a public protest with other progressive members. In a few generations the family had made a transition from wealthy traders and pearl merchants to extremely wealthy modern contractors. Simultaneously their political status declined from central political positions of power and influence, to peripheral political posts, and finally to opposition and disillusionment.

The merchants' withdrawal from formal politics has been accompanied by the development of new ties. These include the establishment of direct links between the state and its citizens, through social programs and public employment, and new ties between the state and historically weaker non-merchant political groupings – Islamic groups, Sunni and Shia, tribal groups, notably in the Assembly, and the progressive opposition. The most important new ally, however, has been the ruling family, which has developed from a recruitment pool to a new, centralized and streamlined protoinstitution. Sabahs continue to dominate, but the mechanisms of Sabah control are now more refined. Overall, one-quarter of Kuwait's seventy-five ministers have been Sabahs. Sabah cabinet representation has never fallen below one-quarter (Assiri 1988: 49–50). Gradually the amirs have become more selective, placing Sabahs only in key positions: the prime minister post, interior, defense, foreign affairs, information, and, with a brief intermission, finance. Although there have been fewer Sabah ministers, they continue to dominate the cabinet by holding more important posts and holding them for longer periods of time. Sabah Ahmad, for example, foreign minister and deputy prime minister, has been in the cabinet since it was first established over twenty-five years ago. The more selective patterns of control also appear in the areas of public political prominence the ruling family avoids, generally the less important posts. Outside security, few second-echelon Sabahs are in the government. There have been no Sabahs in the Assembly – clearly a deliberate omission.

The centralization of the ruling family has also been selective. Power is concentrated in a few branches, primarily the Jabir and Salim branches. With one exception (1966, when Sabah succeeded his brother) there has been an alternation of these two sides through all six amirs (seven, counting Saad) starting with Jabir Mubarak in 1915. Since independence the constitution has stipulated that the amir be a descendant of Mubarak the Great. With each alternation the second most powerful post of crown prince/prime minister has gone to the alternate and often hostile side. With the exception of this post, the branch in power has not compensated the other with cabinet seats but instead consolidated its own hold through these posts.

These historical transformations, while almost invisibly slow and gradual, help account not only for the broad sweep of Kuwait political history in this century, but also for the concrete dynamics of domestic politics today. They help explain why certain political problems have arisen and what in Kuwaiti politics makes an interest a political issue. They also explain how outside political events are assimilated into the system and translated into domestic political issues. The key issues of Kuwaiti politics under Jabir – the Suq al-Manakh crisis, administrative reform, the response to the revolution in Iran – have all grown out of these historical transformations.

The mechanisms employed by successive Kuwaiti amirs have largely worked. Nonetheless, despite the apparent successful adaptation of the regime to a radically changed environment, new problems are emerging as the consequence of these earlier policies. In particular the policies of the last few decades have almost inadvertently produced a large public administration to handle the more complex chores demanded by the new wealth and the new alliances. These emerging problems, of bureaucratic capacity and control, may be the most challenging for Kuwait in the future.

5 Qatar

At the beginning of this century, Qatar's settled population was 27,000; by the mid-1980s it had grown to over 350,000 (Lorimer 1908–15, vol. 2: 1532; Qatar, Central Statistical Organization 1987: 10). From a sleepy pearling village, Doha had become an ambitious capital of shining buildings and palm-lined boulevards. Oil was at the heart of this change. By mid-century Qatar's dependence on oil had replaced its earlier dependence on pearling. Oil production rose rapidly, from 2000 b/d in 1949, the first year of exports, to a peak of 570,000 by 1973 (el-Mallakh 1979: 41). In the late 1980s Qatar was exporting about 250,000 b/d.

As in Kuwait, important domestic political transformations accompanied oil, key among them the emergence of new groups, new coalitions and new state institutions. Qatar's pre-oil economy and society resembled Kuwait's in its dependence on pearling and the ruler's consequent dependence on the merchants; but it also had important differences: a weak trade sector and a concomitantly weak grouping of merchants. These differences had political consequences. Oil's broad impact was the same; its revenues prompted similar economic, social and political policies wherever they occurred. But variations also emerged, within the constraints set by oil, as a result of the pre-oil differences. In Qatar these variations produced a ruling coalition in which the Shaikh far more thoroughly dominated the merchant community, and in which he ruled in a more troubled alliance with his large and often contentious family. This uneasy relationship with his family left him, in turn, far more dependent on British support. Oil allowed the ruler to increase his distance from the merchants, but to distance himself from the shaikhs, he needed British support. To balance the ruling family, the ruler also turned, although more reluctantly, to the national population, developing allies through distributive policies, policies which in turn produced a large, distributive state. Unlike Kuwait, however, Qatar's inherited political structures, in particular its large ruling family, weakened the ruler's control over this new bureaucratic state. Oil thus prompted the formation of similar state institutions, but in Qatar the ruler's control of these institutions remained much weaker. As oil revenues declined, these weaknesses became more apparent.

Economic and social structures

At the beginning of the twentieth century Qatar was a poor, small set of villages dependent on the pearl banks, some camel breeding, and fishing. In 1907 its settled population of 27,000 was predominantly tribal and nomadic, consisting of twenty-five major clans, largely concentrated in Doha and Wakra. The population was Sunni, save for 500 indigenous Shias and 425 Shia Persians, mostly boat-builders. There were no British subjects (Lorimer 1908–15, vol. 2: 1530–1; GB, Admiralty 1916–17: 327). The population was highly mobile and even nominally settled clans moved frequently. Most tribes had branches elsewhere in the Gulf. One consequence of this frequent migration is that the major social distinction in Qatar today remains the pre-oil distinction between beduin-identified tribes and descendants of Arabs returned from Iran. The political consequence of this social structure was that it limited the ruler's power. Clans using these outside ties could and frequently did leave. Tribal mobility severely restricted the extent of the ruler's fiscal control.

The economy was based on the pearling industry. Agriculture was impossible; even date palm production was limited. Qatar's meager resources in 1907 consisted of 1430 camels, 250 horses, and 817 pearl boats (Lorimer 1908–15, vol. 2: 1533). The pearl boats employed 12,890 men, most of the adult male population. In 1917 the British Admiralty described the economy:

The chief occupation in El-Qatar is pearl-fishing, supplemented in some places by the breeding of camels. The interests of the peninsula are essentially maritime; the men live by the sea, and for much of the year upon it; the towns and villages turn their backs, as it were, on the barren land. There is hardly any agriculture and date-groves appear to be confined to half a dozen towns and villages.. Little live stock is owned by the settled inhabitants, but the Bedouins have the average amount possessed by nomadic tribes. Boat-building is carried on by carpenters from Bahrein and Persia, and the scanty foreign trade is with Bahrein . . . and with Lingeh on the Persian coast. Pearls form almost the only export, but until quite recently . . . the arms traffic provided a profitable re-export.

(GB, Admiralty 1916–17: 328)

For revenues the Shaikh taxed the pearl boats. In 1907 the boats of Doha and Wakra paid four Maria Theresa dollars annually for each captain, diver, and hauler. The shaikh of Wakr collected MT$3400 annually, the shaikh of Doha MT$8400. Some tribes were exempt, however, as were the al-Thani shaikhs – the Shaikh's control over his family was already tenuous. The northern and eastern towns claimed independence from the Shaikh and paid no taxes. Other ports had no set tax, but the pearlers paid the beduin who guarded the villages in their absence (Lorimer 1980–15, vol. 1: 2288). In addition to the pearling taxes and a customs duty (4–7 per cent) at Doha, the Shaikh also had income from personal investment in pearling. In the 1930s Dickson observed, "Ibn

Thani is a merchant prince, he derives his power from wealth accumulated by his father and grand-father from pearling and trading."[1] Because customs revenues could not cover government expenses, rudimentary as they were, the Shaikh's investment income was perhaps as important as the income he extracted through taxes (al-Uthman 1980: 23).

Compared to Kuwait, the most notable attribute of this economy was the weakness of its trade sector. Because of Qatar's small size, its distance from the overland trade routes, a settled entrepôt economy never developed. Qatar's trade sector was small; among its traders the ruling family loomed large. One social structural consequence was that, although Qatar had merchants, it never developed a merchant class. The powerful trading families of Dubai or Kuwait were unknown here. A second consequence was that Qatar had, before oil, no emerging working class. The local divers did not double as sailors, as they did in the more settled merchant towns. Some were slaves; they returned to their owners' households when the pearling season ended. Others returned to the desert economy. There were thus no economically organized groups in society with sufficient autonomous power and identity to challenge the ruling family. Because workers were not as deeply obligated to the merchants as their counterparts elsewhere, the indigenous merchants lacked the control over the workforce that Kuwaiti merchants enjoyed. The merchants' weakness, in turn, limited the extent to which the ruler could rely on them to extract and remit revenues from the population. The economy reinforced the highly fluid social structure, one that generated no enduring political institutions, save perhaps that of the ruling family. Qatar on the eve of oil had few institutionalized political structures. Its regional position reinforced its weak institutional development. Tensions in the nineteenth century included recurring problems with Bahrain, which episodically laid claim to part of the peninsula; with Saudi Arabia, which exercised sovereignty over some tribes within Qatari territory; with the Ottoman Empire, which sent an occupying force; and with Britain. These interventions all served to further weaken local authority.

In the interwar period, three events transformed Qatar's economy and society, allowing the ruler to consolidate and extend his rule. The first was a new international constellation of power. The second was the collapse of the pearl market in the 1920s. The third was the discovery of oil. World War I brought a new alignment to the Gulf. Following the Saudi reconquest of Hasa in early 1913, Ottoman forces left Qatar. The Ottoman withdrawal meant that Britain could now easily bring Qatar into the trucial system. Then in July 1913, Shaikh Qasim died and his son Abdalla came to power. Abdalla's claim, however, contested by twelve brothers and many cousins, was tenuous. Up to his father's death, his relatives had refused to take an oath endorsing him as governor of Doha.[2] With the Ottomans gone, the Saudis were now the local power; his brothers and cousins could and did turn to them for support. The Political Agent in Bahrain wrote in 1914, "there is no doubt that Bin Saud would find a considerable following from the malcontents among the Qatr Shaikhs."[3] When he did, Abdalla had to find his own external ally. World War I offered new possibilities in the international arena. Reluctantly, Abdalla welcomed Britain. For its part, Britain was anxious to consolidate its power in the area now that the Ottomans had gone. In November 1916 the two parties signed a treaty (reprinted in Zahlan 1979: 144–7).

This agreement, resembling the trucial, Omani, and Kuwaiti treaties of the 1890s and replacing the 1868 treaty, finally brought Qatar into the trucial system and established the framework for the British presence. In the treaty Abdalla agreed to suppress slavery, piracy, and gunrunning, and to keep the maritime peace. He agreed not to undertake relations with other powers, nor to cede land, pearling or concession rights without British consent. Customs dues were to be no higher for British subjects than for Qataris. He also agreed to receive a Political Agent, a British post and telegraph office, and to allow British subjects to trade in peace. In exchange Britain promised, at Abdalla's request, to protect Qatar from aggression by sea, to use her good offices against aggression by land, and to let Abdalla import some arms. In foreign affairs Britain would now limit the reach of Qatar's neighbors, Bahrain and Saudi Arabia. In a concession to Abdalla's fragile domestic position Britain agreed, in a separate letter, to temporarily ignore the articles on slavery and British subjects, agents and telegraphs. These unenforced articles promised a greater domestic role for Britain, but first the ruling family disputes would have to worsen, giving Britain more negotiating leverage. In the meantime, Britain's presence was limited to infrequent visits by the Political Agent or Resident in Bahrain.

Abdalla hoped the treaty would constitute a guarantee of his domestic power. He was particularly concerned about a joint threat from his relatives and the Saudis. In 1914 the Political Agent had written, "I have not a doubt that Bin Saud could eat up Qatar in a week & I am rather afraid that he may do so."[4] Yet when Abdalla asked Britain in 1921 if he could expect protection against a Wahhabi attack, especially one accompanied by an internal uprising – his dissident brothers were now receiving Saudi support; some villages were refusing him tribute – he was told he would receive diplomatic help; Britain did not interfere in internal affairs.[5] By the late 1920s his relatives were appealing directly to Ibn Saud whenever disagreements arose. Abdalla asked the Political Agent explicitly, "I want to know if I were to punish such people, whom I mentioned, and they went to Bin Saud and asked his help would he (bin Saud) be prevented (by British Government) from interfering in my internal affairs?"[6] The answer was still no. With British help not forthcoming, with Saudi opposition tied to his internal political problems, Abdalla worked out his own arrangement: he secretly agreed to pay Ibn Saud 100,000 rs a year.

It took the oil negotiations to bring the parties to an understanding. The economic dislocations associated with the Ottoman evacuation, with World War I, and with the loss of revenues resulting from the activities of his dissident relatives, all left the Shaikh more open to negotiation. The discovery of oil in the region had renewed Britain's interest. The 1916 treaty, like similar treaties with Kuwait (1913) and Bahrain (1914) contained a clause constraining the Shaikh's ability to grant concessions. So it was that Abdalla turned to Britain. In 1926 Abdalla, at British urging, granted an exploratory option to the D'Arcy Exploration Company, a subsidiary of the Anglo-Persian Oil Company (APOC), predecessor of British Petroleum. In the 1930s British interest in the concession negotiations deepened. Britain and Abdalla had now become more aware of US competition – an American company had acquired the Saudi concession. However British officials were not yet convinced the area would produce an interesting amount of oil and in the meantime they wanted to avoid stepping on any toes: "the Foreign Office has always made it clear that they were anxious to walk very carefully in this part of the world, so as to avoid an oil war with American oil interests over what was on a long view a relatively unimportant area."[7] Saudi Arabia, aware of possible oil in Qatar, also took a new interest in the peninsula and its borders. In 1933 negotiations for a long-term concession began. Throughout the talks, the possibility of linking protection to concessions recurred. In 1934 Britain offered Abdalla the first firm, if still qualified, protection: "His Majesty's Government are prepared to give Shaikh a guarantee in respect of unprovoked aggression by land in return for grant by him of an Oil Concession to Anglo-Persian Oil Company . . . but are anxious to confine it to major aggression, i.e. to an unprovoked attack by Ruler of a neighboring State and to major Bedouin raids."[8] At this Abdalla became more interested in APOC. He agreed to extend the exploratory option. In May 1935 an agreement was signed.[9] The concession gave APOC seventy-five years exclusive oil rights in Qatar, whose borders it defined in an attached map. Abdalla received 400,000 rs down and 150,000 a year. In June, Petroleum Development Qatar Limited (PDQL) was formed (later becoming the Qatar Petroleum Company, QPC). Abdalla also requested, but was refused, machine guns and armored cars as well as a firmer promise of protection against internal uprisings. Britain did however throw its weight behind the Shaikh's faction in the family struggle, recognizing his son Hamad as heir apparent after he, too, signed the 1916 treaty.[10] Britain also demanded jurisdiction over non-Muslim subjects. Abdalla refused to renounce rights over Gulf subjects and on this Britain relented.

The windfall was shortlived. In the 1920s competition from Japanese cultured pearls devastated the market for natural pearls. As pearl prices dropped dramatically, customs revenues followed. As if that weren't enough, Qatar now had to face an embargo from Bahrain as a result of a standing dispute over Zubara, a contested area in the north. This dispute had its origins in the settlement the al-Khalifa built when they migrated to Qatar in 1766. Even after leaving for

Bahrain in the late eighteenth century, the al-Khalifa asserted a claim to Zubara and exercised some control over the Naim tribe of that area. Continuing al-Khalifa claims prompted a series of disputes with Qatar which several Residents and Agents failed to settle. Following an 1873 ruling by the Political Resident that Bahrain, while enjoying some customary rights over Zubara, had no sovereignty there, the al-Thanis occupied and then destroyed Zubara in 1878. The Naim came to transfer their allegiance to Qatar. The matter resurfaced in the economically troubled interwar years. In 1937 when an oil representative visited Zubara to survey its port potential, Bahrain protested. Shortly after, two Naim factions at Zubara had a dispute. One side turned to Abdalla, the other to Bahrain, which sent guards and a flag. When British mediation failed, Qatar's Shaikh attacked and defeated the Naim; Bahrain countered with an embargo. Shaikh Abdalla had already lost tribute from his rebellious brothers' villages, from the pearl crash, and the depression. The embargo on top of this was devastating. Although oil was discovered in 1939, World War II prevented its exploitation. In 1942 oil operations stopped. During the suspension the Shaikh received 300,000 rs a year and the pay for a few salaries. Money was tight and Abdalla had debts. To repay them Abdalla mortgaged his home.[11] A British observer wrote, "the dispute over Zubara seems to have accelerated the decay and depopulation of the Northern end of the peninsula, which the decline of the pearl industry had begun, and the villages of al Fuwairat and al Ghariya, which were formerly inhabited, like other small hamlets in the area . . . are now almost deserted and in ruins."[12] Qataris left for Bahrain, Hasa, and other points, depopulating the area by migrating as entire clans: families and retainers. The retinue of one pearl merchant, Khalifa bin Hitmi, for example, came to 200 people.[13] When the Political Agent visited in 1945 he found that many inhabitants of Doha and the villages had left. So many Qataris left that the population fell dramatically, from 27,000 at the beginning of the century to 16,000, possibly lower, by 1949 (Lorimer 1908–15, vol. 2: 1532).[14] The Political Resident described Doha at the end of the 1940s as "little more than a miserable fishing village straggling along the coast for several miles and more than half in ruins. The *suq* consisted of mean fly-infested hovels, the roads were dusty tracks, there was no electricity, and the people had to fetch their water in skins and cans from wells two or three miles outside the town" (Hay 1959: 110).

The few merchant families were badly hurt. Most migrated, those who remained faced hard times. This was even true of the two most prominent trading families: al-Mani and Darwish. In 1934 the Political Agent wrote, "Salih al-Mani is reported to be at the end of his resources financially and his wife's brother has taken her back to Zubair . . . [Salih] was hawking his motor launch round the Trucial Coast when I was there recently."[15] The migration removed the last vestige of a local trading community. The ruling family, however, survived. The political consequence of this exodus was to leave the shaikhs as the most important players when oil arrived. Thus, at the end of the interwar period Qatar had an economy badly weakened by a series of crises;a social structure, already fluid, now devastated by those crises; and a political authority that was vested in a Shaikh, but contested by his relatives, the ruling family – the only group to survive the interwar economic crises more or less intact. Even it was weakened, riddled with dissension, and propped up in part by British recognition.

The transformation with oil

In 1947 the oil company returned. In 1949 oil exports began. Production and revenues rose quickly. As they rose the Shaikh and the oil company negotiated a series of new agreements, beginning with a 50:50 agreement, modeled on similar Gulf agreements, in 1952. These agreements were handled by appointed negotiators, two leading merchants, first Salih al-Mani, then Abdalla Darwish.

Offshore oil had a separate history. In 1949, shortly before abdicating, Shaikh Abdalla gave an offshore exploration concession to the US company, Superior Oil, the first offshore concession in the Gulf. This concession prompted a crisis between the Shaikh and PDQL, which saw it as an infringement on their concession, but Superior prevailed in the subsequent litigation. In 1952 it transferred its concession to Shell. For a long time Shell's revenues were not significant. Operations were plagued by a series of practical problems and equipment disasters and Shell did not discover oil until 1960.

To PDQL the scale of operations was modest. In the 1950s the company believed that oil would last about twenty years. It did not take Qatar's oil or its ruler very seriously and made no effort to disguise this attitude. First it kept a physical distance. Operations were relatively far from the capital, at Dukhan on the west coast and at Umm Said, the oil terminal and company port south of Doha. The company representative did not live in Doha, nor did he maintain lines of communication with either the Shaikh or the company personnel. One result was years of angry confrontation with the ruler and with the Qatari labor force. Each oil agreement was painfully negotiated, each article held up for later recrimination. From 1950 on PDQL had to deal annually with at least one major strike.

To Qataris, from the Shaikh to the shaikhs to the merchants to ordinary nationals, oil, or rather oil revenues, were now everything. At first oil seemed a blessing. It brought money and, with it, freedom. Oil rapidly changed the face of Qatar:

Large investments had to be made before the first drop of commercial oil could be produced in Qatar. Practically everything, including labor and even satisfactory drinking water, had to be imported. A jetty for the unloading of cargoes, the first in this part of Arabia, was built in Zekrit . . . and nearly a hundred thousand tons of cargo had to be discharged over this jetty before the commercial production of oil could begin in 1949.

(Melamid 1953: 202)

As in Kuwait, oil rapidly replaced preexisting industry. In 1955, for the first time in Qatar's history, no pearling ships set sail.[16] The only non-oil economic activity was some small overland trade with Saudi Arabia. The oil industry itself, however, had limited impact. As in Kuwait, the operations were located outside the capital (where the bulk of the population lived). Workers stayed by the oilfields, returning to Doha in a weekly bus.

The most important change the oil company brought was money. A small amount bypassed the Shaikh and went directly into the economy through jobs and contracts, bringing with it inflation. But the bulk went directly to the Shaikh. This income triggered renewed dissent in his family of unprecedented seriousness. As in Kuwait, where Ahmad Jabir ruled from 1921 to 1950, Abdalla's long rule from 1913 to 1949 had kept the peace, but below the surface family disputes simmered. Abdalla's rule was personal and autocratic. He granted political access to court favorites and to the domestic merchants on whom he relied for money, excluding his own family, and certainly the bulk of the population, from the political process. Abdalla made one exception to this exclusionary policy. He included his second and favorite son Hamad in all important decisions, until by the early 1940s he had become virtual ruler. Hamad, however, was diabetic and his illness made him increasingly unable to handle the tasks of government.

In May 1948 Hamad died. His death sparked a succession crisis that continued in muted form for decades. With Hamad's death, the political situation deteriorated rapidly. The two strong candidates were the Shaikh's disfavored first son Ali and the late Hamad's teenage son Khalifa (who became ruler in 1972). A tradition of primogeniture would have given it to the former, a tradition of regency to the latter. Lacking both, the Shaikh settled on an uneasy compromise. Ali would be the new Shaikh, Khalifa heir apparent. At the insistence of Hamad's branch, Ali wrote a letter stating that Khalifa would succeed him. To force this compromise the Shaikh needed new allies. In November Abdalla had the notables sign a statement approving the succession decision. But once politicized, the family was harder to contain. They had their own grievances which they now wanted addressed. Oil revenues had brought rapid inflation, several hundredfold increases in the price of basic commodities. Oil also brought expectations of distribution. In July 1949 Abdalla received the first payment for offshore rights. That focused the issue. In August several al-Thanis petitioned the Shaikh for allowance increases. When that failed, they took stronger action: buying arms and threatening to riot if the Shaikh did not raise allowances.[17] So strong was the family opposition and so weak were Ali and Abdalla that they were forced to turn to Britain.

Unlike Kuwait, where a pattern of succession developed early in this century and consequently Britain was largely content with a low domestic profile so long as maritime peace prevailed, in Qatar Britain now began playing a direct role in assuring the throne. Oil made the situation more critical as Jakins, the Political Agent in Bahrain, noted: "it is obviously in our interest that the local situation should be stabilised before big money begins to pour in."[18] The succession crisis of 1949 provided the opportunity. The situation seemed critical; Britain responded quickly and forcefully.

In early August the Residency first secretary visited Qatar to assess the situation. He learned that a few days before, the Shaikh's relatives had threatened to riot if they did not receive more of the oil income. Under these threats, the Shaikh agreed to raise family allowances.[19] On 15 August Jakins received an urgent message from the Shaikh, saying that his situation was critical. Lermitte, a PDQL representative, delivered the message, adding his own embellishments. He reported that security was failing and Indians and Pakistanis were being robbed (which was not true), that the ruling family was buying arms and that the Shaikh was sending his money abroad (which almost certainly was). When Jakins visited Qatar to see for himself he found the Shaikh desperate, ready to abdicate to Ali, "on condition that he was 'protected' by His Majesty's Government. By 'protection' he meant from exterior and interior attack." Abdalla asked Britain to recognize Ali as heir apparent. In return, Jakins suggested activating the dormant articles of the 1916 treaty regarding slavery and the British presence. Jakins observed, "they both seemed to me so scared that they will agree to anything."[20] They did. On 20 August 1949, with Jakins presiding, the Shaikh granted new allowances and formally abdicated, turning the crisis over to Ali, informing Britain:

As I have attained an age at which I am unable to carry the burden of ruling I desire to abdicate in favour of my son Ali bin Abdullah who was previously acknowledged as heir apparent as stated in the letters exchanged between me and Your Excellency in this connexion and on which I obtained the approval of the British Government through you. I, therefore, declare that I have actually abdicated and throw all the responsibilities and obligations off my shoulders after which I shall not be responsible for anything. I assign the rule to my son Ali. Let this be known to Your Excellency.[21]

Both Ali and Abdalla agreed in writing to adhere to the 1916 treaty in its entirety. Ali also agreed to request an advisor. Jakins agreed to a 400,000 rs pension for Abdalla. When these matters were settled Jakins assembled some fifty members of the Shaikh's family in the palace and read them a statement on the abdication. In the afternoon he made a further announcement to a crowd of family members, notables and "a very large, representative gathering of the local population." At this ceremony Jakins, flanked by an honor guard from the HMS *Flamingo*, oversaw the reading of Abdalla and Ali's letters, along with Jakins's reply.[22] To these statements Jakins added his own announcement that, in accordance with the 1916 treaty and Ali's request, Britain would be appointing a Political Officer and Advisor to Qatar.[23] The event concluded with a salute from the *Flamingo*. Jakins was intent on dramatizing both the importance of the succession and Britain's new role. The incident was, to him, "the first public ceremony ever to take place in Qatar and I felt it desirable for reasons of security if for no other reason to impress the occasion on the public mind."[24] To guarantee the succession, Britain sent a landing party ashore – a scaled down version of the original plan (Jakins had suggested flying in a small Arab Legion detachment, but the Foreign Office decided a naval landing party would suffice).[25]

Abdalla had achieved the succession he wanted and had also rid himself of his troublesome relatives. The price Britain exacted was the activation of the dormant articles of the 1916 treaty. In a few short years British subjects, Political Agents, and telegraphs arrived and slavery was finally abolished. As in Kuwait, where in the 1950s Abdalla had reluctantly allowed in the first British advisors to contain his relatives, so too the new Shaikh turned to Britain in a family crisis. But Ali's position was more tenuous than Abdalla's in Kuwait. Britain, knowing this, exacted a higher price in fiscal and political control.

Britain and the bureaucracy

Despite the abdication, Abdalla continued to exert considerable control over his son, with whom he met daily. Ali refused to make any important decisions without his father's approval. Abdalla maintained strong ties with the Darwishes, the most important commoner family, and with other notables. He also exercised indirect control; when he abdicated he so thoroughly sacked the treasury that Ali was unable to entertain any serious new commitments. Abdalla took not only the state funds, but also the 700,000 rs advance from Superior Oil which had set off the agitation in the first place, the palace cars, furniture and anything else he could move. After abdicating, he continued to claim not only his 400,000 rs pension, but also money paid by the oil company for guard salaries, and even the accounts receivable for the period up to the abdication. Ali was forced to turn to PDQL for an advance, but by September he had spent most of it on allowances, debts, cars, furnishings and basic state expenses. For a time the British despaired of the situation, hoping to somehow maneuver Abdalla's departure from the country.[26]

That was not necessary. The 1949 succession crisis quickly gave Britain the leverage it needed to impose advisors and set in place an administrative structure. Britain started with a virtually blank slate. Hay, the Political Resident, wrote with little oversimplification, "before 1949 there was, practically speaking, no administration and Shaikh Abdullah's rule was entirely patriarchal" (1959: 109). Britain now wasted no time, beginning in late August 1949 with Wilton, a Political Officer. Plant, the new advisor, started in February 1950. His instructions from the Political Agent in Bahrain were plain:

One point however should I think be made perfectly clear and that is that His Majesty's Government's interest in the Persian Gulf Arab States is *NOT* confined merely to conducting their "external relations" even if in the case of these States a sharp dividing line could be drawn between "external relations" and internal affairs . . . Marked examples of the principles I have tried to state are finance, relations with the oil company, slavery and smuggling.[27]

Once Britain had its foot in the door, it then proceeded to introduce standard colonial institutions: a fiscal and coercive apparatus. It introduced little in the way of administrative structures beyond this.

The initial phase of bureaucratic development centered on finance and security. Plant's first duty was to get hold of the money. Hay was clear about this: "unless we can exercise some control over the ruler's financial affairs we shall never make any progress in introduction of a proper administration."[28] The problem was that Ali had no revenues to speak of. Abdalla had left him no funds. Britain estimated that two-thirds to three-quarters of the customs dues went straight to Muhammad al-Uthman, the customs director, but when Ali hired a man to watch al-Uthman, "whose style of living would arouse the suspicions of a babe in arms" his father sent the man to Persia to buy hawks.[29] Meanwhile, Ali had acquired new financial obligations: a large civil list.

Another problem was PDQL. From the start there was some tension between the British administration and the company. The differences were not fundamental, but they were real. In part, they were differences of style. Hay noted in early 1950, "owing to the absence of a Political Officer the Company have in the past, been dealing direct with the Sheikh and they no doubt resent our interference."[30] Under Foreign Office pressure the company advanced the ruler money, but then, to the Foreign Office's displeasure, continued to pay him when London wanted the money held up as leverage. Hay wrote,

Pelly [Political Agent, Bahrain] is anxious that we should try to induce the company to with-hold payments for so long as may be necessary in order to bring pressure to bear on the Ruler to agree to joint financial control by the Adviser . . . Unfortunately, it is most unlikely that the company would agree to with-hold payments at our request in this manner and I do not think we have any means of compelling them to do so.[31]

The company also fought with the Foreign Office over release of the budget, reducing the Foreign Office to dire warnings that if the company didn't cooperate, Qatar might just become like Saudi Arabia or Persia, where the government could pressure the companies.[32] The Foreign Office was also anxious to stake an independent claim on development. In 1950 Hay wrote Wilton:

I must revert again to the question of becoming independent of the oil company . . . if the State is to be dependent upon the company for medical and other services, then the company's participation in politics in absolutely inevitable; and we cannot blame them for interference . . . The state *must* have its own transport, medical services, communications, Customs, and other administration independently of the company.[33]

In the long run, Hay needn't have worried. The company resisted every opportunity to involve itself in local development.

The Shaikh, sensing the tension between the company and the Foreign Office, insisted on dealing directly with the company when the Foreign Office caused problems and *vice versa*. To influence the Shaikh, the Foreign Office depended locally on Plant. Plant, however, lacked administrative experience. He was the best they could get for the post on short notice, but he was an embarrassment from the start. When Wilton asked him to draw up a rough budget, Plant "went off the deep end."[34] In 1950 under repeated pressure Plant drew up a budget so rough it horrified them.[35] His incompetence of course endeared him to the Shaikh who, despite repeated promises, did nothing about drawing up a budget himself. As long as Plant procrastinated, so could he.

Ali, however, needed money. That meant he needed the oil company. In the end the comapny agreed to grant Ali advances only at the price of introducing some fiscal control. Reluctantly, Ali agreed in March 1950 to establish a distinction between public and private revenues and take a set share of the revenues – one-quarter for himself, three-quarters to an account held jointly with the advisor.[36] After discussion with the family, allowances were settled and checks signed. A similar agreement was worked out over customs revenues. That was Plant's one accomplishment. In April 1952 he was asked to resign to make way for a more experienced administrator. There were lawyers involved, but he left. In late 1952 Hancock, the new advisor, arrived in Doha. In 1953 he drew up the first real budget. Other fiscal measures followed, such as tax laws to cover the oil companies. By 1954 Hancock had "succeeded in setting up the nucleus of a sound system of government accounting and financial control."[37]

The next area to develop was security. Hay felt that "the first necessity in building up an administration is to create an efficient and reliable police force."[38] Jakins shared his view. The existing force consisted of beduin supporters, palace retainers, and slave and ex-slave bodyguards. Once Britain had Ali's permission, it wasted no time. In August 1949 the Shaikh reluctantly agreed to the appointment of a police officer. In early September Cochrane, the police inspector in Bahrain, arrived, followed by a consignment of rifles.[39] Cochrane's arrival "took the Sheikh somewhat aback at first. He evidently had not realised when he agreed to the appointment, that it was likely to materialise so speedily."[40] Hay gave Cochrane a broad mandate: "I have told Cochrane that if given the opportunity he should not confine his activities to the police but assist the State in every branch of the administration."[41]

The Shaikh struggled against this new force in every way possible. First he tried simple obstruction. Cochrane immediately ran into trouble when the Shaikh tried to fire a favorite guard and prevent Cochrane from going on rounds with the night guard and talking freely to people. Police finances were precarious, but when he tried to earmark a vehicle tax Ali at first refused. In 1950 at the advisor's suggestion, the Shaikh tried to ban guns on Doha, but to no avail; the ban was simply ignored.[42] Whenever serious trouble threatened, the Shaikh refused to use Cochrane's force, relying instead on his beduin. The Shaikh also offered Qataris no encouragement to join the force. Few did, the notable exception being Muhammad al-Attiyya, the one Qatari officer, and he had his share of problems.

As a result Cochrane was initially only able to put together a weak force, comprised almost entirely of foreigners, which he could only use effectively against foreigners. This force was not strong enough to maintain internal security in those areas of concern to Britain. To Britain the force's primary function was to protect the oil company. The company's security concerns included labor disturbances and theft from beduin forces, often instigated by ruling family factions. However, each time Cochrane actually tried to *use* his force, the Shaikh failed to back him and the police were forced to either retreat or face a public defeat.

The first crisis occurred in 1951 when an oil company strike pitted Qatari workers against Dhofaris. Virtually half Cochrane's force was Dhofari and when, to resolve the strike, the company Dhofaris were deported, the Dhofaris on the force also quit. The force was reconstituted, but it never received the Shaikh's backing. When the police intervened without it, as happened in 1955 against striking workers at Dukhan, they lost.[43] This strike saw the police at perhaps its least effective. The Political Resident summed up the problem:

The unfortunate thing is that the police force, which is very young, only having been in existence three or four years, knows it can rarely count on the Ruler's support against the Qataris, and therefore shrinks from action . . . It is an alien force, for apart from its British officers, its rank and file, though Moslems, are Gulf Arabs of different kinds and Adenese with some Palestinian warrant officers.[44]

Qataris knew this and used it. Generally, when crowd control was required the ruler used his beduin forces.

The force also had responsibility for routine police functions in Doha and for keeping the peace there. This peace, however, was most frequently threatened by the ruling family itself and, again, the Shaikh resisted using the force against his own family. In 1952, for example, an incident occurred between the police and Suhaim, a nephew of the Shaikh (and later foreign minister) when one of Suhaim's slaves nearly ran down Plant's wife in a truck with faulty brakes. When Cochrane impounded the truck, Suhaim, armed with a submachine gun and backed by beduin followers, stole it back. Although the Shaikh did not fire Cochrane, as Suhaim demanded, neither did he carry out what Cochrane considered appropriate action. Suhaim's punishment was to accompany the Shaikh to Beirut, where he could keep an eye on the headstrong boy.[45] By 1953 Cochrane was forced to take an extended leave from Qatar. On his return the Political Agent noted, "although supposedly fully recovered from his nervous breakdown, Mr. Cochrane still does not look well . . . "[46]

For the first five years Cochrane simply struggled with the Shaikh. Two factors changed Cochrane's position. The first was a relentless pattern of strikes that was emerging at the oil company. The Shaikh first called out the police during a strike in March 1950 when it looked as though the strikers, who numbered about 1000, would descend on Doha.[47] Although he was generally reluctant to use the force against Qataris, the pattern of strikes finally wore him down. After a major strike in 1955 in which the police were clearly bested, Ali agreed to form a Qatari riot squad for use against Qataris.[48]

The second factor was Ali's inability to contain the growing tension within his family. Reluctant as he was, in desperation, he would occasionally turn to Cochrane. The Political Agent drew this connection directly for the Shaikh, pointing out that if he didn't back the police in general, they might be of no use when he needed them against his family.[49] Britain had its reservations about using the force against the family, as Burrows, the new Political Agent in Bahrain, noted, "it would also of course be most awkward if the British-led police force had to act against Khalifa bin Hamad and he then or subsequently became Ruler," which he did.[50] But it was the only way Ali would let the police in. This first occurred in June 1952, after a dispute involving an attack by a few young men of the Ahmad faction, one very active faction, on al-Uthman, the customs director, who had accused them of importing alcohol.[51] The dispute escalated when al-Uthman, backed by the Hamad faction, took his complaint to Ali, who ordered the surrender of the Ahmad faction, which had meanwhile "mustered some 12 tommy-guns and 300 rifles in the Palace."[52] Ali was now desperate enough to turn to the police. He authorized Cochrane to give the Ahmad faction a twenty-four hour surrender ultimatum. Fortunately Weir, the new Political Officer, and Cochrane were able to negotiate a resolution which included the surrender of the youths, who were later exiled. This was particularly fortunate since they were outarmed – the police had only rifles against the family's automatic weapons. On agreeing to intervene, the Foreign Office wrote: "we consider that we should not lose the opportunity of hinting to the Ruler that if he takes advantage of our assistance in circumstances such as the present, we expect him to be receptive of our advice when it is proffered on matters affecting the good of his state."[53] This was a key incident in establishing the status of Cochrane and his force. It was the first time the Shaikh used the police against his own family. And it was a precedent; later that year Ali also turned over a nephew to the police, the first time a shaikh was imprisoned, after he had shot a former slave in a fight over a prostitute.[54] In 1954 when the police intervened in a family quarrel, arresting a shaikh, the Resident could write with some optimism, "somewhat to everyone's surprise the Ruler supported Mr. Hancock in the action which he took and there is now good hope that the police may become powerful and independent enough really to maintain public order in Qatar."[55] A final precipitant occurred in 1955 when a shaikh, on learning the police had entered a house he rented during a burglary investigation, went, armed and angry, to the police station to protest. The officer on duty was Muhammad al-Attiyya, the sole Qatari officer, who promptly complained to the ruler.[56] Following this incident Ali proposed a special police detachment for Qataris. Ali's need to rely on the police was reconfirmed in 1957 when detonators were discovered in the home of a shaikh amid rumors that Ali's new palace had been mined.[57] Family indiscipline also earned the police some support in the general population. Burrows wrote in 1956, following a number of violent incidents involving shaikhs, "as a result of these three incidents the people of Doha except members of the Ruling Family and their tribal henchmen wish to see the Ruler take a much firmer line with the young shaikhs than he has done in the past; some of the semi-educated Qataris who are normally critical of British influence have said in private conversation that colonisers have their points."[58]

Both these factors, strikes and shaikhs, came together in 1956, prompting Ali to rely more heavily on British security. In 1956 Ali faced a sudden coalescing of what had been previously disparate and muted opposition: from the shaikhs, who continued to demand allowance increases, from the oil workers, who struck repeatedly, and finally from the wave of pan-Arab opposition blowing through the region. As the regional anti-British fervor increased along with the tension following Nasser's nationalization of the Suez Canal in July, opposition in Qatar coalesced. Up to now Ali had not had to deal with mass opposition outside the oil camps, or with ideologically organized opposition. But in 1956 well organized oil strikers joined with dissident notables to forge a pro-Arab, anti-British front. At first the opposition centered on the Islamic Library, a gathering place for reformist Qataris, under Abdalla Hussain Naama. In February 1956 a Library lecture series on cultural and religious affairs took an anti-British turn, prompting Ali to ban the series and admonish the education director who had organized it. Naama now joined with other opposition leaders, including two radical, pan-Arab al-Attiyya brothers, Hamad and Khalifa (brothers of Muhammad al-Attiyya, the Qatari police officer). When they now began putting forth timid participatory demands, they were told that Qataris were still too inexperienced to take part in politics. As for expatriates, in June the government began inserting a ban on political activity in labor contracts. In July Ali sent the erring education director around the Middle East to recruit less politicized, non-Egyptian teachers.[59]

As the opposition at home grew, taking an increasingly anti-British bent, the shaikhs joined in. Many, including Ali's son Ahmad, had their own reasons for opposing Ali's British-associated commoner advisor Abdalla Darwish.[60] Seeing an opportunity to attack Darwish, they joined in, as did Darwish's other enemies – some workers and small merchants. The nationalists, seeing an opportunity to broaden the coalition, also took on Darwish. Opposition came to a head on 16 August when a crowd of 2000 marched through Doha waving Egyptian flags and shouting anti-British slogans. Ahmad, acting ruler, dispersed the crowd with his retainers, as the British summoned a landing party from a ship standing by. These events led Britain to express more concern over security. Unpredictable crowd control by royal retainers alarmed them.[61]

For Ali the 1956 demonstrations were a turning point. In September he began talking about retiring, handing more responsibility over to Ahmad. He also began spending more time at Rayan, his father's palace outside Doha. More demonstrations erupted in October, led by the Attiyya brothers who were now suspected of oil pipeline sabotage, as well as other anti-British, anti-regime activities. In October after an armed attack on al-Uthman, the customs director and a Darwish ally and in-law, Ali began arresting the opposition leaders, including Abdalla Naama (although no link was alleged to the al-Uthman attack), who was flogged, "the Ruler himself taking part in the operation," with the support of the shaikhs.[62] The Attiyya brothers were detained but released on popular demand in November.[63]

The combination of events in 1956 – the attacks on the British, on Darwish and al-Uthman – turned Ali around. These events made it clear that public security threats were emerging outside the family that were not contained in the distant oilfields. The role of the shaikhs also led Ali to reassess family discipline. In October Ali called the family together and told them he was going to see that public security was maintained and announced that the police had his backing. In late 1956 an ordinance was issued regularizing the police, along the lines of a similar Kuwaiti regulation.[64]

From then on the force grew. In 1957 Carden, the Political Agent in Qatar, could report that "the Police carried out their duties and had the necessary overt support from the Ruler."[65] By the late 1950s, Cochrane had "an efficient and well-equipped Police Force of about 1000 men under British officers, which maintains law and order throughout the peninsula and among other things guards the oil companies' camps and installations" (Hay 1959: 110). Outside Doha, the British, perhaps having learned a lesson from Jordan, also began controlling the beduin by hiring them, recruiting police from the beduin, against whom the force was originally, in part, established. Bibby, who worked for the oil company under Abdalla and carried out archaeological work in Qatar under Ali spoke highly of the force:

The network of police radio-communication in Qatar was to save us much anxiety and even expense in later years. Originally set up by Ron [Cochrane] as an Early Warning system against Bedouin raids, it soon proved its more day-to-day worth as a saver of lives. More and more the Arab uses the automobile in the desert . . . wherever he goes the police radio network follows him . . . Wherever we stopped . . . within two or three hours a police truck would nose over the horizon.   (1969: 124)

As for Cochrane, he became a Muslim and, as Muhammad Mahdi, went on to oversee the establishment of Qatar's army. Once the police were established, the British also gained some control over the courts, following company complaints that offenders, once caught, were soon released.[66] In addition to the expatriate courts, a weekly court composed of the advisor, Ali, and his son, Ahmad, was established. So by the end of the 1950s a security apparatus of sorts, backed up by a court system, was in place.

   General administration, social services, and infrastructure developed far more slowly. Plant, the first advisor, was reluctant to assume any large projects. In the early 1950s only a few development and distributive policies emerged. Under Plant a new corniche was begun, along with a new customs warehouse and jetty, police headquarters, a new airstrip, and a water supply system. In health care, he inherited a one-doctor hospital which opened in 1945 and an American Mission hospital. Ali now agreed to a British doctor who arrived with a small staff in 1951. Until the 1950s education was provided by several small mosque-based Quran schools. The first modern school, Islah al-Muhammadiyya, opened in 1949, offering history, math, geography and some English (al-Uthman 1980: 22). In 1956 the government introduced modern primary education.

   Compared to Kuwait or Bahrain the early projects were limited. The most charitable thing one could say about them, as Hay did, was that they were not carried out in chaotic haste (1959: 110). As one observer described Doha:

Even as late as the 1950s the most ordinary modern amenities had not yet arrived. Water was still brought in by tanker . . . There was no drainage of any kind . . . The weekly plane which brought the mail often did not bother to land; it would circle around two or three times and then drop its load by parachute. In the harbour there were only two small jetties. One belonged to the ruler.   (Moorehead 1977: 83–4)

Infrastructure developed under the supervision of a British engineer, appointed in 1952. The government had acquired a small refinery in 1948, in 1953 it built another, which processed 600 b/d. In 1953 Hancock drew up a cautious development plan, mindful, on the Resident's advice, of Kuwait's experience: "it is most important that Hancock should know as soon as possible where he stands, since otherwise there is a danger that he may overspend in the first year, as has happened in Kuwait."[67] In 1953 the first telephone exchange opened. In 1954 a desalination plant was built, followed by a power plant in 1957, providing subsidized electricity and, for the first time, local drinking water. Administrative organizations followed: a mechanical equipment department, a water department, new administrative offices. Much of this development spending, little though it was, targeted the poorest Qataris. Education, health care, drinking water, these services were all progressive in effect. It was, perhaps inadvertently, the Shaikh's first effort to develop allies in the popular sector. These policies also started the first spurt of state growth: state employees rose from six in 1949 to forty-two in 1954 (al-Kuwari 1978: 115).

The ruling family

Development plans, however, had to compete with the ruling family for funds. In time oil would bring the Shaikh independence from the merchants. It bought him no such distance from his own family. The long-term impact of oil was just the opposite: it actually increased the role of the shaikhs. Oil quickly politicized the family. As revenues trickled into the economy, the shaikhs became vocal in demanding a share. At first there was simply widespread but uncoordinated family opposition over the disposition of revenues. Then, as new alliances emerged and the ruler was forced to come to terms with these new groupings, a process occurred which was similar to that in Kuwait. In the early 1950s, the limits of the ruling family, both in membership and power relative to the ruler, were set. In the course of a few years, the family and its position was formalized. This was not an easy process, for the family was large, politicized and discontented.

Through struggling with his relatives and with Britain Ali worked out several principles. The first was that the ruling family, and no other, was entitled to allowances. Even this prompted dissent from at least one commoner family, the al-Attiyya, which had long and close ties of marriage and friendship to the al-Thanis. Shaikhs Abdalla and Ali counted al-Attiyyas among their wives and mothers. The al-Attiyya now put forth an unsuccessful claim for shaikhly allowances.[68] The next principle was that familial proximity to the Shaikh was the first criterion for financial claims. This principle was contested by the ruler's cousin, Saud Abdalrahman of Wakra, who for a time claimed parity with the ruler based on his father's status as Ottoman provincial representative. His family had once enjoyed some autonomy in the area: as a Qatari noted in 1914, shortly after Abdalla's accession, "at present Sheikh Abdulla is ruling over all Gatar, but in Okra there is his brother Sheikh Abdurahman who administers justice there. If however there are any important cases they go to Sheikh

Abdulla. Sheikh Abdurahman also enjoys the Customs of Okra and the tax . . . same as Sheikh Abdulla does in Doha."[69]

Saud was able to create a nuisance by interfering with the operations of the oil company (located in his territory), bringing himself to the repeated attention of the British. In the end they resorted to threats of force: "he was discouraged by the appearance of HMS *Flamingo* off Wakra, and he subsequently made his submission to the Shaikh and received 7,000 rupees . . . Sa'ud appears to have decided that co-operation . . . is more profitable than trying to squeeze the Company."[70] Saud remained troublesome from time to time. While visiting Ali in 1953, Hay commented that Saud walked in and demanded two cars – it was no wonder Ali was in debt. In 1957 on finding his house robbed Saud asserted local authority by setting up roadblocks, searching cars, and even firing toward two company vehicles which refused to stop.[71] To this day, Wakra remains a source of opposition to the ruler.[72] But in general Saud accepted the discipline that accompanied his allowance.

The relative weights of various claims were painfully sorted out. Some were prompted by the payment to Saud which produced complaints based on differing principles,

The "Bani Ahmad" complain that Ali has given Sa'ud of Wakra 7,000 rupees, and that he intended to give him only 3,000, but the Darwish intervened on his behalf. Also that Ali bin Jasim has had 6,000 rupees for a motor car, while Khalid bin Ahmad has had only 1,000 rupees, although he is "Akbar." He may be older than either of the other two, but he comes of a collateral branch, and his father was a younger brother of Jasim the Ruler, the former being his son and the latter his grandson. The question of seniority is going to provide many headaches once the money begins to flow.[73]

As in Kuwait, it did. Allowances were calculated roughly on the degree of consanguinity with the ruler, with distinctions for seniority, different mothers, and sometimes leadership potential.[74] Gradations were worked out among the various ranks.

The first big push for allowance increases came with the 1949 abdication crisis. The crisis began when one family faction, catalyzed by the prospect of revenues from the recently granted offshore concession, pressed Shaikh Abdalla for new allowances. The effort failed when Abdalla hijacked the movement by abdicating, taking the money with him. The Hamad faction, family of the late heir apparent, led by his son Khalifa Hamad (who would eventually rule) were the strongest force behind the "movement for no allocation without representation."[75] They wanted more money and confirmation signed by the ruler, the Political Agent, and Resident of Abdalla's promise that Khalifa would succeed Ali. The ruler's view, wrote the British, "is that he signed the original document under compulsion and it not going to commit the folly of repeating it as a free agent."[76] Abdalla's longevity (he died in 1957) and open support for Hamad fueled this faction's claim.

Other factions were rooted in the contested succession of 1913. The most important was the Ahmad faction, associated with the sons of Ahmad, brother of Shaikh Qasim (who ruled until 1913). The Ahmad faction played a key role in pressing for new allowances during the abdication crisis. Their spokesman was Nasir Khalid, head of security at Dukhan and later, until his death in 1986, economy minister. The Political Agent wrote, "the Bani Ahmed consider themselves rulers, and have little respect for the police."[77] Although this line never produced a ruler, it did produce two ministers, Nasir and Ahmad Saif, minister of state for foreign affairs.

Against these factions Ali stood almost alone. His father was no help: before abdicating he promised allowance increases, then left Ali with the obligation but no funds. Ali's only support was his son Ahmad, who would succeed him, and his advisor and supporter Abdalla Darwish. From the abdication on, Ali faced opposition and demands for increased allowances from these various factions in fluid alliance. Repeatedly Ali complained to the Political Officer that his family came to him whenever they wanted money and constantly sent him petitions and letters (four or five a day, at times) asking for increases. Ali also spent large amounts on presents – houses, cars – for his relatives in addition to the allowances, keeping him in constant debt. In 1950 the Ahmad faction circulated a family petition calling for a municipality, customs reorganization (to remove Darwish power) and more jobs for the ruling family. But when Ali appointed Nasir Khalid municipality director, Ali's brother Hasan and supporters walked out of the meeting in anger. In May 1951 the Hamad faction's successful negotiation of an allowance increase prompted similar demands from Hasan's faction. In July 1951 as oil workers struck and the ruler negotiated a new royalty agreement, Hasan led a family protest over allowances, threatening violence. In October Ali agreed to double allowances.[78]

New oil negotiations in 1952, leading up to an agreement with Shell in May and a new agreement with PDQL in September, forged an alliance among the various branches. In March and again in August the family presented the ruler with petitions demanding a quarter of the revenues. In March the family staged its most vocal protest yet, submitting a petition to the Shaikh with 158 signatures, almost the entire civil list, demanding their quarter of the oil revenues.[79] In October Ali sent Hay a proposed civil list doubling allowances, reminding Hay that he had promised the family an increase on completion of the oil agreement. He justified the rates citing inflation, precedent (it was, he said, still below the Bahrain civil list and his family had no private date garden income) and stability: "as long as the family is angry and dissatisfied with their situation and as long as their allowances do not meet their expenses they will continue to press their demands, a matter which will waste both your time and mine."[80] The ruler "insisted that the new allowances proposed were the lowest he could get his family to accept. He could only do that by telling them that they were what the Hukoomah [British government] ordered and they would have to acquiesce."[81] Reluctantly Hay approved.

But family demands only continued. By 1956 they had led Ali to the verge of abdicating. There were rumors that he was ready to retire from public life completely, certainly that he was prepared to hand over more and more day to day administration to Ahmad. The Political Resident placed heavy blame for the 1956 events on the subversive tendencies of the Hamad faction and the general instability of the ruling family: "it was no doubt partly this disunity among the Ruling Family, contrasting markedly in this respect with family affairs in Kuwait and Bahrain, which gave so good an opportunity to hostile propaganda and subversion from outside."[82] Ali had had enough. In August when the Ahmad faction demanded a 150 per cent increase, Ali joined his father in seclusion in Rayan.[83] In October Ali apoproached Burrows, now Political Resident, with a request for moral and, if necessary, material support against the Ahmad faction. Burrows obliged: "after a stormy meeting between the Ruler and this faction in my presence they all made submission to the Ruler."[84] Material support, in the form of rifles for Ali's retainers, followed.[85]

The family pushed Ali one way; the British the other. When protests reached a peak, Ali turned the matter over to the Resident, arguing that either Britain should set the allowances and take the flak, or allow him to grant whatever allowances he liked, however high, a position the Political Officer conceded had "a disturbing element of logic."[86] Escalating demands for allowances, factional disputes that broke into violence, all brought Britain in more thoroughly. Britain was interested both in extending control and in the ramifications if it did not intervene and family quarrels broke into open fights. The shaikhs were heavily armed and often took the law into their own hands, on several occasions shooting, and from time to time killing, other Qataris in various quarrels. This proclivity reinforced Ali's tendency to acquiesce. Because revenues were rising, Ali was able to both increase dollar allowances and limit percentages, but it was a constant struggle. Ali refused to negotiate on his own quarter saying this included family gifts. However, he waffled when it came to resisting the shaikhs' claim for their quarter, the share they were promised during the abdication. As long as revenues increased, everyone could be accommodated. But in 1958 PDQL stopped raising production. Revenues stopped rising and then started falling – from 287 million Qatari riyals in 1958 to 253 million in 1959 (al-Kuwari 1978: 117). Something had to give; it was Ali. Unable to meet or halt his family's financial demands, Ali again reached, and this time passed, the verge of abdication. In October 1960 he turned the affairs of state over to his son Ahmad.

The merchants

Through all this, the merchants remained quiet. Before oil, the Shaikh's relationship with the merchants was, as in Kuwait, conditioned by his need for revenues: customs duties and pearl taxes. Oil, by providing a new income, changed this. As in Kuwait, the revenues enabled the ruler to strike a tacit deal with the merchants, a trade of wealth for formal power. But in Qatar the Shaikh was able to strike a better bargain because the economic crises that preceded oil – the pearl crash, the depression, the Bahrain embargo – removed, through bankruptcy or migration, most of the trading families. Of the two important families who initially survived – al-Mani and Darwish – both had made their fortunes through pearling, trading and smuggling. Both were important socially: in 1939 the only buildings with electricity were those of the Shaikh, Salih al-Mani, Abdalla Darwish, and Muhammad al-Uthman (al-Uthman 1980: 22). Darwish and al-Mani survived the interwar period by parlaying their ties with the palace into ties with the oil company.

Al-Mani was a merchant family with Najdi roots. The patriarch was Salih, the Shaikh's secretary in the 1920s. When British agents and oil representatives met with the Shaikh, Salih was present. He was there at the signing of the 1935 treaty, after which he became PDQL's representative. When the new Political Officer and Shaikh Ali met, they met in Salih's house. When Bertram Thomas crossed the empty quarter in 1931, Salih's uncle Muhammad, a major pearl merchant, hosted him (Thomas 1932: picture f. 298). The Salih family was Qatar's welcoming committee. One draw was doubtless the fact that until after the war Salih owned Qatar's only radio (Moorehead 1977: 93).

When the war interrupted Salih's liaison work with the oil companies, he returned to smuggling. After the war he took up oil work again, taking several salaries as local representative, as well as a fee (1 rupee to Qataris, 40–50 to foreigners) for work certificates.[87] During the abdication crisis Salih sided with dissident shaikhs, hoping to extend their hostility to Darwish, his main competitor. In 1949 Salih gave Jakins "a very lurid account of the unsettled conditions in Qatar," and told the Residency that a permanent British representative in Qatar would be most desirable.[88] After the abdication, Salih happily backed Ali. When Ali needed to furnish the palace (his father having taken the furniture), Salih supplied some. When the new police force needed supplies, Salih handled the orders. For a time Salih was able to achieve real financial power through contracts from the company and the state.

But by the late 1940s, the al-Mani political and economic position was declining in favor of the Darwishes, to whom they were indebted, in part because of their own loans to the ruling family.[89] The decline began during World War II as Shaikh Hamad developed a smuggling alliance with Darwish. Salih petitioned Shaikh Abdalla with complaints, but to no end. The showdown came in 1949 when Abdalla Darwish got the Shaikh to block an al-Mani contract to build a canteen at Uma Said on which Salih, with oil company approval, had underbid the Darwishes. Abdalla pressured Ali to force Salih to let him in as a partner, "or rather to a share in the profits, as there appears to have been no influx of fresh capital."[90] Next, Darwish obtained the Shaikh's veto on Khalid al-Mani's request to rent a house to the British firm, Gray Mackenzie. In 1952 in the Shell negotiations Salih was not appointed local agent. Salih's ascendancy was over. Darwish had won.[91]

The Darwish family was originally Persian Arab. In Qatar it came to wealth through pearling and trade. Three brothers formed the family's core – Abdalrahman, Qasim and Abdalla – sons of a small food importer. The family survived the interwar period through their palace ties. The Darwish children had grown up with the Shaikh, attending palace Quran class together. As adults they connected Shaikh Abdalla at his palace to the rest of the world. Qasim, the eldest, was his pearl buyer. Abdalla was his general confidant. The Political Agent, who was not a fan, described him in 1944 as:

a bearded, one eyed man of between thirty and forty, clever, and with a really remarkable capacity for smooth lying. He is Shaikh Hamad's man of affairs and carries through practically all his smuggling ventures with no little profit to himself for he is as willing to deceive his master as he is anyone else. He follows the legitimate profession of a wholesale trader and holds no official position with the Shaikh of Qatar.[92]

From the Darwishes' personal and administrative connections, financial benefits followed. Because of his palace proximity, Abdalla was able to pick up 150 rs a month from Britain for information on US companies (Field 1985: 250). In 1932 Abdalla and Qasim got the kerosene concession from APOC at Abadan. When PDQL started in 1939, the Darwishes got some building contracts. During the war they handled rations profitably: "most of the 'tamween' commodities pass through the hands of the Darwish brothers at some stage, after which their disposal becomes a matter for speculation. Very little appears to reach the populace at reasonable prices."[93] During the war Abdalla Darwish worked closely with Hamad in smuggling operations, making blackmarket profits so large that Britain took over the distribution and confiscated the Darwish travel papers after several Qataris petitioned the Agent with complaints. This shocked the Darwishes when they heard it on the radio while visiting Muhammad al-Mani.[94] Salih, seeing an opportunity, suggested he take over the rationing; but the offer was declined. After ruling family intercession, the travel ban was lifted in 1946 (Field 1985: 252–3). Britain attributed to the Darwishes great influence over the Shaikh and his sons. Hamad, shortly before his death, reportedly wrote a letter naming Darwish the sole supply agent to the oil company.[95] Despite the alliance between the al-Manis and disgruntled shaikhs, the Darwishes survived the abdication crisis, "swiftly recovering from the blow which Salih had hoped would prove fatal to their influence, achieved a degree of control which seriously threatened Salih's few remaining powers."[96] During the crisis Abdalla Darwish was instrumental in moving Shaikh Abdalla's money to Dhahran. After abdicating, Abdalla spent his visits in Doha with Abdalla Darwish, not his son. As long as Shaikh Abdalla was in the picture, the Darwishes served as his go-betweens. When the Resident visited, Abdalla Darwish was the old Shaikh's interpreter. When Abdalla was ill, Qasim Darwish issued his bulletins.[97]

The relationship continued under Shaikh Ali, who never did businsss without Abdalla Darwish. Having backed Hamad until his death, Darwish lost no time in switching allegiance to Ali's side of the family. The desperate financial situation Ali inherited left him still more dependent on Darwish. Jakins noted the situation just after the abdication:

Shaikh Ali has for only income at present the custom receipts normally about thirty thousand rupees but this month less than half this. He is having to borrow from the Manis and the Darwishes. By agreement of three weeks ago members of Al Thani family will be expecting monthly allowances aggregating some fifty thousand rupees, which Ali will not be in a position to pay . . . It would be of interest to know when next PDQ payment is due.[98]

Along with Muhammad al-Uthman (married to a Darwish sister) Abdalla Darwish controlled the Shaikh's expenditures. Each month al-Uthman would draw up "a summ which he describes as the Customs receipts for the month," and turn it over to Abdalla, to whom Ali would then turn for bills and purchases.[99] Ali himself saw neither cash nor books. No accounting system existed, nor was needed since Darwish was usually both buyer and seller. He also supported the Shaikh with direct loans, making himself especially available when Britain was being difficult. In 1949 when the company told Ali it would give him an advance only if he drew up a budget and allowed Britain to supervise expenditures Ali dropped the request and borrowed from Darwish. Within eight months of his accession, Ali owed Abdalla 200,000 rs.[100] While Abdalla handled business, Qasim, who held himself out to be knowledgeable in theology, ran religion and education, later supervising the new state school system. Abdalrahman functioned as a sort of palace chief-of-staff.

When PDQL resumed operations, the Darwishes became their agents and intermediary with the Shaikh. PDQL allowed only the government and Abdalla Darwish to use its Umm Said port facilities. The Darwishes sold housing, water, and goods to the oil camps. By 1949 the Darwish store in Dukhan had a monopoly on most lines. Like the al-Ghanims in Kuwait, they also supplied labor. Abdalla charged 11.5 rs per worker and paid 3.75 rs (plus food and water). With a workforce of 1500, Abdalla made over $1,000,000 (*Mideast*

Markets, 19 November 1979: 15; Field 1985: 255). The key to Darwish's power was his negotiation on behalf of the ruler with the oil company. Once oil revenues began arriving, Darwish made most of his money through the state, which placed all its purchases through Darwish, who took a 12 per cent commission.[101]

Britain maintained some useful ties with the al-Manis, but at first had nothing but ill to say of the Darwishes. They were among the reasons Britain gave for needing a local advisor. The Foreign Office wrote, "the monopolistic position that Darwish appears to be creating for himself in Qatar is causing us some anxiety. He behaved in a very overbearing and self-advertising way while here and made no secret of the fact that he felt he had the Ruler in his pocket. His interest (contrary to our own) seems to be to spend Qatar's income as fast as possible on projects in which he takes a large cut."[102] But Hancock, the advisor, found the only way he could accomplish anything was by overlooking his commissions. As Britain learned to work with him, its opinion of him improved. Rose, in the Foreign Office, called him "a clever and thoroughly unscrupulous merchant who, with his family, is a force very much to be reckoned with. He is classed as an asset because his cleverness cannot be ignored and must therefore be used."[103] And he had his uses; as long as they played by his rules, he welcomed British firms. By the mid-1950s the Foreign Office had come to accept and work with Darwish. That would accelerate his downfall.

The oil company, however, remained hostile to Darwish. PDQL saw him as nothing but trouble. Darwish's position with the ruler was built in part on the argument that PDQL was out for everything it could get and only Darwish's vigilance kept them honest. The company did little to dispel this view, but still it could hardly see Darwish as an ally. It never succeeded in working out any kind of happy arrangement with him. Typical was the reaction of Jackson, their local representative who "got into an almost psychopathic state of mind in which he automatically opposed anything put forward by Darwish."[104]

By the late 1940s the Darwishes were very wealthy. In 1950 when the Eastern Bank opened in Doha, Darwish made the first deposit.[105] From 1953 on the Darwishes worked on bigger projects with the Lebanese Contracting and Trading Company (CAT), for a time the only foreign contracting group in Qatar (Finnie 1958: 174–5). CAT did the work for the oil company; Darwish took 50 per cent of the profits plus a charge for labor.[106] It got the contracts for the first hospital, desalination plants, roads, and palaces. In the 1950s a visitor wrote, "posted up on newer building were huge signs indicating that a variety of businesses were owned by Abdullah Darwish, in fact so insistent were his signs that it was difficult to see what businesses weren't owned by him. He seemed to be agent for the universe" (Owen 1957: 131).

However, by the early 1950s Darwish had begun acquiring enemies among the shaikhs because of his power over the Shaikh, and among the small merchants, because of its monopolistic tendencies and the economic advantages of his ties to the ruler. Frightened of assassination, he surrounded himself with guards and never slept in Doha.[107] By 1956 Abdalla had reached the height of his power. Having alienated many Qataris, he had meanwhile improved his relations with Britain and this clinched his downfall. In 1955 anti-Darwish leaflets began appearing which the Political Agent attributed to the Ahmad faction.[108] In 1956 as Nasserist, anti-British demonstrations swept the Gulf, his enemies accused him of being pro-British, citing his ties to the Agency and to British firms. Shaikh Ali's son Ahmad, trying to strengthen his position *vis-à-vis* his rival Khalifa, put himself forward as an ally of the enemies of Darwish. The few traders, seeing an opening, joined in. Finally, Darwish lost the support of labor. In February and March Darwish encouraged Ali to refuse to back rigmen and equipment workers in a company dispute. Shortly after, anti-Darwish pamphlets began appearing: "Abdullah bin Darwish, the broker of colonialism in Qatar" and "it is a disgrace that bin Darwish remains ruling over the people's heads with his sword and exercises, in your name, authority and power . . . If you just raise up your head and use your power this English rat, bin Darwish, together with his masters the English, will vanish forever."[109] By 1956 Darwish was opposed by small merchants with an eye on his businesses, oil workers angry at his reluctance to meet all their strike demands, anti-British nationalists and dissident shaikhs. It was dangerous to attack the ruler; Darwish provided a vulnerable local target. Then in September, following anti-British and anti-Darwish demonstrations in August, Ali began talking about retiring. One rumor was that he had agreed to hand day to day administration to Ahmad on condition that Ahmad settle his quarrel with Darwish and accept him as advisor. Darwish was reportedly visiting Ahmad in Beirut trying to effect just such a reconciliation when they were interrupted by Ahmad's brother Khalifa Ali, brandishing a gun and threatening to kill Darwish. For this Khalifa was briefly banished from Qatar, but Darwish was too frightened to return. The Shaikh did not encourage him to. Burrows suggested that Ali may have struck a deal with the shaikhs: the exile of Darwish in exchange for their acceptance of the 1956 security measures.[110] In September the Ahmad faction submitted a petition demanding the removal of al-Uthman, a Darwish ally, from customs. Then in October someone fired shots into al-Uthman's home. Darwish power was fading fast.[111]

In October 1956 Darwish was told his appointment as oil representative was terminated and that the government would be ending its arrangement with him as state purchasing agent. In 1957 the government signed an agreement with the British firm from which Darwish had bought supplies, designating them as buying agents for the state, with a 2 per cent commission.[112] Darwish retired to Saudi Arabia, leaving his brothers to manage the business as best they could. They stayed on for a time, but in 1973, following Khalifa's accession, Abdalrahman moved to Abu Dhabi and the family formally divided the business. The

Darwishes had been at odds with Khalifa's branch since shifting their loyalties to Ali's side on Hamad's death in 1948. Khalifa also continued to nurse some concern over the division of business assets between Darwish and the Hamad estate in 1948. Finally, Qasim Darwish had helped arrange the marriage between Miriam, daughter of the Shaikh of Dubai, and Shaikh Ahmad, who Khalifa deposed in 1972 (Field 1985: 262). The family was welcome to stay in Qatar, but not that welcome. With Abdalla in Saudi Arabia, Abdalrahman in the UAE, the Darwishes decided to divide the company.

At its peak, the business included Atlas Insurance, International Aeradio, Darwish Engineering, the Oasis Hotel, Bos Kalis Westminster, Qatar National Travel, Darwish Travel, Qatar Tours, agencies for Austin, Pirelli, Union Carbide, Philips, Dunlop, Friedrich Air Conditioners, General Electric, Hobart, Volkswagen, Audi, Fiat, as well as general trading and contracting firms, retail outlets, and real estate (in the late 1940s the Shaikh gave the Darwishes large seafront tracts in Doha).[113] With the departure of Darwish, the circle turned one last time. In October 1956 Ali tracked down Salih al-Mani in Beirut and asked him to return as an advisor, which he did.[114]

In the transitional period when oil first arrived, the trading families were able to hold their own by providing political and administrative services that freed the Shaikh from any need to rely on his contentious family, and by demanding conditions for loans less onerous than those of the oil company (notably the British demand for formal budgets and accounting which the Shaikh took, correctly, as a step toward financial control). In the first years of oil, Ali's financial situation was strained. Abdalla had looted the treasury, expatriating the contents, leaving Ali with new financial commitments but few resources. Merchant loans were critical. But eventually, as in Kuwait, oil revenues allowed the Shaikh to bypass the merchants. Because the merchants had some value, at least in the transition period, the Shaikh did not ignore them entirely. In exchange for their support, he made sure some of the oil revenues trickling into the economy trickled their way. For a few years they enjoyed protected access to the new oil wealth: through local agencies for imported products, lucrative liaison work with the company, and real estate.

Both Darwish and al-Mani were also skillful in maintaining their positions by exchanging political and financial power. Both were adept at exacting financial concessions for administrative services. In 1949 Wilton remarked, "it is to be hoped that Salih the merchant is not at cross-purposes with Salih the 'Prime Minister'."[115] Abdalla Darwish too, was advisor, confidant, and travel companion to the Shaikh, who referred to him occasionally as his prime minister. The Resident observed, "he is the only outsider, that is the only man not a member of a Shaikhly family, to have aimed at and achieved political power. His ambitions appear to be power and money."[116] But ultimately the merchants could not compete with the oil company. By 1952 the Shaikh was able to cut customs revenues.[117] The merchants were bypassed and bought off; as in Kuwait they benefited from the new revenues, but the deal they arranged was not as advantageous and the Shaikh moved more quickly to renege on it. Already in the early 1950s, Abdalla Darwish was airing protests that would not be heard in Kuwait for another decade: calling for regular consultation between the government and representatives of the merchant community and complaining that the ruling family was taking over parts of the trade sector, unfairly, as their allowances gave them an income.[118] That was true. Already by the early 1950s Nasir Khalid and other careful shaikhs were becoming rich through trade. By the mid-1950s the merchants were being eclipsed. In his last year Darwish tried to stave off the inevitable by hiring Heseldin, PDQL's former general manager, as state oil consultant and as a member of the CAT board.[119] But the tide had turned. Darwish could no longer compete with the oil company for money and with Britain for influence.

Class formation and national identity

Oil had an immediate and radical effect on the base as well as the peak of Qatar's social structure. Within a short time oil turned unemployed pearl divers and slaves into a politically significant and volatile concentration of workers, then into a working class, and finally into a nationally identified working class. This new identity was the result of a combination of oil company policies and an unusual workforce. In Qatar the workforce comprised two important segments: expatriate and local. The expatriate workers were largely Arab, with a significant Indian component and British senior staff. The Qatari workers came from two different groupings: Qatari slaves and free Qatari nomads and pearl divers.

Qatari laborers, across this divide of free and unfree, shared one common characteristic: they were both a workforce untamed to wage labor. This produced an unfortunate tendency, from the company's viewpoint, for them to strike. At work these two groups came to have similar interests and find common cause against the company and the expatriate workforce. In this new identity they were joined by the few wealthy Qataris, who had an interest as slaveholders and contractors in seeing that Qataris received preferential treatment from the company. For a time their national identity was also encouraged by the ruler, who used Qatari labor disturbances as leverage to extract concessions from the company. In the end, however, the alliance between the Qatari rich and poor became too great a threat and, under growing abolitionist pressure from Britain, Ali relented and freed the slaves, thus breaking this unfolding alliance and developing a new bond between himself, as ruler, and the poorer Qataris – the freed slaves.

The first oil workers came from the pearling industry. In the early 1950s Shell even used pearl divers to set up offshore oil rigs (precipitating environmental protests over fears that the company would strip the oyster beds; Moorehead 1977: 89). In Kuwait, when pearl divers became laborers, the transition was mediated by the state. In Qatar, workers took this into their own hands. The local non-slave divers who formed the core of the indigenous labor force were already more independent financially than divers in neighboring areas. In Qatar, three-quarters or more were out of debt (Harrison 1924: 170). Harrison observed:

The most conspicuous example, however, of-divers who are out of debt and therefore out of bondage, is to be found in Katar. Here is a small diving community where practically all of the men are out of debt, and the atmosphere of freedom and equality, good fellowship and comfort is a refreshing contrast to the conditions of Bahrein. The men show real independence and self-respect. These divers can change their employers if the treatment they receive is not satisfactory. They can move to another city to live. In a word, they are free men. Yet the system under which they work is no different from that obtaining in Bahrein. It is the divers who are different. They are Bedouins or descended from Bedouins. (1924a: 93)

They had a history of resisting what they considered unfair labor practices in the pearling industry. Three factors gave Qatar's divers more freedom. First, their continuing ties to desert tribes gave them mobility. Second, they had a weaker merchant class above them. In Kuwait the merchants colluded; no one would think of hiring a diver indebted to another merchant. Third, the ruler's power was weaker. Harrison wondered about this:

I asked, "how does it happen that divers in Katar keep out of debt while here in Bahrein almost every diver is heavily in debt to his captain?"

"The trouble is this," replied the merchant, and I thought I could discern in his tone a little envy of the wealthy Bahrein merchants. "We have no powerful ruler in Katar. It is no use to lend a diver money. He will borrow all you are willing to lend and then go to work for some one else in spite of the debt. If at the season's end you try to arrest him or to compel him to pay, he simply leaves the city and returns to his tribe in the desert, and it is impossible to get him back. At least our sheikh does not get them back and recover the money. So the money lent is a complete loss. The merchants will not lend money under such circumstances and so nobody is in debt." (1924a: 94)

These were free workers, but what about the slaves? In practice their situation left them just as untamed a workforce, just as likely to strike as the free labor. Slaves were not, after all, in danger of really becoming unemployed. More importantly, slaveholders had almost as much to gain by any strike-negotiated wage increase as free workers. When the oil company arrived, there were many slaves in Qatar – in 1951 Jacomb, the Political Agent in Qatar, estimated 3000 (Lorimer estimated 4000 earlier in the century; 1908–15, vol. 2: 1531).[120] PDQL employed slaves from its first year. In 1949, 250 local slaves worked for the company, many at the personal request of a slaveholder, often a shaikh. Slaves were paid directly, but immediately turned in 80–95 per cent of their wages. In 1950 Jacomb voiced his disapproval to the Shaikh who, after some argument, issued a decree allowing slaves to keep half their waves.[121]

Qatari workers, free and slave, soon found common enemy in the oil company. At first they focused exclusively on wages, benefits, and conditions. As competition from expatriates increased, however, they began focusing on foreign labor. Opposition increasingly organized along national lines. The first factor prompting national identification in the industry was the 1935 concession which required PDQL to give hiring preference to Qataris. From early on, hiring preference for nationals was an issue in Qatar, as it was in the other Gulf states. At first, with Salih al-Mani's collusion in granting nationality papers to anyone for a fee, PDQL was able to evade this commitment. The result, however, was to compel the Qatari laborers themselves to define and defend their identity. The second factor was the growing number of foreign laborers. Initially Qataris could not provide enough labor, especially skilled labor, for the company. By one estimate in the mid-1950s Qatar had only 630 indigenous literates (Finnie 1958: 120). So the company hired expatriates. In 1951 PDQL employed 2891 workers and staff, of whom 1252, less than half, were Qatari (with another 328 non-nationals holding Qatari papers).[122] The company thus had enough foreigners to anger but not intimidate the Qataris. There were still enough Qataris to lead a good strike. From these conflicts the first stirrings of Qatari consciousness arose.

Trouble began with the first oil shipment. In February 1950 at the opening of the Umm Said terminal Salih al-Mani gave a speech criticizing PDQL's housing and pay policy and calling for contract preferences to local merchants and better pay for Qatari laborers, "as they, being the sons of the soil under development, deserve, more than the others employed, the Company's special consideration."[123] This speech gave organizers the go-ahead. In March laborers in Dukhan and Umm Said held a one day strike. The immediate precipitant was the company's failure to issue coffee rations and an announcement that Indians would replace some Arabs. Other factors besides nationalism played a role: working conditions, growing expectations – a feeling that because oil was again flowing, raises were due – but the solidarity along Qatari lines was notable. The strike ended with a compromise worked out by Ali and the Political Officer. From then on strikes were the norm. Houseboys struck over sweeping porches. Bakers struck over baking bread. Children struck over discipline in the schools.[124] The most important strikes, however, were the oil strikes.

The next big strike was in 1951. This time the nationalist tone was unmistakable. Discontent crystallized around Dhofari workers who Salih al-Mani had originally recruited and given Qatari papers. In June 900 Qataris at Dukhan, then Umm Said, struck demanding the Dhofaris' deportation. This time conditions of work and wages were not even an issue. When the organizers were arrested, 900 Qataris who had gone to Doha for the holidays refused to return to work until the June strike organizers were released and the Dhofaris deported. Local shops closed in solidarity. A court was set up under Ali's son Ahmad and Plant. Plant, however, found the organizers guilty; Ahmad found them innocent. They settled on suspended sentences. As for the Dhofaris, Ali found no alternative – and Plant agreed – but to get rid of them. Shortly after, 250 Dhofaris were sent to Dubai and the Qataris returned to work. Afterwards Hay wrote, "had it been possible to despatch one of His Majesty's ships to Dohah the Ruler might have been willing to take a firmer line and the strikers would probably not have adopted such a defiant attitude."[125] Perhaps. Ali, for his part, had an interest in seeing some strike activity; during this period he was actively negotiating with PDQL over a new oil agreement.

The Qatari workers found temporary allies in odd places: in the Shaikh, who wanted to pressure the company for more money, in the slaveholders, and in the merchants. Increasingly, Ali and his son Ahmad took on the role of mediating the strikes, giving them some power to manipulate them to their own ends. In September 1951 drivers at Dukhan struck, objecting to cleaning cars and complaining that Indians were favored over Qataris. Following a written complaint the Shaikh met with a delegation and worked out an agreement. The company, in compliance, hired car cleaners, but then in October fired six drivers, among them the strike leaders, saying they were no longer needed now that car cleaners had been hired. When Ali then asked the company to rehire the strikers, it refused to take back the organizers and the others refused to return. In the end, Ahmad personally hired the organizers at the palace and the others returned to work.[126] Following short-lived strikes over the summer which Ahmad mediated, 2000 workers struck again in September 1952 at Umm Said and Dukhan, in a very coordinated, non-violent labor action over wages, precipitated by the company's plan to charge for meals. When the company dropped the plan and agreed to a raise, the workers held out for still more pay and here Ahmad drew the line. When he threatened to deport the non-Qataris, they returned to work. The Qataris were harder to handle. A delegation went to the palace demanding a raise or passports to leave. When Ali refused, a small skirmish in the market followed, but it was put down and the strikers returned to work. This was the first strike where the workers did not get all their demands. Ali had his new oil agreement, signed 1 September 1952; he no longer needed the strikes to pressure the company.[127]

The strikers found allies among the many slaveholding shaikhs who wanted better wages from their slaves. Slaveholders were among the first to call for hiring preference for Qataris. They also played a role in negotiating strike settlements.[128] The cleverer shaikhs were able to manipulate the strikes so as to simultaneously pressure Ali for allowances and the company for increased revenues.

The March 1952 strike, for example, was immediately followed by a family petition for new allowances.

The strikers found allies in the merchants for whom a policy of local preference was a way to pressure the company to use local contractors. In the 1950 speech that precipitated the first large strike, Salih al-Mani called on the company to "prove co-operative where the interests of the Qatar Government, local merchants and contractors are involved, giving these local men preference over those from foreign lands."[129] Local merchants stood to gain from any blanket policy favoring nationals. Both Darwish and al-Mani grew wealthy from their contracts with the oil company. As Darwish supplied the contentious labor, he also came to play an occasional role in strike mediation. When he stopped backing the strikers in 1956 they turned against him, publishing the anti-Darwish pamphlets which hastened his downfall. Like the ruling family, some merchants were also slaveholders – Abdalla Darwish had twenty-three slaves in 1951.[130]

The ruler, the shaikhs, the merchants, and the Qatari workers, free and slave, thus formed a working coalition against the company. These groups, however, had little in common save their Qatari identity, so that is what they emphasized. The political value of Qatari labor to the merchants and the ruler and his family exacerbated tension along national lines, producing a series of angry strikes and a specifically Qatari cohesiveness. The alliance proved successful, so successful that it gave the Shaikh pause. Ali found the labor tensions useful as a way of pressuring the company. However, when the strikes had achieved his purposes, when they further threatened to forge a working alliance between labor and family factions, he withdrew his energetic support. In 1952 he freed the slaves. By May he had paid 1500 rs compensation each for 660 slaves (this may include a few emancipated slaves who were reemancipated for the money; the Political Officer reported turning back a chartered plane full of freed slaves from Bahrain, "willing to renounce their freedom for a day").[131] This policy served to break the emerging nationalist alliance among slaveholders, slaves, merchants, and dissident shaikhs against PDQL. Manumission was also one of the first welfare policies, distributing oil wealth not only to large slaveholders, many of them shaikhs, but also to relatively poor villagers from the north, with one or two slaves. It was certainly a benefit to the slaves who, judging by the stories of those who fled, found the relationship very unsatisfactory.[132] The Political Officer reported, "this has been by far the widest distribution of wealth that has yet resulted from the oil royalties."[133]

British pressure also played a role. After 1949 Britain made some effort to discourage slavery, manumitting those enslaved in their lifetime who appeared at the Agency and condemning slave traffic, but making less effort to halt ongoing practices. Jacomb, the Political Agent, in particular pressured Ali about slaves.

He got him to increase the amount of pay employed slaves could keep. He actively supported the Agency policy of manumitting slaves who approached the Agency, freeing fifty-seven in 1950.[134] He faced practical problems, however. With the decline of pearling many shaikhs had few income sources beyond the slave trade. Local opposition to an advisor grew mostly from the fear that he would interfere with slavery. Once oil arrived, the Political Agent in Bahrain toyed with the idea of directly linking abolition to new allowances. Indirectly, that is what happened. It was only the oil revenues that allowed Ali to compensate slaveholders. A final problem was finding employment for the slaves. Again, expanding government and oil operations answered that in time.[135]

The abolition of slavery may have broken the common interest between slaves and slaveholders. It did not, however, eliminate strikes. If anything it increased the bonds among Qatari workers and the sense of local identity. Ali and Ahmad repeated their formula of encouraging strikes during oil negotiations in 1955. In August Qatari drivers at Dukhan, then Umm Said, struck. When the police tried to retrieve company cars taken by the strikers, a clash ensued in which the police lost. At Umm Said strikers took matters further, forcing the staff to leave their offices, then cutting off utilities. The strikers took their complaints directly to the ruler who took up their defense. The grievances included standing complaints over housing and the quality of water and food. The strike was finally settled with several concessions from the company. An oil agreement was reached on 17 August 1955.[136]

Labor tensions were also fanned by the oil company's incompetence. Hay wrote in 1951 that PDQL "appear to be generally inept in their dealings with both local labour and the local government."[137] Burrows wrote in 1954 that "they have more arguments and disputes with the Qatar Government than all the other Oil Companies in the Gulf put together."[138] Part of the problem lay, as the company argued, with Abdalla Darwish, but much of the blame lay with the company itself. It refused to concede anything not in the contract, refused to make any public relations gestures, and refused to build anything for the community, such as schools, as was the custom with other Gulf oil companies. In 1955 the Political Resident noted, "I do not think that the company's idea, as it struck me . . . that it is a sort of sovereign power able to talk down to the Ruler, is wise or practical . . . There is still too much of the 'take it or leave it' attitude." The ruler, he thought, would not respond well to this: "after all it is his oil."[139] It was; he didn't. In every instance where a gesture might have helped, the company failed to offer one. A few examples: in 1949 as oil operations deepened, PDQL, whose relations with Ali were poor, still had no full-time representative for Qatar and handled its relations with the Shaikh through a busy representative in Bahrain. When they did get a representative in Qatar, they posted him, not at Doha, where he could talk to the Shaikh, but at Dukhan. In 1954 when the palace cooks all quit and the Shaikh asked the company to lend him a few, they refused. "Shaikh Ahmad has fulminated against the Company ever since," wrote the Political Agent, who offered the Shaikh the Agency cook.[140] In 1955 a company driver ran down the ruler's blind prayer caller. When Ali demanded the driver's dismissal, the company balked, citing its contractual right to handle personnel. Labor relations were equally inept. In 1950 PDQL prompted a strike by forgetting to issue the month's coffee rations for three weeks. In 1952 PDQL mixed up its calendar and tried to force men to work on the Id holidays. Whenever workers organized, the company fired the spokesmen, then complained at the next strike that no spokesmen would come forward to negotiate with. The company's incompetence helped Ali and Ahmad play the role of mediator. Since the workers couldn't put forward spokesmen out of fear of retaliation, Ahmad filled the gap.[141]

The most important consequence of these strikes was the development of a Qatari consciousness. In the course of these strikes, Qataris forged an identity as citizens and then pressured the company and the state to institutionalize this identity and give it legal worth. The strikes forced the company to reiterate its commitment to a preferential policy for Qataris. In 1955 the company promised to give nationals preference and to employ qualified nationals in jobs held by foreigners.[142] In 1956 the Shaikh issued a proclamation forbidding non-Qataris from opening shops or businesses without permission.[143] This laid the basis for a series of protective nationality laws in the 1960s, beginning with Qatar's first labor law in 1962 which stipulated that Qataris, followed by other Arabs, were to have hiring preference.

By 1957 labor troubles began receding. The Shaikh started taking a harder line against the strikers, ruling that they would not be paid for strike days and ordering strikers not to molest or intimidate people, or harm property.[144] Ali also began looking at mediation procedures. In 1957 the Beirut labor counselor visited Qatar and drew up labor legislation. In 1959 a labor department was established for oil industry workers. The 1962 labor law codified arbitration procedures. The labor disputes of the 1950s succeeded then in both winning Qatari workers significant concessions, especially preferential employment, and in forging a national identity among disparate Qatari workers and, in a larger sense, among Qataris – workers, merchants and shaikhs alike.

The pattern of rule after oil

In a few short years, oil had transformed Qatar. Oil not only changed the size of the population, but also its composition: by creating a class of Qatari workers, by accelerating the manumission of slaves, by introducing a large concentration of expatriates, and by forging something of a Qatari identity. The government has released little hard data on the population's composition today. As el-Mallakh so charitably puts it, "Qataris are, by nature, modest people: hence they do not immediately volunteer extensive data" (1979: 13). The only censuses, taken in 1970 and 1986, were never officially published.[145] The population has grown tremendously since oil, that much is clear. Officially it stood in 1987 at 369,079 (Qatar, CSO 1987: 10). Of these, an estimated 35,000–70,000 are Qatari.[146]

The transformations with oil have radically changed Qatar's social composition. The larger distinction between Qatari and non-Qatari has been added to the old distinction between Arab Persian and beduin. A class structure and new classes have appeared. The population has become urbanized and sedentarized (although the beduin, often with several passports, still leave for the desert from time to time, maintaining tribal ties with Saudi Arabia and other Gulf states). The population is increasingly well educated. In 1951 Qatar had one school, 240 students and 6 teachers; in 1960 it had 5965 students and 494 teachers; in 1985 it had 52,050 students (Qatar, CSO 1987: 95; Qatar, Ministry of information 1982: 49). The population is also healthier. Three large hospitals, dozens of clinics, 514 state physicians and many health care professionals provide exceptional care (Qatar, CSO 1987: 123–44). Nuclear family residences are replacing extended family housing; polygamy has declined; bride prices have risen; intergenerational conflict has increased. Qatar has changed a good deal (El-Islam 1976, 1978; Graham 1980; Melikian 1981; Melikian and al-Easa 1981; Abu Saud 1984).

Yet despite these radical social and economic changes, Qatar, like Kuwait, has maintained a high level of political continuity. It continues to be ruled by al-Thani shaikhs. As in Kuwait this precarious continuity at the top has been achieved by a series of policies aimed at placating the old groups politicized by oil with oil-funded state largesse and developing new allies among newly politicized groups using these same revenues.

The first group to be placated was the ruling family. They had the highest historical expectations. With oil, Shaikhs tried to buy their support using three mechanisms – allowances, land, and state jobs. Finally, the rulers took a similar approach with the merchants, giving selected merchants profitable access to state contracts and legal protection from foreign competition. The rulers also tried to develop new allies in the national population using social programs and state employment. These policies all helped create an almost inadvertently large and bureaucratic state. When these policies proved insufficient for maintaining domestic peace in the family, the Shaikhs reassessed their relationship with the merchants and began allowing shaikhs to invade their economic territory. The merchants, weaker and more dependent than their Kuwaiti counterparts, were unable to block this. Yet even these policies did not quiet the family. In Kuwait, in the interwar period, the key family factions – the Jabir and Salim lines – were institutionalized into a succession mechanism. With each new Shaikh, power reverted to the other faction. The faction out of power received interim posts (prime minister, crown prince, and a handful of lesser posts). Even more distant family lines (e.g. descendants of Mubarak's brothers) received secondary posts. In Kuwait, family descent was institutionalized and controlled. In Qatar, however, the ruling family never became the institution that it became in Kuwait. No institutionalized tradeoff of key posts emerged. Techniques that worked well in Kuwait failed in Qatar. Succession was never regulated. Unlike Kuwait, Qatar's Shaikhs were unable to turn the family into a ruling institution because of the weaker inherited institutional legacy – the absence of succession mechanisms, a weakness that grew out of the nomadic economy. The ruling family's larger size contributed, as did the lack of a politicized merchant bloc to encourage family solidarity. The weakness of the family as a political institution has been demonstrated in the succession crises of recent decades. Family dissent forced Abdalla's abdication to Ali in 1949, Ali's to Ahmad in 1960, and Ahmad's to Khalifa in the 1972 coup. It was only with Khalifa's succession that a partially successful effort was made to limit the financial advantages of the shaikhs and develop policies that would create significant support among the citizen population.

The ruling family and the merchants

The first mechanism for placating the ruling family was direct allowances, supplemented by loans and gifts. The civil list in the 1950s gave outright grants to over 150 adult male al-Thanis. As the family grew, so did the number on the list. As revenues rose, so did the family demand for more money. Throughout the 1950s family protests prompted repeated allowance increases. In the 1960s, the mechanisms of distribution became more sophisticated. Allowances continued, but now a second mechanism for distributing money to the family through bureaucratic posts appeared. In choosing this policy, the Shaikh responded not only to the shaikhs' nuisance value but also to the opportunity they provided: he hoped to reinforce their stake in continuing al-Thani rule and to use his relatives to control claims from the rest of the population. This policy began when the British advised Shaikh Ali to give relatives state jobs in the hopes of cutting back their financial claims.[147] This role for the family was new. In the 1950s the Political Agent wrote, "there is no regular method of consultation even with the other members of the family. Normally the Ruler is glad to see as little of them as possible. They flock around him when they want more money or when some critical event occurs."[148] From the 1950s on, shaikhs began to move into high and mid-level government posts. A process of centralization at the apex of the political system occurred which transformed the ruling family into an elite recruitment corps and broadened its political functions. While this policy served both to provide a recruitment pool and to buy some peace, it had its limits. Qatar has one of the largest ruling families in the region, certainly the largest relative to its population. Estimates of the family's size range up to 20,000 (or perhaps over half the national population), their ranks augmented by longevity and large families (encouraged by the policy of granting stipends to every new member). The higher estimates include all who can claim any family tie to the al-Thanis. Most estimates are more modest, but still large, with the number of shaikhs (adult men) ranging from 500 to 2000 (*MEED*, 3 March 1972: 232; Anthony 1975: 77, 85; London *Times*, 12 November 1985: 17). It is hard to employ so sizable a family; it is particularly hard in times of shrinking oil revenues. By the late 1970s, one observer noted "many of the [al-Thani] sons are accused of unproductively occupying government sinecures and living extravagantly off state revenues. The fact that they have no hope of directly exercising power also gives rise to frustrations, which from time to time break through the surface of family and state solidarity" (*MEED*, April 1977: 40).

The third mechanism for distributing wealth predominantly, although not exclusively, to the ruling family was through land. By the early 1950s many al-Thanis, especially the Hamad branch, were already large landowners. As development occurred, the value of land rose rapidly. In the early days of oil real estate was, throughout the Gulf, the fastest way to wealth. The shaikhs quickly recognized this, competing with each other in piling marker stones on vacant desert stretches. Shaikh Nasir Khalid, recognizing the power of state positions, used his municipality post to distribute land, prompting a family crisis in 1953 that led Ali to issue a decree forbidding the appropriation of vacant land.[149] Ali also deprived Nasir of his power to allocate land, turning the question over to the Advisor, who was not entirely pleased with this authority: "all land questions, including registration and distribution, have been passed by the Ruler to the Adviser – a most unwelcome burden as no records exist and claim jumping is a universal recreation."[150] Ali, however, was ultimately unable to prevent shaikhs from claiming land; in the end he decided to allow land claims to appease the shaikhs. In 1956 when the Advisor crossed Khalifa by ordering the removal of stones staking land claims, Khalifa responded by staking a much larger tract of land with concrete posts. When the Advisor asked Ali for support, Ali said he was unable to evict Khalifa.[151] After oil revenues arrived, many shaikhs also began moving, with retainers, from the coast to the less populated interior, building weekend homes and state-subsidized farms. These fortified farms enjoyed considerable autonomy (9th June Studies 1974: 27–8). They constitute virtual private police forces,

Among the more powerful segments of the population upon which the Al Thani are dependent for their survival are the armed retainers, synonymous for all practical purposes with the defense, internal security and police forces . . . living in tent and *barasti* settlements near the numerous shaykhly palaces are entire tribes subsidized by the ruling family and who could be called on to help defend the regime if the need arose.

(Anthony 1975: 85)

They could also be called upon to defend their particular patron shaikhs. This policy of encouraging shaikhs to settle outside Doha explains the government's strong support for agriculture, support which primarily benefits shaikhs. Compared to the rest of the economy, agriculture has been very free of state control. While industry is state-owned, Qatar's 400–500 farms are private. The reluctance of their owners to invest in commercial agriculture has forced the government to backpeddle on its earlier plans for agricultural self-sufficiency, despite the rapid depletion of the aquifers which irrigate the land. The landowners have too much influence for the government to pursue more aggressive agricultural policies (London *Times*, 22 February 1983: 14; *MEED*, August 1983: 41).

In the early 1960s land distribution was coupled to a state housing program and institutionalized into a major distributive policy. In a pattern reminiscent of Kuwait, old houses were demolished, with generous compensation for the owners and grant of alternative sites. Land speculation drove prices still higher, so high that when Doha began expanding in the mid-1970s, the government literally created a new suburb, West Bay, because land speculation made reclamation cheaper than purchase at market prices from landowning shaikhs. Today West Bay land sells for $11 a square foot (*MEED*, August 1983: 34). Episodic attempts to contain land speculation have been ineffective. *MEED* writes, "there is no legal mechanism for compulsory purchase of land in Qatar and government departments often run into serious difficulties with landowners who demand exorbitant prices or simply refuse to sell at all" (August 1982: 33). A vague land acquisition law was in fact promulgated in 1966, but rarely enforced. Only after Khalifa came to power in 1972 was land registration introduced to curb speculation and new controls placed on land loans from banks. Even so, in the early 1980s a housing plan at Umm Said was delayed because of opposition from Doha landowners who feared it might prove cheaper for people to live there and commute to Doha (*MEED*, August 1981: 23). These policies – allowances, state employment, land grants – bought the Shaikh less respite from his family than he had hoped. Their continuing economic demands prompted him to begin allowing the shaikhs to play a greater role in the private sector.

In Qatar, as in Kuwait, the arrival of oil revenues also changed the nature of the alliance between the Shaikh and the trading families. As the ruler began to rely more on his family for administrative services, he encouraged the merchants to retreat into the economic realm. In the 1950s the merchants grew wealthy through their contracting relationship with the oil company, through foreign product agencies and through real estate. In each case, the ruler's intervention made this wealth possible. In the 1960s new mechanisms were introduced which resembled those adopted in Kuwait – a series of nationality and commercial laws which served both to guarantee wealth to Qatari merchants and to give the government leverage over foreign companies. First, nationality laws defined who Qataris were. A 1961 law gave citizenship to those who had settled in Qatar before 1930. Then other laws gave Qataris commercial advantages. Laws in the early 1960s required foreign firms to place orders through Qatari merchants, regulated shareholding companies, and set visas and entry requirements. A 1963 law recognized the Chamber of Commerce and empowered it to issue certificates of origin and nationality and settle some commercial disputes. Other laws in 1963 banned foreign real estate purchases and regulated work visas and sponsorship. Law 20/63, the most important of the series, regulated foreign commercial and industrial activities. Non-Qataris could do business only in partnership with Qataris and only with 51 per cent Qatari ownership. A 1964 law stipulated that all new commercial businesses must be wholly Qatari owned, industrial businesses 51 per cent (Qatar, Department of legal affairs 1975).

These laws secured the wealthiest merchants' wealth. As in Kuwait, however, as these families grew wealthier, their political power declined. With oil, the merchants began to lose their access to the Shaikh. They were peripheralized politically, placed in new but unimportant institutions. Paramount among these was the Advisory Council established in 1972, an appointed body composed of notables (Qatar, Advisory council 1981). Its members included such once notables as Yusif Qasim, Abdalla Darwish's nephew, a Council vice-president.

The general impulse behind the economic legislation of the 1960s was the same as in Kuwait: to give Qatari merchants economic advantage. In Kuwait established wealthy merchants became richer; in Qatar however many of the merchant families made a transition from merely well off, or better off than average, to quite wealthy in the 1960s and 1970s. Their rise was both more dramatic and more completely dependent on the state. Unlike the Kuwaitis, they had far weaker independent power bases, the result of their smaller size and weaker historical role relative to the large ruling family. Unlike Kuwait, where the merchants were well established, in Qatar the established indigenous merchant community was almost nonexistent. As a result they were less able to set the terms or hold their own against the ruler on such issues as reclaiming ruling family debts, labor law, and price and rent controls. Following the first spurt of protective legislation, laws limiting prices and profits were enacted in the 1970s which restricted the merchants.

At the same time, and unlike Kuwait, the ruler has also tried to control the ruling family's continuing financial demands by allowing it a greater role in the private sector. One reason this was possible is that Qatar had never had as sharp an historical division of labor between the ruling family as political leaders and the leading families as merchants. From early on, the al-Thanis were actively engaged in trade. Compared to Kuwait, Qatar's Shaikhs were merchants first, rulers second. That was true of Abdalla of whom the Political Agent wrote in 1914, "it was with difficulty that he was persuaded to undertake the duties of

Chief of Doha . . . as he preferred pearl dealing to responsibility; and he more than once during his father's life time threatened to resign."[152]

With the Shaikh's encouragement, family members now began to join commoner merchants as the leading traders. The most successful merchants were those with shaikhs for partners: "operations [of the ruling family] are usually undertaken in partnership with a merchant, and the result has been the emergence of a kind of comprador class of merchants who hitch up with a sheikh for mutual profit. In such arrangements the sheikh remains a sleeping partner" (9th June Studies 1974: 28). Smaller merchants, with no palace ties, did not fare well. In the early 1950s the Darwishes, in particular, began facing growing competition from the al-Thanis. Nasir Khalid, a successful trader and later economy minister, led the al-Thani opposition to Darwish. First his faction tried to get Darwish out of government by reorganizing customs and putting Nasir forward to head the new municipality. Then they tried to compete economically. The turning point came in 1956 when Abdalla Darwish clashed with Shaikh Ali's son Khalifa in Lebanon. After that Abdalla left for Saudi Arabia and the ruling family moved in on his territory. In the late 1950s Nasir, in partnership with lesser merchants, and with the support of Shaikh Ahmad began bidding on company contracts (Field 1985: 262–3).[153] By the 1980s his group, now Nasir Khalid and Sons, with almost 500 employees, had invested in a broad range of Qatari firms (*Euromoney*, May 1985: 252–4). Other shaikhs from the Ahmad branch followed suit, joining with merchants to form companies to compete for oil company favors. The Jaida merchant family got its start in the 1950s this way as partners with the Ahmad faction, as did the al-Attiyya. The Ali ibn Hamad al-Attiyya merchant group does very successful contracting work through such connections. Its QPC Prefabs has several large housing contracts. The al-Mannai family, one of the largest merchant groups in Qatar, holding among other businesses the General Motors agency, has likewise expanded through shaikhly ties, including ties to Shaikh Khalid Hamad, the interior minister. Ahmad al-Mannai, Bahraini-born, moved to Qatar in the 1940s, after oil operations resumed and in the 1950s and 1960s began acquiring foreign agencies, key among them General Motors. It was only after Khalifa's accession that his fortunes rose dramatically through his connections with the shaikhs and with the prime minister, Khalid Abdalla al-Attiyya. With a newly developed engineering firm, al-Mannai began bidding on government projects. He has since extended his investments outside Qatar, to Saudi Arabia, the UAE, and even the US: in 1984 both al-Mannai and Shaikh Khalid were named as co-defendants in a Securities and Exchange Commission insider trading case (*Wall Street Journal*, 16 July 1984: 3). Among the more visible al-Thani traders is Ghanim Ali Abdalla (brother of Shaikh Ahmad), owner of the $8,500,000 Doha Center which opened in 1978. Ghanim also owns the Ramada Hotel, the Ghanim Gardens villa complex, and holds agencies for BMW and International Harvester. His company's turnover is $40,000,000 a year; its registered assets $44,000,000. In 1981, when the company had difficulty repaying foreign loans (including $25,000,000 for the hotel) the state bailed it out. Ghanim is also a landowner whose property assets alone might well have covered his commercial debts (*MEED*, 20 July 1979: 35; *Financial Times*, 16 February 1981, III: 8). These shaikhs are far more visible commercially than their Kuwaiti counterparts.

Despite the policies introduced to placate the ruling family, ranging from allowances, to land, to preferential access to the private sector, family opposition to the Shaikh's rule continued unabated. Unable to combine delegation of power with continued control, Shaikhs have retreated to a highly personal style of control. As they gave more and more money to the family, they also alienated segments of the larger Qatari population, thus giving dissident family members allies.

Family opposition has continued through three contested successions: 1949, 1960, and 1972. The 1949 succession crisis was handled by a compromise that only postponed family disputes. When Abdalla abdicated to Ali, he named Khalifa heir apparent, promising that Ali's successor would be a son of Hamad. However, Ali quickly came to favor his own son Ahmad as successor. Until Abdalla's death in 1957 Ali did not come out in the open with this. But tension between Ahmad and Khalifa was never far below the surface. Khalifa tried various ways of undermining Ahmad. In 1955 he tried to make himself a labor advocate, Ahmad's historical role. During the annual strikes, pamphlets appeared in the mosques calling for Khalifa to come forward on the workers' behalf.[154] Khalifa also put himself forward as a mild pan-Arabist, crossing Ahmad by trying to collect funds for arms to Egypt. When Khalifa was named education minister in 1957, replacing Qasim Darwish, he began using that position to enhance his claim, aligning himself loosely with the Nasserists and using his responsibilities for finding foreign teachers to dabble in foreign affairs. In 1956, Khalifa, taking advantage of the troubled local environment – Abdalla Darwish's ouster, anti-British agitation – confronted Ali directly, asking to be appointed his deputy and successor: "the Ruler replied that he would appoint as his deputy whom he thought fit and he thought fit to appoint his son, Shaikh Ahmed."[155] Ali, in turn, asked the Political Agent to give Ahmad his full support. After 1956, with Darwish ousted and Ali left without his counsel, Ali began turning more and more ordinary tasks over to Ahmad, strengthening Ahmad's position in the succession struggle. In 1957 Ali again requested and received the Political Agent's assurance that Britain would give all necessary help to Ali and Ahmad.[156] Burrows wrote in 1957: "Her Majesty's Government will make available prompt military aid to support Your Highness if you are confronted with trouble in Qatar with which you are unable to deal by means of your own forces."[157]

Despite challenges from Khalifa and the rest of the family, the 1949 compromise held for a decade. However, by the late 1950s, the compromise was beginning to unravel. In October 1960 Shaikh Ali finally abdicated – to his son Ahmad, not to Khalifa. The abdication was the consequence of a decade of family pressure for increased allowances, coupled with a drop in revenues that left Ali unable to meet family demands. The system stuck together until in the late 1950s oil revenues began falling, resulting in cutbacks (al-Kuwari 1978: 117). The family was unhappy with this, especially the Hamad faction. In 1960 Nasir Hamad (Shaikh Khalifa's brother), dissatisfied with the cutbacks, expressed this anger over "unsettled financial differences" by trying to kill Ali in Lebanon, leaving five bullets in his car.[158] Shaikh Ali decided it was time to retire. The abdication was also the product of cumulative popular dissatisfactions, among them Ali's financial excesses and his concomitant policy of devoting few expenditures to development. Ali spent his oil money personally, extravagantly, and usually abroad. His relatives (including his father, until his death in 1957) ate up much of the remainder. So Ali abdicated to Ahmad. In deference to the 1949 promise, Khalifa was now named heir apparent and finance director.

Ali had groomed Ahmad for the position for some time. Ahmad had served as police chief as well as deputy ruler. Still Ahmad took the post somewhat reluctantly. He faced a family revolt that had driven his father and grandfather from office. Ahmad now had two choices: confront the family or comply. He chose the latter, placating the family by raising allowances. Ahmad's first move was to divide the revenues equally between the family and the state: the ruler took 25 per cent, the shaikhs another 25 per cent and the state 50 per cent (al-Kuwari 1978: 117). This division, however, necessitated radical cutbacks in development and social services, which did not sit well with the bulk of the population.

The tension of the abdication exploded in 1963. On 19 April a group celebrating a proposed union of Egypt, Syria, and Iraq blocked the car of a nephew of the Shaikh, Abdalrahman Muhammad, who then fired on the crowd, killing one. Opposition leaders quickly organized a National Unity Front and called a week-long general strike. The Front's demands were popular demands: the reduction of shaikhly privileges, expansion of social services, reduction of foreign labor in the government and oil company, establishment of a budget, creation of a representative municipal council, recognition of trade unions, better utility rates, a movie house and a broadcasting station (*Middle East Journal* chronology, 1963: 305; Stoakes 1972: 197; 9th June Studies 1974: 30–1; Nyrop *et al.* 1977: 262; al-Kuwari 1978: 205).

The strike coalition had different factions. First were the Qatari oil workers. In the 1950s they had gained considerable organizational experience striking against the oil company. From 1956 on they had turned that organization and experience into more explicitly political opposition. In 1963 they were now able to hold a strike for nearly three weeks. Second were the dissident shaikhs, especially those connected with the oil company, with a stronghold in Khawr. These were second and third rank al-Thanis, outside the inner circle of high allowances. Third were a handful of notables led by Abdalla Misnid in Khawr and Hamad al-Attiyya. Both had a history of opposition. Abdalla Misnid's complaints against the government went back to the early 1950s when he felt the expanding state had usurped his historical role as local leader of the Muhanda tribe.[159] Al-Attiyya's opposition was more complex. He came from a family with historical ties to the Shaikh. Several Shaikhs, including Abdalla and Ali, married al-Attiyyas. As oil had increased the shaikhs' power, the al-Attiyya position, once near equal to the al-Thanis, began to decline. Having tried and failed to get shaikhly allowances, family members adopted two different strategies. Some decided to cut their losses and join the government. The best example of this was Muhammad, who became Qatar's first police officer and later army chief of staff. Other al-Attiyyas became public works minister, director of the heir apparent's office, ambassador to Iran, and other high posts. Muhammad's brothers, however, took the opposite approach and began actively opposing the Shaikh, leading demonstrations and engaging in a variety of legal and illegal opposition activities in the late 1950s (including the suspected sabotage of an oil installation). In 1963 Hamad became a leader in the popular uprising.

The government's response was swift. Although some family members wanted to shell Khawr, calmer heads prevailed. At the end of April the ruler jailed fifty notables and exiled the leaders. When Ahmad refused to allow Misnid to return, his substantial clan followed him to Kuwait. Hamad al-Attiyya was arrested and died in exile.

The uprising prompted Ahmad to institute some belated control over the family. He put some restraints on family allowances including his own (agreeing to forgo his quarter of the Shell revenues). The shaikh who had fired on the crowd was exiled (and in the late 1960s, for other offenses, executed). In 1968 Ahmad announced that all shaikhs must settle their debts and submit to ordinary law in disputes with other citizens (Declassified documents 1978: 19A). Even so, the events of 1963 suggest how little progress had been made in institutionalizing a system of dispute resolution in the ruling family. The shaikhs were still undisciplined. Old tactics (resort to gunfire) in turn met old responses – as in the past the dissidents were exiled. It is evidence of Qatar's late, and limited, centralization of political power that exit was still a viable political choice. The one difference in 1963 was that the Shaikh recognized and in small measure responded to the popular opposition. The strike met not merely with repression but also with popular reforms. The strikers conceded to a general promise of reform and specific promises on a municipality and on hiring and promoting Qataris. By May the strike was over. In May the Shaikh issued an "Explanatory statement on the comprehensive program for the advancement of the country" in which he promised reforms to achieve justice, equality, stability and production. He also introduced a few popular measures. A 1964 law gave low income Qataris land and loans. By 1971 1065 subsidized and 260 free houses were distributed (UN 1972: 74). After the 1963 disturbances, workers' committees were also established to hear complaints and settle disputes. Still, it was too little, too late. As discontent increased, Ahmad now simply spent more and more time abroad, leaving daily administration to Khalifa.

Khalifa's accession

Khalifa's role in day-to-day affairs of state had grown steadily since Ahmad's accession, as Ahmad displayed no particular desire to rule, preferring Europe, Asia, indeed anywhere to Qatar, leaving Khalifa *de facto* ruler, a status to which Khalifa never fully acclimated. In his mind, his legitimate rule had been usurped. He nursed this claim for years. Beginning with the 1963 demonstrations, Khalifa and his supporters had begun taking on more and more duties. By the late 1960s Khalifa was handling more state affairs than Ahmad. The final break between the two arose over the issue of independence and federation. In 1968 Britain announced its intended withdrawal from the Gulf. One of the options Qatar faced was that of joining with the other shaikhdoms that would form the United Arab Emirates. Ahmad advocated this position; Khalifa wanted independence. After disagreements between Ahmad and Khalifa became so pronounced that Qatar began putting forward "debilitating" proposals, Qatar withdrew from talks, paving the way for Qatar's establishment as an independent state (al-Rumaihi 1983: 61). In September 1971 this occurred. Shaikh Khalifa made the announcement; Ahmad, in Switzerland, did not return for the celebrations. On 22 February 1972 while hunting in Iran, Ahmad learned that Khalifa had deposed him. Ahmad had by then lost the support of the family, the Saudis, who backed the coup "financially, politically, and with a show of armed force at the border" (Cordesman 1984: 595), and Britain. Britain had long had little positive to say about Ahmad, "a singularly useless individual." His "poor performance" as acting ruler in the 1956 riots led Burrows to conclude that Khalifa would be the best successor.[160] In the 1963 crisis Britain resisted Ahmad's appeals for help (Monroe 1964: 72). Britain was now prepared to back Khalifa.

An immediate factor in the coup was the apparent move by Ahmad to make his son, health minister Abdalaziz, heir apparent, thus reneging, still again, on the 1949 agreement. Truckloads of arms were found at Abdalaziz's palace, as well as an electric chair and a list of fifty prominent Qataris and expatriates in the government (thus giving the new amir at least fifty allies). Abdalaziz was accused of using state health programs to assure his own succession at the expense of development. Over 5000 Qatari supporters of Ahmad, many in apparent good health, were sent abroad for luxurious, but not rigorous, health care by Abdalaziz. In 1970 his expenditures had grown so large that Ahmad was dipping into his personal allocation to cover the health budget. In the following years Khalifa moved ahead with particular speed in health care, providing the services that effectively eliminated much of the need for Qataris to travel abroad for treatment and setting up a medical committee to evaluate those genuinely in such need. Abdalaziz now joined his father in exile (*Arab Report and Record*, 1–15 March 1972: 119; *MEED*, 3 March 1972: 232; August 1983: 48; 9th June Studies 1974: 33; Anthony 1975: 94; al-Kuwari 1978: 119).

Since Khalifa had been promised the post, his position was that the coup was simply a restoration of his legitimate rule. He had the chief judge defend the coup's legality in the Friday mosque sermon (9th June Studies 1974: 25). Khalifa arrived in the position with substantial government experience. He had been head of oil security, the civil courts, the education department, and the finance department. Because Khalifa was already prime minister and *de facto* ruler the transition was easy.

Khalifa now faced the same choice that Ahmad had: contain the family or comply with their demands. The strategy he chose was the opposite of Ahmad's. He decided to rein in the family and devote more revenue to development and building popular support. As in Kuwait the ruler now introduced a series of policies aimed at bypassing the ruling family and the merchants and developing new ties with the national population. Social services had seen little development under Ahmad. The first state hospital opened in 1959, followed by a maternity hospital in 1965. Educational facilities had grown some in the 1960s. In the early 1960s a social security system was introduced. But with so much of the revenue going to the shaikhs, development was necessarily constrained. Not that much had changed since 1952 when the Foreign Office wrote, with some exaggeration, "the Ruler is afraid of his family and will always, I suppose, yield if they make enough noise. The family say: 'How can you spend money on roads and hospitals and such like nonsense when we haven't even got a decent Cadillac to ride in'"[161]

Khalifa's first policies signaled a shift in the support base from his predecessor. In a major break with his predecessor's policy, Khalifa decided to confront the family rather than comply with their financial requests. He cut family allowances and increased spending on social services. In 1970 Ahmad had taken a quarter of the revenues, his relatives another quarter or more. Extravagance was abundant. Now Khalifa announced he would curb the shaikhs' extravagance. He detailed a new division of revenues. He transferred the ruler's quarter to the state budget, almost half of which now went to public services. Popular measures included a 30 per cent increase in social aid, a 20 per cent raise to the armed forces and civil servants, and a 25 per cent increase in old age pensions.

The amir canceled outstanding public housing payments, and within a year 2500 new, free housing units were built. Khalifa also introduced price controls on consumer goods and set up subsidized food cooperatives (*MEED*, 14 April 1972: 412; 29 December 1972: 1511; 2 March 1973: 242). Where Ahmad had been criticized for not implementing the Provisional Constitution, Khalifa now promulgated an Amended Provisional Constitution and established an Advisory Council. In the following years Khalifa poured large amounts of money into education, health care, and other programs that would benefit the less wealthy Qatari. He also redoubled state efforts to provide government posts for Qatari nationals. When the University of Qatar produced its first graduates in the early 1980s, they received high state posts despite their relative youth and inexperience. In 1985 legislation put new limits on the placement of non-nationals in state jobs.

Khalifa also reorganized the government, purging his cousin's side and using his own family faction as an elite recruitment corps. One son became finance and oil minister, another commander-in-chief of the army, another deputy commander. A brother became interior minister, a nephew police commander. By the late 1970s, the amir seemed in better control of the family. By 1977 he felt confident enough to name his son Hamad, now defense minister, heir apparent. Nonetheless, as in the previous succession crises, Khalifa's rule carried with it the danger of family opposition. Hamad's appointment as heir apparent did not sit well with many. One source, until his death in 1977, was the deposed Shaikh Ahmad. Although Ahmad and Khalifa reached a reconciliation of sorts in 1975, Ahmad's faction continued to stake a claim. By some accounts when Ahmad took power in 1960 he agreed to an arrangement similar to Kuwait's, whereby the succession would alternate between the Hamad and Ali factions (*MEED*, 3 March 1972: 232). By this logic, Khalifa's successor should come from Ali's line. Whatever was agreed, and by whom, no institutionalization occurred and so dissent remains. Another source of opposition was the amir's brother Suhaim, who in the 1950s had crossed Cochrane so defiantly. In exchange for his support in the coup he became foreign minister and felt he was promised the succession. When Khalifa instead backed his son Hamad, Suhaim expressed his opposition by boycotting cabinet meetings. The amir then created the ministry of state for foreign affairs, thus avoiding actually firing Suhaim, but contributing to bureaucratic proliferation. Suhaim's claim ceased only with his death in 1985. Indications that opposition continues appeared in 1983 when the government announced that it had foiled a plot to blow up the Doha Sheraton during the forthcoming Gulf Cooperation Council (GCC) summit. Dozens of arrests followed, including some in the security apparatus. Some sources linked the plan to continuing family disputes over the succession (as well as to Libyan backed domestic opposition – the Libyan Charge d'Affaires was ordered out of

Doha; *MECS*, 1982–3: 406; 1983–4: 417; *Wall Street Journal*, 7 November 1983: 38). Like Ahmad, Khalifa succeeded in placing his own family supporters in high positions of state. He could not, however, eliminate family opposition.

Bureaucratic growth and bureaucratic control

The policies of the last few decades – the use of bureaucratic posts as shaikhly sinecures and the expansion of social services and development – have produced a large and, for Qatar, complex state bureaucracy. Unlike Kuwait, where the shaikhs have managed to exercise sufficient, if incomplete, control over this bureaucracy by manipulating reinforced family ties, in Qatar the rulers have been unable to exact predictable control over the bureaucracy because they lack the requisite control over their own family.

The first state structures to appear in Qatar were the financial and security administrations developed by Britain. The second phase of administrative growth, in the 1950s and 1960s, focused on infrastructure. According to the 1962 Arthur D. Little (ADL) study which began this phase, government organization at the time was quite limited: "major defects of the present system are that there is sometimes confusion and over-lapping between departments and that an unduly heavy burden is placed upon the Deputy Ruler and the Director General" (ADL 1962: 29). ADL felt it was important for Qatar to develop a proper state staff. It called for the immediate appointment of experts to work with Khalifa in development. The report also expressed concern over Qatar's overwhelming dependence on oil which would, it projected, run out by 1982. It urged Qatar to diversify by developing natural gas, foreign investments, and fishing – the only local industry they thought had potential. The government moved broadly on ADL's recommendations. In 1964 the ruler announced plans to create a state reserve, to establish gas-based petrochemical industries, and to develop a handful of local industries and agriculture. The first major industry was the Qatar National Cement Company, established in 1965. This venture was one of the few joint public/private concerns; subsequent major industrial projects were state owned. In the late 1960s the government established a number of new state organizations to run the industries. The decade ended with the drawing up of Qatar's first five-year plan for 1970–5. Projects included a refinery, a gas plant, a salt plant, a bag factory, a plastic plant, and expansion of the fertilizer facility. Administrative reorganizations followed, along with training programs to bring Qataris into the government. With the inauguration of the *Official Gazette* in 1961, laws were regularly published. As the state's functions grew, so did its staff. By 1971 11,719 people, 13 per cent of the workforce, worked for the state. Two-thirds were Qatari, but concentrated in lower-skill jobs (UN 1972: 83–4).

This growth was largely uncontrolled. In the early 1970s one observer described it,

Continuous enlargement of government and the extension of its functions and services led to the growth of administrative units. [This however] occurred without adequate efforts to coordinate them with each other or with already existing departments. This proliferation and fragmentation of governmental activities resulted in poor coordination and not infrequent duplication . . . the administrative structure of Qatar was composed of 33 major departments, all placed at the same level and reporting directly to the ruler . . . Since similar and related functions and activities were not grouped together . . . the number of separate units was relatively large and, hence, the span of control of the ruler became unduly wide and difficult.   (Sadik and Snavely 1972: 158)

Britain's withdrawal and independence created the next administrative burst. With independence, the thirty-three departments were reduced to ten ministries (under seven shaikhs) and given formal jurisdictions. When Khalifa took over he changed the individuals in power, but not the basic organizing principle of bureaucratic rule. He removed Ahmad's supporters only to replace them with his own.

After the 1973 oil price increases Khalifa initiated a phase of rapid industrialization. He brushed aside both the concerns of the ADL team and those of a UN team brought in in 1972 which, like ADL, was pessimistic about diversification prospects (UN 1972). Under Khalifa, Qatar's industrial ventures have been in three areas: fertilizer production, begun in 1973; a steel mill, started in 1978; and petrochemicals, with production starting in 1981. These industrial ventures have not been very successful. Qafco, the fertilizer company, has had relatively good output, but Qapco, the petrochemicals company, came on line in 1981, just when falling oil production necessitated cutbacks. The steel industry has fared even worse. The $275 million plant that opened in 1978 could produce steel only at three times the selling price (*Wall Street Journal*, 18 July 1983: 22). World steel prices have fallen in the 1980s. These setbacks came to an economy already depressed by the oil price decreases of the 1980s. Although Qatar has substantial foreign assets – $7–8 billion – it still lacks Kuwait's investment cushion (London *Times*, 22 February 1983: 13).

Oil remains the only highly developed sector. In 1976 Khalifa nationalized the oil industry, giving service contracts to the former concessionaires. Under the Qatar National Petroleum Company, Khalifa has made some effort to expand up and downstream, but Qatar lacks the resources to attempt anything on Kuwait's scale. With only a few years of oil left, Qatar has now put its hopes in gas. But if producers have been unable to hold to agreed oil prices, they have not even set gas prices. Moreover, gas has far higher transport costs. Qatar's gas production came on line only after serious setbacks (including a 1977 explosion which nearly destroyed the Umm Said gas plant) about the time oil prices started seriously dropping. Qatar has also had problems expanding sales and Japan, its primary market, is locked into long-term contracts with Asian suppliers. Hence, ambitious, but expensive, plans for developing the North Field, which contains 10 per cent of the world's proven gas reserves have had to be scaled back (*MEED*, August 1984: 15).

All these policies – distribution, employment, development – have contributed to bureaucratic expansion. Their unintended consequence has been to produce a large and nearly uncontrolled bureaucracy. In 1986 32,549 people worked for the state in thirteen ministries and fifteen major departments, councils and committees. State employment is clearly one form of welfare: 44 per cent of these were Qataris, almost half of whom were illiterate or could barely read and write (Qatar, CSO 1987: 56, 62). There have been efforts to address the policy confusion this bureaucratic proliferation had produced – episodic expert advisory commissions, repeated administrative reforms. However, the problems of central control have not abated. The amir continues to try to control this bureaucracy personally. Aside from some delegation of authority in the more technical areas, he and a few advisors run state affairs closely. A US embassy official observed in 1983,

Individuals are more important than institutions in Qatar, and personal relationships among Government officials often carry more weight than lines on an organization chart would suggest. Most government agencies are highly centralized; authority to commit funds is in the hands of a relatively small number of individuals and is rarely delegated. One result of this lack of institutionalization can be that decisions are often delayed if the responsible individual is away from Doha or preoccupied with other matters.

(US Embassy, Doha, "Doing Business in Qatar," 1983: 1)

The *Financial Times* reports that "money supply is sitrictly controlled by the amir in such a personal way that bankers claim to be able to tell when he is on holiday, through no other way than the effect that three weeks of his now signing any cheques has on liquidity" (16 February 1981, III: 2). The patterns of control that evolved never solved the problem. Their failure can be seen in the history of administrative reforms, usually heralded by teams of foreign experts, followed in a few years by another spurt of reform. When administrative reforms fail the amir returns to more autocratic and personal methods of control. Khalifa himself personally signs all checks over $50,000 (*MEED*, August 1983: 27). The unintended outcome of a decade of development and distribution had not been a tightly controlled state, but rather a larger machine for distributing revenues to Qataris. State employment itself is now one important form of welfare. The long-term result may well be a loss in popular loyalty to the ruler. As welfare functions become the norm they are increasingly seen less as examples of the ruler's largesse and more as arrangements that clients can claim from patrons or as rights that individuals, as citizens, can claim from the state. These are the direct, although unintended consequences of state policy.

As oil prices fell in the 1980s, problems began to appear. Budget deficits prompted a series of austerity measures: freezes and cutbacks in departmental expenditures, reductions in state employment, and the delay of several major development projects. Following the April 1983 austerity budget the government announced in May that it would introduce some charges for health care, water and electricity. In November the government announced plans to fire 3000 employees, mostly expatriates (*MEED*, 27 May 1983: 47; 23 December 1983: 31). When prices dropped again in 1986 austerity measures increased. Unlike other Gulf states, Qatar did not initially increase production to compensate for the revenue loss. Instead it cut back on existing expenditures and put several new projects on hold, ranging from the university expansion to the North Field gas project. The one budget area to emerge unscathed from the austerity measures was defense, which soon became the major source of contracting work. Cutbacks could not help but increase opposition in the population, among the poorer Qataris whom Khalifa, until now, had courted. The 1983 plot to assassinate GCC heads may have reflected this, following not only a year's recession which had virtually brought the economy to a standstill, but also substantial government cutbacks in services, for example in the health ministry, which cut clinic staff by almost 10 per cent (*MEED*, August 1986: 16). By 1986 dissent had even spread to the ruling family. Following cutbacks there was talk "of dissatisfaction among the ruling family, most of whom fill senior positions in government, over cuts in their normally generous allowances for personal expenses" (*MEED*, August 1986: 4). The dependence on outside revenues, bountiful as those revenues could be, was leaving the ruler in a vulnerable position.

The development of a civic myth

One response to the problem of bureaucratic growth and the tensions tied to cutbacks in state services has been for the amir to lay greater stress on normative socialization. When Khalifa came to power in 1972 he faced a dilemma. His accession had inaugurated an era of great change. Not only were new policies emerging, but the pattern of rule had decisively shifted, he hoped, to his side of the family. Yet he felt obliged to stress publicly that nothing, really, had changed. The same firm hand, at the helm since 1960, was still there. There had been no coup, no change of government, only a reform movement. The formal change was primarily symbolic. Just what it symbolized, however, remained unclear.

The amir's accession speech of 22 February 1972 suggested the ambiguity of the transition in the realm of symbols. He thanked the ruling family and the armed forces, alluded to the harm he had prevented, cursed the previous administration for ignoring his advice, and promised a new era of prosperity, justice and stability. Although he wanted to form "an illuminating bridge that links the glorious present with the ancient past," he clearly didn't know what symbolic spans to use (Qatar, Ministry of information 1976: 29). Although his accession was, at best, irregular, neither had it broken decisively through the past to a brave new era.

No clear symbols were evoked for none were evocative. Qatar was sadly lacking a civic myth: it was a polity suffering from a severe shortage of symbols. The only solution was to create them. In the next years the amir gave high priority to developing symbols that would clarify and legitimize his claim to rule. Fortunately, the new amir's resources were almost boundless. His first task was to take stock of his meager symbolic legacy. A few resources were at hand. First, the rudiments of a Qatari identity were forged, like any other, through conflict, in this case economic conflict. In the 1950s the oil strikes that had pitted Qatari laborers against Dhofaris and Pakistanis had finally merged into a conflict of Qataris against expatriates. This emergent Qatari identity was strengthened by alliances of convenience as merchants grasped the national symbol as a weapon against foreign contractors. The ruling family also found it opportune to recognize and encourage this struggle to pressure the oil company and the Shaikh. This new identity was then buttressed by a series of nationality and commercial laws that defined Qataris and granted them special status and rights.

The second legacy Khalifa inherited was more recent. Independence defined Qatar's place in the family of nations, giving it international status and recognition, providing the amir with the most overt trappings of state, augmenting his meager cache of inherited symbols with new ones: flags, coins and anthems. The third legacy was a founding myth. Qataris already knew to trace themselves back to Arabia through migrations in the eighteenth century, a connection firmly implanted in official history. This defined the people and tied them to their land. As a myth it was adequate but not illustrious. It was not an ancient myth, nor was it an inspiring myth, forged from revolutionary or anticolonial struggle, full of heroes and heroic acts. Compared to Kuwait, it lacked the unifying power of the story of a single migration that forged the Bani Utub and justified their leading institutions.

The most pressing problem with the myth was that it left a gap between the desert past and the present. It did not explain how the Qataris' life today, a life of oil and money, was tied to the lives of those in the desert myth. Oil, especially, was as unintegrated symbolically as it was economically, an enclave myth of its own. Oil never developed myths because oil itself touched fewer people than its revenues. The one exception, the oilfield workers, were occasionally inclined to immortalize their experiences in poetry, for example, the poem by one worker "On the occasion of the oil company's reneging on its promise to raise wages after completing excavation work on well number two" (al-Uthman 1980: 217). If the myth could not make sense of oil, it also did not explain why the al-Thanis, let alone Khalifa, should rule. That link would have to be forged through a new myth. Fortunately, the time was propitious. The desert past was too close to be myth to the oldest, who actually remembered it, or even to their children who, like those of any immigrants, wanted little to do with the embarrassing old country. The poverty and deprivation of the desert could only be romantic to the new generation which had never experienced it. But they were ascendent.

There were also practical problems with creating a new myth. First, there weren't enough Qataris to do it. Much of the myth-making would have to be contracted out to expatriates. Second, the nation-state myth had larger rivals: a Gulfian identity, kept alive by ties of trade and family and the geographic mobility of a wealthy population, a pan-Arab identity, kept alive in part by the rulers' legitimizing dedication to Palestine; and a broad Islamic identity, an attachment that needed to be handled carefully since Islam provided the most accessible, evocative, but also flexible and volatile set of symbols.

The amir's first step into the past was to commission an archaeological study. Work had already begun in the 1950s with a Danish expedition, but it had only produced stone age sites, fragments of someone else's past. In 1973 a British archaeological expedition arrived. Its mission was to produce something appropriate for the amir: a national museum. As the expedition's chronicler described the task:

In terms of the Museum project the immediate need was to provide a broad chronological framework to give meaning and coherence to Qatar's past by using, and wherever possible extending, such limited material as was already available. This fact needs to be stressed because it explains the number and unusually wide range of projects undertaken and described in this volume as a means of recovering as much evidence of Qatar's past as possible in a relatively short time. (deCardi 1978: 3)

The mission had the highest level of cooperation, including army drivers and equipment from the heir apparent. It produced a wealth of artifacts and history for the museum and even unearthed more appropriate evidence of eighteenth-century mercantile settlements along the coast. The project's next phase, collecting pieces for the museum, was a national acquisition effort, organized by the information ministry, supervised by a committee of Qataris, and categorized by a team of researchers. It used the new state media to call on Qataris to bring in materials of possible relevance. The museum also drew on older Qataris for its staff. Thus Qataris participated collectively in writing their history. The museum opened in 1975, a beautiful and accessible, prize-winning success, popular above all among Qataris. The heart of the museum was the old Shaikh's palace, first occupied by Shaikh Abdalla early in the century. The selection of the palace as a centerpiece linked the ruling family to all the other pasts displayed within: the stone age, the nomadic days, the Islamic era, the pearling days, the oil boom, the state projects. Lest the lesson be lost, exhibits included poems by the founder of the dynasty, Shaikh Qasim, as well as later ruling family photographs.

The museum was the first and most important step. It defined Qatar's basic history. Continuing work on that history was now placed in a new institution, the information ministry, established in 1972. The ministry controls the ongoing process of writing history through the national archives, housed in the palace. It controls the media, used extensively since Khalifa's accession to cover high and popular culture. The ministry also controls the entry and movements of foreign journalists and writers. The ministry's goal is to guard history, but this is an ultimately impossible task. Unlike non-oil states, where the citizen is tied to the state through taxation and participation, the amir must rely on normative socialization. But this normative socialization does not have an ideology behind it. This is neither for lack of imagination nor talent, rather it is because Qatar must integrate deeply conflicting local myths of the state. It is hard to reconcile a monarchist ideology (for the ruler) with a capitalist ideology (for the merchants) with a social entitlement ideology (for the population). The tensions inherent in this project have not been resolved. They manifest themselves in a deep distrust of research, a tendency to take refuge in the more distant past and in *turath*, or cultural heritage, a heavy hand in censorship, and an ambient ill-ease about the recent past.

Oil and the regional environment

Qatar's new reliance on outside sources of revenue has not, then, eliminated all the political problems the Shaikhs hoped it might. To the extent that oil has allowed Qatar's Shaikhs to distance themselves somewhat from internal sources of opposition – merchants and relatives – it has been at the price of increased dependence on outside forces. As in Kuwait, the rulers in Qatar are finding they have exchanged one kind of dependence for another.

Qatar has long had to rely on larger powers in its conflicts with its neighbors, especially with Bahrain. Throughout the nineteenth and twentieth century, foreign powers and intrigue reinforced the weakness of local institutions; as local factions, who could always appeal to Saudi Arabia, Bahrain, the Ottomans, were never forced to set up strong local structures to settle their differences. This was one reason the Shaikh welcomed Britain. Britain's presence did not so much introduce a new foreign dependence as deepen it and change the actors. Britain limited but did not eliminate the involvement of other powers. Saudi Arabia continued to collect taxes from tribal sections in Qatar into the late 1940s. Through the 1950s Britain remained concerned that its untimely action might drive the Shaikh into Saudi arms.[162] Saudi Arabia also continued to play its historical role as refuge for Qatari dissidents. The Saudis have been a haven for a long line of Qatari exiles, ranging from deposed rulers to ruling family members, to merchants, to ordinary dissidents. Shaikhs, unhappy over allowances, went there after the war. In the 1950s, troublesome shaikhs were banished there (although often only temporarily, for as one observer noted, "this only means that they are given a good time by the Saudis and are very soon allowed back as a result of Saudi intervention").[163] Long after borders were settled, dissident Qataris traveled there easily. Abdalla Darwish, who long maintained ties with Saudi Arabia, settled there after his ouster. Saudi Arabia welcomed such contacts. In 1955 Burrows wrote that "when King Saud visited Qatar recently he said, in the presence of the Political Agent, that Qatar and Saudi Arabia were as one, that there was no boundary separating them, and that the Ruler could always depend on him for help."[164] Britain worried about:

the possibility that King Saud regards Qatar as the thin end of the wedge that would split the Persian Gulf States open to his ambitions. The Ruler of Qatar has long held the Saudi Ruling Family in that veneration which the Arab feels for the powerful . . . Nevertheless, the Ruler appears fully aware that but for the British connexion his State might soon be swallowed by Saudi Arabia, a consummation he shows no sign of wanting. To ensure that he does not weaken, there is a British Adviser in his service as well as a Political Agency in Doha.[165]

Once Britain withdrew, Qatar had little choice but to turn again to Saudi Arabia. The Saudis appear to have since involved themselves in a number of major decisions. There were rumors in the late 1960s that Saudi Arabia backed Khalifa in his disputes with Ahmad over federation, and in the 1972 coup (although this support was offered in the context of a renegotiation of the Saudi borders; Cordesman 1984: 410–11). Saudi Arabia has tried to integrate Khalifa's development projects with their own and to work together in joint defense planning.

With Britain gone, Qatar has also relied more heavily on Saudi Arabia in its disputes with Bahrain. The Zubara dispute had reached something of a settlement in 1944 when the Political Agent negotiated an agreement between the two Shaikhs which acknowledged some of the al-Khalifa's customary rights, such as grazing and visitation without customs formalities. But when Shaikh Abdalla broke the accord by building a fort at Zubara, Bahrain imposed prohibitively high transit dues on goods for Qatar in retaliation. Ali's accession in 1949 produced hopes of a *rapprochement*. Ali approached Bahrain's Shaikh Salman on friendly terms and Salman reciprocated with a loan of thirty rifles. In 1950 a settlement was achieved after much difficulty which removed the transit duties and reconfirmed the al-Khalifa right to visit Zubara. The next year many Naim who had fled during the dispute returned to Zubara. With the embargo and trade restriction lifted, trade from Bahrain grew rapidly. But it didn't last. In

1953 Bahrain sent a party of students and teachers to Zubara where they proceeded to write "Bahrain" in huge letters on the fort walls. The Bahrain education department also published maps giving Bahrain sovereignty over Qatar's entire northwest coast. Ali responded by posting police at Zubara, to the consternation of the Political Resident. In 1954 when Bahrain revived its claims Shaikh Ali responded by reoccupying the Zubara fort, adding police in 1956. The British suspected Ali had Saudi encouragement. And indeed, in 1957 the Qataris accepted a Saudi offer to mediate over Zubara. In the following years Qatar tightened its control over Zubara, where it now exercises effective sovereignty, but it never really settled its dispute with Bahrain.[166]

These tensions, and Saudi interventions, reappeared most recently in 1986 in a dispute between Qatar and Bahrain over Fasht al-Dibal Island. Fasht al-Dibal was a new source of contention: until March 1986 when it was reclaimed it wasn't an island at all, but a coral reef, submerged at high tide. It was however part of a larger zone of disputed territory which also included the Qatar-claimed, Bahraini-controlled Hawar Islands. This had been a source of contention for years. In 1982 Saudi Arabia had intervened when Qatar accused Bahrain of provocative naval maneuvers near Hawar (which included a Bahraini patrol boat named *Hawar*). The conflict over Fasht al-Dibal followed on this dispute. It erupted when Bahrain had a Dutch firm send workers to the island to build, variously, a coast guard station, industrial installations, or GCC naval monitoring posts. Qatar interpreted the creation of Fasht al-Dibal, certainly its fortification, as a violation of a 1978 agreement to maintain the status quo. In April, Qatari soldiers arriving by helicopter opened fire and seized twenty-nine workers. As the conflict grew, both Bahrain and Qatar reinforced their military forces. Qatar began building a causeway toward the Hawar Islands, but stopped after Saudi intervention. Saudi Arabia, anxious to arbitrate, sent high level delegations to both states. In May it announced an ingenious solution to the crisis: the parties agreed to dismantle the island.

The Gulf war also kept the Saudis involved in Qatari affairs, although the war itself had little effect on Qatar. Qataris have some family ties, Sunni and Shia, to Iran, the result of many migrations. Historically Iran and Qatar have had good relations. Iran was among the first states to recognize Khalifa in 1972. In 1986 it backed Qatar on Fasht al-Dibal. Courted by Iran, interested in maintaining a balance between Iran and Saudi Arabia, Qatar remained for some time reluctant to follow the Saudis more closely. But following the Iranian pilgrimage clashes with the Saudis in July 1987 Qatar moved more firmly into the Saudi camp. The Saudis however have not been able to keep the Qataris completely in line. They were unable to prevent a 1988 dispute with the US over Qatar's purchase of twelve blackmarket US manufactured Stinger anti-aircraft missiles, bought in reaction to the US decision to sell Bahrain Stingers.

Oil, then, has made Qatar, like Kuwait, more dependent on the outside world. This dependence takes two forms. The first is an economic dependency. Qatar relies on major foreign powers for the purchase of its oil and gas. The second is a security dependency. Qatar, like Kuwait, is a small state whose security rests in part on the particular regional configuration of power, in which oil also plays a role. The revolution in Iran and the Gulf War have changed that regional configuration. Although Qatar, like Kuwait, has been able to exercise a degree of maneuverability within these constraints, it remains vulnerable to other powers, regional and global, for its security.

Conclusion

At first glance, Qatar seems to be a political anachronism. It is ruled by a monarch, odd enough these days, but by a monarch whose style of rule seems more autocratic and less restrained by social and political institutions than his neighbors. The government, it is said, stops when he leaves town. The fact that so little is publicly known of Qatar, that the internal political dynamics are so shrouded in mystery, only reinforces this image of a regime that has accidentally survived into the modern age. Nothing could be further from the truth. The seeming anachronisms that characterize Qatar today are in fact quite modern. Those institutions that seem to cling most strongly to the past are among the most recent creations. Qatar's politics, its strengths and weaknesses as a state, make sense only when viewed in the context of its formative influences, key among them oil.

That Qatar, as a monarchy, has survived by accident, because nothing has shaken it, is a supposition most easily dispelled. Qatar has in fact been shaken with great frequency since its creation: all of its modern successions have been uneasy. Qatar's rulers have been anything but stable. Yet despite these contested successions the issue of power leaving the hands of the shaikhs has never been seriously raised. The regime is stable; its leaders are not. How do we account for this? The primary structural factor is oil: as in other oil states, distributive or rentier states, oil had the effect of weakening the ties between the rulers and society, substituting a short-term independence from social classes with a longer term dependence on outside forces, in this case for a time Britain, which mediated the introduction of oil. However oil revenues were filtered through pre-existing social and political structures. Qatar's historical peculiarities also account for the final form that political rule took. Situational factors include the unsettled economy, a weakly developed class structure, and a large ruling family. These factors explain how this transformation occurred, how Qatar came to be ruled by so shaky yet shaikhly a series of leaders.

In Kuwait the political transformation accompanying oil revolved around two primary actors – the Shaikh and the trading families – and centered on the break-down of the ruling coalition binding the two. In Qatar a similar transformation

167

also occurred. As in Kuwait the Shaikh was, before oil, dependent on the merchants for revenues. Oil, by providing large revenues paid directly to the ruler, freed the Shaikh and the state from this dependence and provided the resources necessary both to financially placate the merchants and to develop new allies – in the ruling family, whose political functions now grew, and among the national population at large. The welfare and development policies the Shaikh chose to bind these groups to the state in turn catalyzed, as it did in Kuwait, a large distributive state.

As in Kuwait, oil revenues restructured political life. But oil was filtered through preexisting social, economic, and political structures. These structures, while resembling Kuwait's, differed in crucial ways. The key factor distinguishing Qatar's pre-oil economy from Kuwait's was the weakness of the trade sector, the result of Qatar's smaller size and distance from the main trade routes. As a result, Qatar depended completely on pearling. This made the population more mobile. Because of this mobility, in an economic crunch the population could leave. That crunch hit with the pearl crash of the 1920s which decimated the population. While Kuwait depended heavily on pearling, it also benefited from the long-distance trade routes to India and Africa and from the overland caravan trade. When the pearling crash hit Kuwait, its merchants had more economic options. Exercising these options, the merchants returned to long-distance trade and diversified by developing land on the Shatt al-Arab. They were weakened economically, but they stayed; those of Qatar, left.

Qatar's fluid economy also shaped the political actors who emerged. The basic groupings were the same – the Shaikh, his family, Britain, the merchants, the national population, the expatriates – but their size, strength, and consequently political role differed. While in Kuwait interwar politics revolved around the merchants and the ruler, with Britain a passive third player, in Qatar the relationship between the ruler and Britain was more important. As in Kuwait, the Shaikh played a pivotal role. But unlike his Kuwaiti counterpart, his rule was new (dating only from the nineteenth century), dependent in large part on external recognition, and contested by his large family. When Britain, then oil, arrived no established succession patterns, as in Kuwait, had developed. Instead, a tradition of family-based factional opposition emerged. Oil revenues only politicized an already contentious family, culminating in Abdalla's abdication to his son Ali in 1949, the first year of oil exports.

Because of family opposition, the Shaikhs turned sooner to Britain for support. The succession crisis of 1949 was resolved only through British intervention. The price for this intervention was fiscal and political control. In the late 1940s the British presence consisted only of occasional visits from the Political Agent at Bahrain. Following the 1949 crisis a Political Officer arrived, followed by advisors. British officials rapidly took control of finance, security and development. Under their watchful eyes, the first bureaucracy was created and the first development and distributive projects instituted, using the new oil revenues.

These new revenues allowed the ruler to distance himself from the merchants, even as he grew more dependent on Britain. Qatar's trade sector was small, the proportion of trade handled by indigenous traders was smaller still and among the indigenous traders, the shaikhs played a larger role. In the nineteenth century the ruler had removed the Indian community and other traders and assumed their role. By the late nineteenth century the Shaikh was one of the largest traders. The sharp economic and political division of labor that characterized Kuwait did not emerge. Then, when the interwar pearl crash hit, the small traders left. Consequently, on the eve of oil, Qatar had no real merchant class, let alone a politically active one. Instead, only two families – al-Mani and Darwish – remained and they were divided by competition. For a few years in the 1950s these families were able to hold their own by manipulating disputes between Britain and the Shaikh, offering terms for loans with fewer conditions than those offered by the oil company. Both families benefited from oil, first by supplying the company with goods and labor, later by moving into construction and imports. But in the end they could not compete with the company's revenues. Gradually the Shaikh's financial dependence on them declined. By using their palace ties, the Darwishes were more successful and in the 1950s able to overtake the al-Mani. But by the 1960s the Darwishes, too, were eclipsed, this time by the ruling family. By then there was no organized trading community left for them to turn to and in 1956 the Darwish patriarch packed his bags and left for Saudi Arabia.

In the following years, oil prompted an arrangement with the merchants, a political and economic division of labor, that resembled the pattern that occurred in Kuwait. But because the merchant community in Qatar was so small and weak, because it lacked experience in political organization, it did not fare so well. As in Kuwait, in exchange for political quiescence, merchants received economic protection: trade monopolies, agencies, and protective economic legislation. But when the Shaikh turned to the merchants, he could, unlike Kuwait's Shaikh, turn to families outside the old trading monopoly. These families were often family retainers, tied to the Shaikh through patron-client networks. The merchants who rose to wealth were dependent clients of the ruling family. From this arrangement, a few trading families grew quite wealthy, but politically they were replaced in key advisory positions by ruling family members and shunted off to powerless political institutions. Because these merchants lacked an independent power base and political organization, the ruler could more easily erode the original deal: he could and did break the rules. In particular he allowed the ruling family to invade their economic territory with increasing frequency.

As in Kuwait, the rulers also tried to develop allies in the national population.

Ali turned to the national population for support in the 1950s in his disputes with Britain, encouraging strikes among oil workers to wrest more money from the oil company. The experience of organized strikes catalyzed a sense of Qatari identification which Ali and Ahmad encouraged and later routinized, as in Kuwait, through protective nationality laws and preferential access to the new welfare state. The presence of an unusually large expatriate population, brought in first to run the oil industry, later to man the development projects, encouraged this Qatari identity. In the 1970s, Khalifa developed his ties to the citizen population by using the increased revenues to rapidly expand social services.

Distributive mechanisms, established originally to create domestic allies, created, as in Kuwait, a distributive state. But unlike Kuwait, where patron-client ties became routinized and even pockets of rational bureaucracy emerged, Qatar remained one large fief. Successive rulers, especially Khalifa, have tried but failed to maintain control over the expanding bureaucracy. The first technique was to give the ruling family new political and administrative roles. As in Kuwait, where once the Shaikh ruled autocratically and rather independently of his family, since oil, rulers have relied increasingly on family members as ministers and heads of parastatals in order to control the bureaucracy. But the same techniques that worked, more or less, in Kuwait have had less success in Qatar. Repeatedly shaikhs have turned their ministries into independent fiefdoms, building on the patron-client ties of family retainers. As in Kuwait, successive rulers have also introduced a series of administrative reforms. Unable to control his subordinates through these reforms, the amir has also tried to maintain the loyalty of the population by direct appeals – laying new stress on normative socialization and the development of a civic myth.

These efforts have not succeeded. The amir is increasingly unable to control the state he has built with oil. Whereas in Kuwait, the bureaucracy functions by incorporating many transitional forms of organization (patron-client, fiefdoms, technocratic) in Qatar it often ceases to work at all. Oil revenues have masked many of the inefficiencies, but in a period of low prices, these problems, of loyalty and control, are beginning to surface.

6 Conclusion

Kuwait and Qatar have presented an enigma: the endurance of almost anachronistically stable monarchical regimes in the presence of overwhelming social and economic change. They raise the question: how did such regimes survive despite the radical transformations catalyzed by oil? As this study has shown, these regimes survived precisely because of those transformations. Beneath the apparent political stability and continuity lie sea changes. This study has sought to identify and explain those changes. The key transformations are the emergence of new coalitions and new institutional structures, the transformation of the regime and the transformation of the state.

The most important regime change has been the withdrawal from formal political life of historically influential economic elites. In both Kuwait and Qatar oil revenues freed the rulers from their historical dependence on the trading families, halting ongoing economic, social and political processes, and catalyzing a new elite arrangement in which the traders renounced formal political influence in favor of a guarantee of economic survival: a trade of power for wealth. In the Gulf the merchants, when forced to choose, chose money over formal political influence. These families were, above all, traders; they knew the best deal had been offered. They were interested in political power for its economic benefits and not the reverse. Since they could have the economic benefits without the direct political influence, they were satisfied. Oil was the reason this choice arose with such clarity. Oil, and the particular power it gave the rulers, allowed the rulers to force the merchants to choose between wealth and formal power in a way they are not normally forced to. It is thus oil which explains the striking political silence of the merchants in a world where newly mobilized groups are elsewhere demanding incorporation into the political process.

The most important change in state formation has been the emergence of new and, for these states, large bureaucratic structures. The merchants' withdrawal from formal politics was accompanied by the development of two new kinds of ties: first, between the ruler and the ruling family, whose political role grew as rulers sought loyal allies for the most sensitive state posts; and second, between the ruler and the citizen population, through social programs and state employment. New institutions have emerged with the primary goal of distributing oil revenues through social services and employment. Oil revenues thus prompted not only the emergence of new bureaucratic states but particular kinds of states: distributive states.

Oil has thus elicited now predictable responses, forcing Kuwait and Qatar into a particular configuration of regime building and state building. This study suggests that the sources of capital and the mechanisms through which it enters the economy are key to understanding its political impact. Oil has produced a patterned response and will to some extent reproduce that response wherever it occurs.

These two processes of regime building and state formation are closely related. Oil gave rulers not only the freedom to turn away from the merchants, their historical allies, but also the capacity to use the new oil-induced bureaucracies to develop new allies among state employees and recipients of the new state services. State institutions were built as part of coalitional politics, to give the rulers leverage against the merchants, by bringing in other groups. In order to exclude the merchants, the rulers also had to include other allies: the ruling family and the national population. The cases of Kuwait and Qatar suggest that exclusionary and inclusionary policies, rather than opposites, are in fact intimately related. The centralization of power in the hands of the ruler demands the exclusion of those who once held power. To accomplish that exclusion and to bridge that transition, rulers must reach out, bypassing the economic elites, to those elites' historical clientele, the popular sector. An appeal for popular support may actually be critical to the centralization of power.

Oil elicited the same general response in both Kuwait and Qatar. But within this larger pattern significant differences also emerged depending on the configuration of economic, social, and political resources available in each state at the onset of oil. This study has not only shown us the similarities in outcomes prompted by oil, but also the differences and the factors that account for those differences. The effect of oil on coalitions and institutions varies depending on a number of determinants, two of which are of particular interest.

One factor is the degree of class cohesion in the economic elite. In those states, such as Kuwait, with an already entrenched and organized economic elite, that elite will be able to negotiate, rather than simply submit to, its withdrawal from politics, thus enabling it to hold on to more of its wealth, to some of its economic influence, and to its organizational structure. In Kuwait, because the merchant class was strong, well organized, and politicized before oil, it was able to strike a better deal with the ruler. This cohesion is important because the dual processes of state formation and coalition building do not cease with oil. Economic elites are more likely to maintain their capability to reenter politics if they negotiate their initial withdrawal. They are more likely to retain this capability if they enter the oil era conscious and organized. Kuwait and Qatar suggest that this cohesion is in turn the result of several factors. First the economic elite must be large. Kuwait's merchants constituted a class; Qatar's were never much more than an economic grouping. These states suggest that there is a numerical threshold that must be crossed before a group constitutes a class and is able to exercise some class capacity. Second, the economic elite is more likely to survive if there is a sharp division of labor between the political and economic realms and if the economic elite has enjoyed an historically high degree of autonomy in economic affairs. Kuwait's merchants enjoyed considerable historical autonomy and were thus capable of more independent action. Qatar's merchants always shared the economic realm with the shaikhs, thus weakening their negotiating power. Third, this study suggests the importance of non-economic factors in maintaining class identity. These non-economic factors allowed the merchants to bridge the economic transition to oil and provided the institutions for maintaining a class memory, and a memory of class tactics that could prove useful in the future. In Kuwait, these mechanisms included the social institutions of marriage and *majlis*. Shared status, a belief in a common, noble history, helped the merchants to remember who they wanted to be. In Qatar, these social institutions were destroyed in the interwar migrations. Their absence accounts in part for the merchants' inability to reconstitute themselves as a class and for their consequent relative weakness in dealing with the Shaikh.

A second factor accounting for the different outcomes in Kuwait and Qatar is the strength of the inherited political institutions or potential institutions, in particular the ruling family. In Kuwait the Shaikh was able to use the ruling family as a basis for a political institution and as an elite recruitment pool because the family had already worked out, on its own, mechanisms for settling internal disputes well before oil. Where such protoinstitutions do not exist, as in Qatar, the ruler will make do, improvising with the family resources available but, working with less flexible institutional material, the end result will be less effective. Rulers' families, let alone ruling families, are not all alike. The extent to which a ruler comes to power with an historically organized family behind him may play a key role in his ability to adapt new sources of revenue to his advantage. Because monarchies are in the first instance based on kinship, because this basis is formally recognized and, even before oil, partly institutionalized, monarchies as regime types may actually have an advantage in coping with the sudden influx of oil.

One of the reasons the rulers were able to force merchants to make choices was because the rulers controlled the state apparatus in a personal way, effective because the bureaucracy was still small. That, however, is changing as the bureaucracy grows. Now, new problems of control and loyalty are emerging. Oil freed rulers from dependency on, and accountability to, other groups just when this accountability was most needed to check the poorly systematized but rapid growth of the new state institutions that formed around the state's new distributive and developmental functions. Distributive policies, designed to ensure domestic peace, have had the unintended consequence of creating distributive states, unusual in that they emerged from the imperative to expend rather than extract revenues. These bureaucracies are now becoming a new arena for politics. The almost inadvertent emergence of these large distributive bureaucracies with capabilities of their own may be a source of weakness for the rulers.

Problems of control

Oil revenues gave rulers the resources for introducing new goals. The welfare and development policies the rulers chose to bind groups to the state in turn catalyzed large and complex bureaucracies. Distributive mechanisms, established originally to create domestic allies, required new state administrations for their implementation, creating distributive states. Today the state is the first employer of working nationals. Its proverbial cradle to grave welfare system as well as its far-reaching development policies touch everyone's life. Because the development of state institutions accompanied the transition to independence and statehood, a process with bureaucratic requirements of its own, the transition was particularly dramatic. In the years since oil, the state's role has continued to grow. The revenues have prompted all the oil states, to some degree, to move from simply distributing capital to creating a return on capital, investing surplus revenues in industries at home and abroad. These states have also assumed a gradually larger role in the oil industry itself. In the 1960s and 1970s Kuwait and Qatar assumed increasing control and finally ownership of the local oil industry. In both countries, but most successfully in Kuwait, the government has followed this control with upstream and downstream expansion, with vertical and horizontal integration. One consequence has been to increase the scope and size of the bureaucracy. Where once the ruler received a check directly from a foreign oil company, today even this receipt of money is mediated by the bureaucracy: a public oil company or an investment board.

The development of this larger state has had ramifications beyond the rulers' original intentions. Oil revenues have allowed rulers to create new state institutions, but bureaucracies are never neutral: as these institutions grow in size and complexity, they are becoming less amenable to control through ruling kinship networks. The ruling houses and the state administrations, though they coexist and exercise jurisdiction over the same populations, are not identical. Bureaucrats have the potential for developing their own centers of power, social relationships, and political ideals and goals. An unintended ramification is a potential loss of control over the population by the rulers as this control is increasingly mediated by a possibly disloyal bureaucracy.

As the state has become increasingly complex, the direct dependence of the population on the ruler has also broken down. Instead this new dependence increasingly involves the bureaucracy. One result is that the bureaucracy may be giving the merchants back in a new form what they lost with oil – independent control over a larger population below them. Gulf bureaucrats are not drawn randomly from the population. Above the expatriate staff the local breaucratic elites, those with the most power, bear a strong familial and social resemblance to pre-oil merchant elites. In part this is because the traders were the first to educate their sons abroad. Thus they initially possessed the technocratic as well as the historical financial skills the state badly needed. As the sons of merchants participated in bureaucratic governance beginning in the 1950s they began to slowly rise in the bureaucracy. Department heads were shaikhs, but the administrators just below them were merchants' sons. Old family loyalties have not disappeared with the acquisition of these technocratic skills. Indeed with oil traditional networks and institutions have been reworked to handle new demands. Today these trading families may be moving back into the second echelon of the bureaucracy, developing independent fiefdoms based on patron-client ties. Patronage links the citizen to the state in a time-honored but risky form of integration, necessarily mediated by patrons. An unintended consequence of the bureaucratic expansion is that merchants, taken out of decision-making at one end, may be gradually reentering through the back door of the bureaucracy. They control administrative fiefs with no necessary loyalty to the amir or his policies.

This bureaucratic growth has, by changing the political and social environment, created new tensions in the original pact. Tension is also emerging as the ruling families and their allies, reneging on that original transitional agreement, are entering the commercial realm. This has been the case in Qatar for over a decade; it is beginning to happen in Kuwait. Merchant protests against the business presence of shaikhs, first heard in the 1970s, were voiced again in the last days of the 1986 Assembly (Muslim students: 59; *The Economist*, 12 July 1986: 34). This process may catalyze political action by the merchants.

If the merchants are one source of tension, another source lies with those who were never part of the original arrangement. Because pacts are built informally, even personally, by particular actors, they may be less readily accepted by a new generation which did not negotiate them. Renegotiation may prove difficult in a changed environment. State distribution and development policies have inadvertently created new actors and new social groupings: expatriates who fit uneasily into established patron-client networks, new local trading families who may want more state contracts than old elites are willing to relinquish. The secret nature and inherent favoritism of the pacts makes them appear illegitimate to these newcomers. The arrangements between the rulers and the trading families have held together so far, but they may be undergoing stress both as a result of this bureaucratic growth and of tensions growing out of the original arrangement.

Problems of loyalty

Below the apex of the system, a loss in popular loyalty to the ruler based on gratitude may also be developing. Affluence is one basis of these regimes' legitimacy, an ideology of progress superimposed on preexisting tribal values of shaikhly responsibility and equality. At first state welfare functions served the ruler: as these institutions offered employment and an increasing variety of services to the citizen, they assumed many of the functions of traditional leaders. But as welfare functions become the norm, as services become legitimate claims on the state, they are seen less as examples of the rulers' largesse, and more as rights that citizens, not subjects, can claim from the state because of nationality (or as arrangements that clients, through *wasta* (connections), can claim from patrons). These policies are thus transforming the citizens' notions of right, obligation, and interest towards the state and the regime. The abrogation of welfare rights as oil prices and state revenues fall may be a source of future instability.

As oil revenues fell in the 1980s and precipitously in 1986, both Kuwait and Qatar began chipping at subsidies and introducing the idea of user fees and taxes. Qatar began introducing health care charges; Kuwait began charging for electricity and introducing "symbolic" charges for some social services. Following the 1986 austerity budget, the health minister raised the possibility of a publicly supported insurance plan. The planning minister called for a taxation system. The finance minister simply announced that Kuwait would no longer be able to continue its policy of providing free services (*MEED*, 30 August 1986: 19; *The Middle East Times*, 31 August 1986).

If this is the path the government chooses, if subsidies are cut and taxes introduced, these policies may well precipitate demands for representation. Among the poorer Kuwaitis the beduins, who form one of the amir's newer popular allies, have already protested at the new charges. The need for such fiscal measures, coupled with a fear of the political consequences, was one factor prompting the Kuwaiti government to close the Assembly, a natural arena for participatory demands, in 1986. The last Assembly went out fighting, among other things, government efforts to raise electricity rates. As one deputy asked, "why should a poor Kuwaiti family pay more for electricity which the country can afford, when the government has already spent four billion dinars bailing out speculators?" (*The Middle East*, February 1986: 9). Fear of such a response may in part account for the great reluctance of these regimes, even in times of substantially reduced revenues, to tax more resources from the population, or to cut back substantially on social services, preferring instead to draw down reserves or flout production quotas.

Rulers' responses

The rulers have responded to the twin problems of bureaucratic control and loyalty in three ways: first, with stopgap measures, episodic administrative reforms that attempt to assure a reliable chain of command from their orders down through implementation. One consequence has been the proliferation of new ministries and autonomous organizations to bypass those over which the ruler has lost control. As this process plays itself out, differences are beginning to emerge. In Kuwait, rulers have been able to exercise adequate, if incomplete, control over this bureaucracy by manipulating reinforced family ties and tolerating some clientelism within the bureaucracy. Kinship and client-based bureaucracies may be serving as a transitional adaptation to a more institutionalized bureaucratic state. Here pockets of rational bureaucracy exist. In Qatar the state remains underdeveloped; it is essentially one large fief. The rulers have been unable to exact predictable control over the bureaucracy because they lack the requisite control over their own family. Despite a series of expert advisory commissions, the problem of central control has not abated. When administrative reforms fail in Qatar, the rulers return to more autocratic and personal methods of control. Aside from some delegation of authority in a few technical areas, the amir and a few advisors control state affairs closely. Power remains uninstitutionalized. There is no meaningful distinction, political or legal, between the person of the amir and the institutions of state. Sovereignty is unchecked.

A second response to the problems of control and loyalty has been the emergence of policies aimed at integrating nationals politically at the mass level. Kuwait's National Assembly was the best example of this. Since its inception in 1963 it enjoyed high levels of support from the enfranchised population (adult male nationals). While excluded from the most important decisions, the Assembly was nonetheless an active forum which functioned both as a safety valve (along with a relatively free press) and as an institution which, by excluding expatriates, reinforced a sense of Kuwaiti identity. The cost to the regime lay in the difficulty in controlling the level and scope of criticism within the Assembly, prompting the Assembly's suspension in 1986.

The final response to the problems of loyalty and control has been a renewed stress on normative socialization, directing state revenues to the development of new civic myths, manipulating *turath* (cultural heritage), in order to restrict or monopolize the loyalty options of the citizen population. These myths aim at legitimizing the regime through a writing or rewriting of national history into a form more compatible with the ruler's public image. These histories aim to reconcile the monarchist and tribalist ideologies (of the ruler) with capitalist ideologies (for the merchants) and with welfarist ideologies (for the people). It is unclear whether these efforts will prove successful. They will only be tested in crisis, when people are forced to choose from among these potentially conflicting loyalties.

If such a crisis were to arise, the rulers' responses would be conditioned by their capacity and that capacity is in turn limited by the kind of state formation and alliance building that occurred under the influence of oil. In key ways state formation in oil states differs from state formation in states dependent on domestic sources of revenue. The origins of most states, certainly most strong states, as Tilly (1975) and others have argued, lie in a fiscal apparatus, a tax gathering structure, which in turn emerged from the development of a coercive monopoly, a military apparatus. Historically finance and defense, extraction and coercion, have played a central role in state formation throughout the world. States built on oil revenues are unusual in that their administrative structures grew originally from the imperative to expend rather than extract wealth. Oil enabled rulers to bypass the historic extractive process. But in bypassing this, rulers also bypassed the process of elite cooptation and coercion that elsewhere accompanied extraction. Unlike European monarchs, forced by the need for revenues to either crush elites or absorb them into the political process, Gulf leaders could simply buy out those elites who historically had had a say in controlling allocation. So oil precluded two kinds of states: in Kuwait, perhaps an oligarchy, possibly with some participatory mechanism; in Qatar, a more authoritarian state. As a result, the oil states also never developed the institutional capability to systematically coopt and coerce, a capacity which they may someday need. The result is that they are not strong states, strong in the sense of an ability to exercise predictable, legitimate control over their territory, bureaucracy, and citizenry, strong in the sense of an institutionalized capacity to implement policy as formulated, strong in any of its conventional usages (Riggs 1966; Cohen, Brown and Organski 1981; Anderson 1987; Salame 1987; Weiner 1988; Migdal 1988).

Today Kuwait and Qatar lack institutionalized cooptative and coercive capabilities, just the capabilities their rulers would need if organized opposition were to emerge. So far, such opposition has not developed on any scale because oil revenues have allowed rulers to buy off opponents. If opposition were more systematic, the state's capacity would be tested and perhaps found wanting. Yet organized opposition remains a possibility precisely because oil revenues have not forced rulers to destroy opposition elites. The merchants are one example. They have been encouraged to withdraw from politics, to avoid pressing their collective interests politically, but the political interests themselves have not been destroyed, nor has the corresponding corporate identity. Merchants maintain a collective sense, especially in Kuwait, where this identity is reinforced by economic institutions such as the Chamber of Commerce and the stock market and the revitalized social institutions of *majlis* and marriage. Through these institutions the merchants continue to recognize and accommodate each other, thus maintaining group awareness and solidarity. Yet they lack class capacity and they have no real assurance that the state will continue to serve their economic interests. They have limited input into decisionmaking and no formal, sustained, institutional mechanisms for stating their case.

Were the basic components of the original pact to change, for example, under the combined pressure of sustained low oil prices and concomitant cutbacks in the level of government contracts and a parallel move by the ruling family into the private sector, then the merchants might move back into opposition. So far the governments have tried to prevent this, making every effort to appease all groups by giving citizens preference. In Kuwait the government followed its 1986 austerity budget and cutbacks with the announcement that it would give local firms priority in state contracts. Likewise in Qatar, the one ministry still generating work, defense, has tried to send as much work as possible to Qataris (*MEED*, 4 October 1986).

The development of oil states has thus far provoked remarkably little domestic resistance. This absence is striking in comparison to both Western Europe and the Third World. It is all the more striking in that the transition occurred in the 1950s and 1960s, at the height of Arab nationalism. This absence of resistance however may be more indicative of weakness than success. The Gulf states are stable, not because they are able to handle opposition, to coopt and coerce, but because they have not yet faced the challenges that produce resistance. They have not been forced to destroy opposition elites; neither have they been forced into the coalitions that might have constrained their power or expanded participation. Thus they have not created allies with an independent stake in their regimes' viability. Oil revenues, by precluding the coalition building that is crucial to stability, have left these regimes vulnerable. Because Kuwait and Qatar are small, virtual city-states, the processes oil induces may have occurred more rapidly. Because of their relatively homogeneous citizen populations, the processes may also have occurred more clearly; they are not masked by sectarian or regional disputes. But the same processes that are occurring in Kuwait and Qatar are also occurring in the other oil-producing states. Saudi Arabia, Venezuela, Indonesia, Iran are all experiencing variations on this theme and facing the tensions that accompany oil.

Oil and the tensions it produces carry the seeds of change. Kuwait and Qatar have achieved a relatively smooth transition into oil monarchies. Yet, the remarkably smooth transition may, on closer examination, prove more apparent than real. In the future, these rulers may find themselves particularly ill-equipped to handle domestic conflict. The transitional adaptation, precisely because of its dependence on oil, is fragile. In fact, it may well be that these states have achieved such a smooth transition only by postponing problems.

Notes

2 History's legacy: Kuwait and Qatar before oil

1 India Office (hereafter IO) R/15/5/18: Hay, Political Resident (PR), Note, 2 September 1910, pp. 179–80. Unpublished Crown Copyright material in the India Office and Public Records Office appears by permission of the Controller of Her Majesty's Stationery Office.

2 IO R/15/5/18: Extracts from Kuwait News, 31 August 1910.

3 IO R/15/5/18: Extracts from Kuwait News, 31 August 1910; 7 September 1910; PR to Political Agent (PA), 2 September 1910.

4 IO R/15/5/18: Extracts from Kuwait News, 7 September 1910.

5 IO R/15/5/18: Hay, Note, 2 September 1910.

6 IO R/15/2/411: Dickson, PA, Kuwait to PR, Bahrain, 18 January 1934, p. 229.

7 While some of Palgrave's other accounts have been discredited, his visit to Qatar is accepted as generally reliable (Johnstone and Wilkinson 1960).

3 Kuwait on the eve of oil

1 Although there is no easy cutoff for the leading families there is substantial agreement on the core members: some thirty key families formed an overlapping economic and political elite, providing the wealthiest merchants and the bulk of the members for the 1921 and 1938 councils and the various *ad hoc* government advisory committees; Lorimer 1908–15, vol. 2: 1051; Dickson 1956: 41; al-Shihab 1980: 72; Kuwait News Agency 1981: 8–9; al-Qinai 1982: appendices. Hickinbotham, the Political Agent, gives an extensive Who's Who for Kuwait in the 1940s, IO R/15/5/179: Hickinbotham, PA to PR, Prominent Persons, 30 May 1942; Amendments, 1943, 26 September 1943, pp. 190–8.

2 IO R/15/5/179: Dickson, PA, Note on Kuwait Principality, p. 29.

3 IO L/P&S/10/1243: Shaikh Ahmad to Dickson, 3 August 1929, p. 80.

4 IO R/15/5/179: Dickson, Note, p. 24; Foreign Office (hereafter FO) 371-91258: PA to PR, Kuwait, Annual Report, 1950, 14 February 1951, p. 25.

5 IO R/15/5/179: Dickson, Note, p. 22.

6 IO L/P&S/12/3758: Kuwait Intelligence Summary (hereafter KIS), 16–30 September 1938, no. 137.

7 IO L/P&S/12/3758: KIS, 1–15 November 1933, no. 124. People were dying to do

business with him. Yusif was arrested for this activity, but was able to draw on the Bahbahani's historically close ties to the Shaikh to have his sentence commuted.

8 IO L/P&S/12/3894A: Fowle, PR to Gibson, IO, 19 October 1938, p. 150. Fowle wrote that Mubarak had taken a rough census in 1910 which put the town's population at 38,000, of whom 1000 were "Persians." Claverley (1962: 41), a physician with the Arabian Mission under Mubarak, put the Shias at 10 per cent of the population in the 1910s.

9 IO R/15/1/303: More, PA to High Commissioner, Iraq, 4 December 1921, p. 36.

10 IO R/15/5/179: Dickson, Note, p. 19.

11 IO L/P&S/12/3894A: Fowle to Gibson, 19 October 1938, p. 151: 10,000 Persians, 3000 from Hasa, 3000 Baharnas (indigenous Shias), 1000 Arabs who had migrated to Persia and returned, and 700 Shias of Iraqi origin.

12 IO R/15/5/179: Dickson, Note, p. 19.

13 IO R/15/5/179: Dickson, Note, p. 19.

14 IO R/15/5/179: Dickson, Note, pp. 6–7; Hickinbotham, PA, Bahrain to Hay, PR, 30 May 1942, p. 194; FO 371-39892: KIS, 16–30 April 1944, no. 130, p. 92.

15 IO R/15/5/180: PA to Hickinbotham, Baghdad, 26 February 1921, p. 7.

16 IO R/15/5/180: PA to Hickinbotham, Baghdad, 20 March 1921, p. 12; IO R/15/5/179, Dickson, Note, pp. 6–7.

17 In 1921 the Political Agent counted six Americans with the Mission and four British; IO R/15/1/303; More to High Commissioner, Iraq, 4 December 1921, pp. 35, 37.

18 IO R/15/5/179: Dickson, Note, pp. 7–9.

19 IO R/15/5/180: PA to Hickinbotham, Baghdad, 26 April 1921, p. 19.

20 FO 1016–142: Jakins, PA, to Rose, FO, 10 May 1951, p. 49.

21 FO 371-21833: deGaury, PA, Administration of Kuwait, to PR, 7 July 1938, p. 34.

22 IO R/15/5/179: Dickson, Note, p. 21.

23 Yusif, described by Dickson as "a schoolmaster and intriguer who is mixed up with every underhand plot in Kuwait" went on to play an active part in the 1938 uprising, serving in the Assembly, IO R/15/5/179: Dickson, Note, p. 11. He was not pro-British; Dickson's successor called him "a snake in the grass," IO R/15/5/179: Prominent Persons, 1943, p. 194. His peers held him in higher esteem. He was an educator who ran a Quran school and then the Mubarakiyya. He later served as education director and as a religious judge until clashes with the ruler led to his resignation.

24 IO L/P&S/12/3894A: deGaury to PR, 7 July 1938, pp. 217–22.

25 FO 371-21833: deGaury to PR, 7 July 1938, p. 37.

26 IO L/P&S/12/3894A: PA to PR, 7 July 1938, p. 217.

27 IO L/P&S/12/3758: KIS, 16–30 November 1938.

28 Muhammad, "the poor descendant of a rich family," was an activist who had already come to the government's attention; IO L/P&S/12/3758: KIS, 16–31 March 1938. He was a founding member of the Literary Club, established in 1924, composed primarily of merchants' sons. The year before the uprising he was imprisoned for leading a taxi driver strike after the ruler, in a period of attention to public morals, had issued a decree forbidding unchaperoned excursions by women outside the city. Muhammad also engaged in anti-government pamphleteering. After the uprising ended Muhammad was one of three opposition leaders specifically excluded by the

ruler in his general amnesty of 1944. He fled to Iraq and from there to Syria, where he was deported by the French in 1940. In 1946 Muhammad finally returned to Kuwait from India and was jailed, but released in 1947. IO R/15/5/206: Assistant Secretary to Government of India. Note on Mu. Bin Barak, 13 December 1946, p. 191; FO 371-52241: KIS, 1–15 November 1946, no. 207; al-Hatim 1980: 69, 150–2.

29 Yusif al-Marzuq came from an old Sunni, Najdi trading family. Yusif organized much of the opposition, including the demonstration in which he was shot in the foot. Although Yusif was anti-British, his brother Khalid was pro-British. The other brothers were less political. Muhammad and Fahad traded and lived in Karachi. Yusif's cousin, Muhammad Daud, a smaller businessman, was also in the 1938 Assembly and notably anti-British. Yusif himself was a leading merchant in India and had already spent time in jail there for smuggling before being imprisoned for his role in the 1938 events. While in jail, his dhows were caught by both India and local authorities for smuggling. He was a man of talent. While the prisoners' families were petitioning the British over prison conditions, Yusif was able to not only continue his shipping operations, but also father a child. IO R/15/5/179: Hickinbotham, Prominent Persons, 1943, p. 195. In 1945, after his release from prison, he was arrested by the Iraqi authorities for smuggling but was able to buy his freedom; FO 371-45178: KIS, 16–31 August 1945, p. 60. Yusif was by all accounts quite wealthy. In the 1940s he was well known for building one of the finest shorefront houses, setting off a spurt of rebuilding among Kuwait's leading merchants. There is a story, no doubt apocryphal, that he won a bride courted by a Sabah by preparing her tea over a fire of 10-rupee notes.

30 IO L/P&S/12/3894A: PA to PR, 19 March 1939, p. 337.

31 FO 371-21832: PR to IO, 18 July 1938, p. 198; IO L/P&S/12/3758: KIS, 16–30 June 1938.

32 FO 371-21832: PR to IO, 18 July 1938, p. 200.

33 IO L/P&S/12/3894A: Translation of the Law Governing the Power of the Kuwait Administrative Council, as granted by His Highness, 9 July 1938, p. 259; deGaury to Fowle, 27 December 1938, p. 118.

34 IO L/P&S/12/3894A: deGaury, Improvements introduced by the Kuwait Council since its Formation, enclosed in Fowle to Peel, IO, 17 November 1938, pp. 131–2.

35 FO 371-21833: Fowle to Peel, IO, 29 October 1938, pp. 116–17.

36 IO L/P&S/12/3894A: deGaury to Fowle, 22 December 1938.

37 IO L/P&S/12/3758: KIS, 16–31 December 1938.

38 IO R/15/5/206: PA to PR, 19 February 1939, Constitution, pp. 54–61.

39 IO R/15/5/206: PA to PR, 12 March 1939, p. 74; L/P&S/12/3758: KIS, 1–15 March 1939.

40 IO L/P&S/12/3758: KIS, 1–15 March 1939.

41 IO L/P&S/12/3758: KIS, 16–31 March 1939; IO R/15/5/206: PR to PA, 11 March 1939, p. 83.

42 IO L/P&S/12/3758: KIS, 16–30 June 1939; the ruler reportedly discussed al-Marzuq's case with the ruling family. Despite some support, his case was shut when the ruler's son Abdalla personally vowed to find and kill al-Marzuq if released; IO R/15/5/206: PA to PR, 1 July 1939, p. 128.

43 FO 371-39892: KIS, 16–30 April 1944, no. 130.

44 IO L/P&S/12/3758: KIS, 6–31 May 1941.

45 IO L/P&S/12/3758: KIS, 16–30 April 1944; IO R/15/5/206: PA to PR, 6 May 1944, p. 183; FO 371-52241: KIS, 1–15 March 1946, no. 64.

46 FO 371-21832: Fowle, Note, 25 April 1938, p. 140.

47 FO 371-21832: PA to PR, 19 March 1938, p. 111; FO 371-21833: Fowle to Gibson, IO, 19 October 1938, p. 101; IO L/P&S/12/3894A: Fowle to Ahmad, 18 June 1938; Fowle to Peel, IO, 18 July 1938, p. 256; 29 October 1938, p. 140; deGaury to Fowle, 22 December 1938, p. 113; Gibson, Foreign Office Minutes, 17 November 1938, p. 134.

48 IO L/P&S/12/3894A: PR to Secretary of State for India, 21 December 1938, p. 124.

49 IO L/P&S/12/3758: KIS, 16 June–15 July 1937.

50 IO L/P&S/12/3758: KIS, 6–31 July 1941.

51 IO L/P&S/12/3758: KIS, 1–15 March 1939.

52 IO L/P&S/12/3758: KIS, 16 June–15 July 1937.

53 FO 371-21858: Suwaidi, foreign minister, Iraq to Butler, Parliamentary Under-secretary of State for Foreign Affairs, 28 September 1939, p. 182.

54 IO R/15/5/126: Air Liaison Officer, Baghdad to Air Staff Intelligence, 10 February 1939, p. 254.

55 FO 371-21833: Boswall, Baghdad to Baggallay, British Embassy, Baghdad, 14 September 1938, p. 65.

56 IO L/P&S/12/3758: KIS, 1–15 April 1939, no. 53.

57 IO R/15/5/126: PA, Kuwait to PR, 25 April 1930, p. 18.

58 FO 371-21859: FO, Record of Conversation with the Iraqi Minister of Foreign Affairs, 4 October 1938, pp. 6–17; FO 371-21858: Suwaidi to Butler, 28 September 1939, p. 182; Eastern Department, FO Memorandum, 1 October 1938, pp. 253–5.

59 IO R/15/5/208: Evans, Air Ministry to FO, 12 July 1938, p. 12.

60 FO 371-21832: deGaury to British Consul, 12 March 1938, p. 118.

61 IO R/15/5/126: Air Liaison Officer, Baghdad to Air Staff Intelligence, 10 February 1939, p. 254.

62 IO L/P&S/12/3758: KIS, 16–28 February 1938; IO R/15/5/126: PA to PR, 24 February 1939, p. 229; IO R/15/5/206: PA to PR, 17 March 1939, p. 105.

63 IO R/15/5/126; Shaikh Ahmad to PA, 9 February 1934, p. 71. When Ahmad tried to plant articles in a Cairo paper to counter the Iraqi propaganda, his Cairo agent refused, saying Iraq's Nuri Said had already bribed him 200 pounds to print *his* articles. IO R/15/1/549: PR to Secretary of State for India, 8 March 1939, p. 40.

64 See, for example, IO L/P&S/12/3758: KIS, 1–15 February 1938.

65 IO L/P&S/12/3758: KIS, 16–28 February 1939.

66 IO R/15/5/126: PA to PR, 23 February 1939, p. 216.

67 IO L/P&S/12/3758: KIS, 16–30 June, 1938; 16–31 July 1938; 1–15 August 1938.

68 IO L/P&S/12/3758: KIS, 16–31 October 1938.

69 IO L/P&S/12/3894A: Fowle to Gibson, 19 October 1938, p. 151.

70 IO L/P&S/12/3894A: deGaury to Fowle, 22 December 1938, p. 13.

71 FO 371-21832: deGaury to British Consul, Bushire, 19 March 1938, p. 112.

72 IO L/P&S/12/3894A: PA to PR, 7 July 1938, pp. 209–10.

73 IO L/P&S/12/3894A: Fowle to Gibson, 19 October 1938, p. 143.

74 IO L/P&S/12/3894: deGaury, Note on a Conversation with HH, PR, 20 October 1938; Fowle to Peel, 29 October 1938, p. 139.

75 FO 1016-142: Jakins to Rose, 10 May 1951, p. 48.

76 IO R/15/5/179: Dickson, Note, p. 34.

77 FO 371-98323: PR to FO, Kuwait, Administrative Report, 1951, 31 October 1952.

78 IO R/15/5/194: PA to PR, 10 May 1942, p. 134.

79 IO R/15/5/179: Dickson, Note, p. 34.

80 IO L/P&S/12/3758: KIS, 16–31 October 1938.

81 FO 371-21833: deGaury, Administration of Kuwait, to PR, 7 July 1938, pp. 26–47. This was the case with a pearl merchant, Ahmad ibn Farhan, who was beaten and fined 5000 rs (later reduced to 2000 through the intervention of other merchants) for responding too slowly to Abdalla's summons. Ahmad paid his fine and moved to Zubair.

4 Kuwait after oil

1 IO L/P&S/12/3894A: deGaury, PA to PR, 7 July 1938, p. 208.

2 IO R/15/5/206: deGaury to Fowle, PR, 6 January 1939, p. 16.

3 IO R/15/5/206: Article 18 of the draft constitution, enclosed in deGaury to Fowle, 19 February 1939, pp. 54–61.

4 IO L/P&S/12/3894A: Prior, PR to Caroe, Government of India, 11 February 1940.

5 IO R/15/5/194: Prior to Caroe, 22 April 1941, p. 25.

6 IO L/P&S/12/3758: KIS, 16–31 July 1945; FO 371-98323: PR to FO, Kuwait, Administration Report, 1951, 31 October 1952.

7 FO 371-68324: KIS, 16–30 June 1948, no. 197.

8 FO 371-98325: Pelly, PA to Hay, PR, 27 May 1952.

9 FO 371-68324: KIS, 16–30 June 1948, no. 197.

10 FO 371-82004: PR to Furlonge, FO, Persian Gulf, Summary of Events, January 1950, 15 February 1950; FO 371-74941: PA to PR, 19 January 1949.

11 The troubles in Iran were quite visible in Kuwait, where Britain used the public beaches to park its tanks. FO 371-98323: PR to FO, Kuwait, Administration Report, 1951, 31 October 1952.

12 FO 371-98323: PR to FO, Kuwait, Administration Report, 1951, 31 October 1952.

13 FO 371-104260: KIS, 6 June 1953.

14 FO 371-98461: LeQuesne, PR to FO, 25 March 1952; FO 371-82004: PR to Furlonge, Persian Gulf, Summary of Events, April 1950, 4 May 1950.

15 FO 371-82005: Hay to Furlonge, 3 June 1950. The reconciliation occurred after rumors that members of this faction had begun organizing opposition in Basra.

16 FO 371-126872: PR, Persian Gulf, Monthly Report, 1–30 May 1957; FO 371-126899: Kuwait Oil Company, Incident on Wednesday, 15 May, 1957, to Riches, FO, 3 June 1957.

17 FO 371-104270: Ross, FO, to Burrows, PR, Foreign Office Minutes, 17 July 1953.

18 FO 371-74959: PR to FO, 14 January 1949.

19 FO 371-74959: PA to PR, 2 January 1949.

20 FO 371-91258: PR to FO, Persian Gulf, Annual Review, 1950, 31 January 1951; PA to PR, Kuwait, Annual Report, 1950, 14 February 1951.

21 FO 371-74941: PA to PR, 19 January 1949.

22 FO 371-98324: Hay to Ross, 16 October 1952.

23 FO 371-98324: Hay to Ross, 9 June 1952.

24 FO 371-98324: Hay to Ross, 1 November 1952.

25 FO 371-98324: Hay to Ross, 5 April 1952.

26 FO 371-98325: Pelly to FO, 28 April 1952.

27 FO 371-98324: Hay to Ross, 9 September 1952.

28 FO 371-98325: Hay to FO, 2 May 1952.

29 FO 371-109810: Logan, PA to Eden, FO, 26 July 1954.

30 FO 371-120550: Bell, PA to Burrows, 11 March 1955.

31 FO 1016-25: Jakins, PA, Bahrain to Hay, 10 December 1950.

32 FO 371-104264: FO to Burrows, 20 November 1953.

33 FO 371-104264: Burrows to FO, 13 October 1953.

34 FO 371-104264: FO to Burrows, 20 November 1953.

35 FO 371-114588: Bell to Fry, FO, 15 August 1955.

36 FO 371-98323: PR to FO, Kuwait, Administration Report, 1951, 31 October 1952.

37 FO 371-114576: Burrows to Macmillan, FO, 15 April 1955.

38 FO 371-82004: PR to Furlonge, Persian Gulf, Summary of Events, February 1950, 6 March 1950; FO 371-98324: PR to FO, 8 January 1952.

39 FO 371-109810: Wilkes, British Bank of the Middle East, Note for Directors, 29 October 1954, p. 110.

40 FO 371-104264: Logan, FO Brief, 9 November 1953.

41 IO L/P&S/12/3758: KIS, 16–31 October 1943.

42 FO 371-109810: Wilkes, Note for Directors, 29 October 1954, p. 110.

43 FO 371-74959: PA to PR, 2 January 1949.

44 FO 371-120541: Burrows to Riches, 19 January 1956, p. 8. In 1955 the ruler agreed to eliminate school lunches after petitions from local merchants. The Resident wrote, "although the Central Kitchen buys its material by tender from local merchants they apparently fear that the provision of meals by the Government would in some way deprive them of a channel of profit."

45 IO L/P&S/12/3894A: deGaury, list of thirty-one improvements introduced by the Council, enclosed in Fowle to Peel, IO, 17 November 1938, pp. 131–2.

46 For the history of al-Ghanim, see Field (1985: 121–32); *MEED*, February 1980, May 1982 and IO R/15/5/179: Hickinbotham to Hay, 30 May 1942, pp. 197–8.

47 In the 1790s an incident occurred between Britain and Ibrahim al-Ghanim, whose boat carried two Frenchmen from Muscat to Basra. Al-Ghanim, despite a large offer of money, refused to release the men to the British until directly ordered to by the Shaikh of Kuwait. Clearly the al-Ghanims were already a prosperous merchant family (Abu-Hakima 1965: 150).

48 IO R/15/5/179: Andrew, PA to Hay, 14 July 1948, p. 234.

49 FO 371-74942: Audsley, Labour Attaché, British Middle East Office, to FO, 9 April 1949.

50 FO 371-82163: Jakins to Hay, 21 February 1950.

51 FO 371-91258: PA to PR, Kuwait, Annual Report, 1950, 14 February 1951, p. 21.

52 IO R/15/5/206: Draft constitution, article 11, enclosed in PA to PR, 19 February 1939, p. 55.

53 FO 371-114576: Burrows to Macmillan, 15 April 1955.

54 Kuwaiti subjects were ruling family members, those permanently residing in Kuwait since 1899, children of Kuwaiti men and, at that time, children of Arab or Muslim fathers also born in Kuwait. Naturalization was possible after ten years in Kuwait, with work and Arabic proficiency and by special order for valuable services. It was revocable within five years for various reasons, among them propagating anti-Islamic ideas. FO 1016-126: Gethin, PA to Pelly, 27 September 1950, p. 15; Order No. 3 of 1948, pp. 23–30; Law No. 2, 1948, pp. 35–49.

55 FO 371-82116: PA to FO, 1 February 1950.

56 FO 1016-431: Logan to Ewart-Biggs, FO, 3 March 1955.

57 FO 371-109947: Logan to Burrows, 16 September 1954, union constitution enclosed, pp. 41–3.

58 E.g., FO 371-109810: Kuwait Democratic League, "Down with the High Executive Committee which does not Represent the People," enclosed, p. 91.

59 FO 371-114588: Rule or abdicate, translation of a circular distributed in the streets by unknown persons, 19 November 1955.

60 FO 371-120555: PA to FO, 15 August 1956.

61 FO 371-120551: Kuwait Diary, 27 August–24 September 1956, p. 86.

62 FO 371-126899: Bell to Burrows, 23 January 1957.

63 FO 371-120557: Bell to Burrows, 9 November 1956, p. 16.

64 FO 371-127008: Chancery, Beirut to FO, 24 September 1957.

65 FO 371-98324: PR to FO, 8 January 1952; FO 1016-362: Kuwait Diary, 22 February–25 March 1954, no. 37. There were 1000 voters in 1951, 5000 in 1954. The election was a complicated affair, with the town divided into several wards, organized by ward chairs and electoral committees. FO 371-109810: PA to Eden, 27 March 1954, p. 16.

66 FO 371-114745: Goodison, FO to Potter, Treasury, 5 July 1955; FO 371-114588: Burrows to PA, 7 June 1955.

67 "While in office a Minister shall not hold any other public office or practice, even indirectly, any profession or undertake any industrial, commercial or financial business. Further, he shall not participate in any concession granted by the Government or by public bodies or cumulate three ministerial posts with membership on the board of directors of any company . . . " *Constitution of the State of Kuwait*, Article 131.

68 FO 371-104264: Logan, FO Brief, 9 November 1953.

69 FO 371-98324: Hay to Sarell, FO, 8 January 1952.

70 FO 371-120598: Bell to Burrows, 23 January 1956.

71 FO 371-114695: Moberly, PA to Ewart-Biggs, 13 September 1955. The first Kuwaiti vessel was formally *flagged* in the early 1950s when the Kuwaiti government bought a yacht to house a dredging company working on the port. When the ship reached the Suez Canal from the Mediterranean, where it had been purchased, canal authorities informed the captain that the ship could not pass through on its old registration. So the Kuwait government registered the ship as the first Kuwaiti vessel so that it could get through the Canal.

72 FO 1016-25: Jakins to Hay, 12 December 1950.

5 Qatar

1 IO R/15/2/411: Williamson, APOC, Qatar, 14 January 1934, p. 230.
2 IO R/15/2/30: Keyes, PA, Bahrain to Knox, PR, Reports of Yusif Kanu, 13 April 1913, p. 25.
3 IO R/15/2/30: Keyes to Knox, 9 September 1914, p. 45.
4 IO R/15/2/30: Knox to Keyes, 15 September 1914, p. 58.
5 IO R/15/2/415: Historical memorandum on the relations of the Wahhabi amirs and Ibn Saud with Eastern Arabia and the British Government, 1800–1934, 26 September 1934, p. 83.
6 IO L/P&S/11/222: Prior, PA, Bahrain to Biscoe, PR, Bushire, 2 August 1930, p. 15.
7 IO R/15/2/412: Laithwaite, IO, Note on conversation with Rendel, FO, on Qatar, 15 December 1933, p. 11.
8 IO R/15/2/412: Secretary of State for India, London, to Government of India, New Delhi, 2 March 1934, p. 124.
9 IO R/15/2/417: Qatar oil concession, 17 May 1935, pp. 52–60.
10 IO R/15/2/417: Fowle, PR, to Shaikh Abdalla, 11 May 1935, p. 20.
11 FO 371-34904: Wakefield, PA, Bahrain, to Shaikh Abdalla, Agreement between the Ruler of Qatar and the oil company, 29 March 1943, p. 18; IO R/15/2/415: PA, Bahrain to PR, 15 December 1934, p. 179.
12 FO 1016-63; Wilton, Political Officer (PO), Doha, to Pelly, PA, Bahrain, 5 June, 1950, p. 10.
13 IO R/15/2/143: Confidential note on Jassim b Muhammad, 23 September 1944, p. 17.
14 FO 371-74942: Audsley, Chancery, British Middle East Office to FO, Persian Gulf Report, 9 April 1949; IO R/15/2/143: Hickinbotham, PA, 26 February 1945, p. 157; Field (1984: 205) estimates the population may have fallen to 10,000.
15 IO R/15/2/415: PA, Bahrain to PR, Bushire, 15 December 1934, p. 179.
16 FO 371-120554: Riches, FO Minutes, 12 June 1956; FO 371-74936: Hay, PR to Burrows, PA, Bahrain, Persian Gulf, Summary of Events, December 1948, 5 January 1949.
17 FO 1016-385: Brant, The Qatar succession, 31 May 1954; FO 371-127009: Riches, The succession in Qatar, 8 April 1957; FO 371-74935: Hay to Bevin, FO, Administration Report, Bahrain Agency, 1948; FO 371-74944: Admiralty to C. in C. (Afloat) E.I., 20 August 1949.
18 FO 371-74944: Jakins, PA, Qatar to FO, 15 August 1949.
19 FO 371-74944: Gethin, Visit to Qatar, 4th to 6th August, enclosed in Jakins to Burrows, FO, 18 August 1949.
20 FO 371-74944: Jakins to FO, 16 August 1949.
21 FO 1016-61: Abdalla to PA, Bahrain, 25 Shuwal 1368 (20 August 1949).
22 The letters and replies from Abdalla, Ali and Jakins are enclosed in FO 371-74944: Jakins to PR, 23 August 1949.
23 FO 1016-61: Statement made by A.P.R. to family al Thani on August 20, 1949.
24 FO 371-74944: Jakins to PR, 23 August 1949.
25 FO 371-74944: Hay, Bahrain to FO, 22 August 1949; FO 371-74944: Jakins to FO, 16 August 1949; FO 371-74944: FO to Bahrain, 17 August 1949.

26 FO 371-82003: Wilton, Administration Report, British Agency, August–December 1949; FO 371-74938: Jakins, Bahrain Intelligence Summary, 1–15 September 1949; Hay to Burrows, FO, 6 October 1949, Persian Gulf, Summary of Events, September 1949; FO 1016-61: Hay to Burrows, 13 September 1949, p. 76.

27 FO 371-82006: Pelly to Plant, 10 June 1950.

28 FO 371-82119: Hay to FO, 7 January 1950.

29 FO 1016-144: Jakins to FO, 3 October 1949; FO 371-74938: Bahrain Intelligence Summary, 16–30 September 1949.

30 FO 371-82119: Hay to FO, 12 January 1950.

31 FO 371-82119: Hay to Furlonge, FO, 15 February 1950; FO 1016-24: Pelly to Manager, PDQL, 29 December 1949.

32 FO 371-82119: FO to Hay, 12 January 1950.

33 FO 1016-162: Hay to Wilton, 25 February 1950, p. 64.

34 FO 371-82006: Hay to Furlonge, FO, 14 June 1950.

35 FO 371-82157: Rose to Hay, FO Minutes, 25 September 1950; FO 371-82054: Evans to Furlonge, FO, 23 October 1950. Rough budget in Pelly to Furlonge, FO, 10 July 1950.

36 FO 371-82004: Hay to Furlonge, Persian Gulf, Summary of Events, 8 April 1950.

37 FO 371-109871: Ewart-Biggs, FO Minutes, 8 April 1954, p. 14; FO 1016-267: Johnston, PA to Burrows, 10 October 1953, budget for July 1953–September 1954 enclosed; FO 1016-165, Plant to Pelly, 8 March 1951.

38 FO 371-74944: Hay to Burrows, 13 September 1949.

39 FO 371-74987: Hay to FO, 6 September 1949.

40 FO 1016-145: Qatar Diary, 1–15 September 1949, p. 8.

41 FO 1016-61: Hay to FO, 8 September 1949, p. 71.

42 FO 1016-61: Wilton to Jakins, 22 October 1949, p. 82; FO 1016-145: Qatar Diary, 16–29 September 1949, p. 12; FO 371-98330: Rose to FO, 2–3 March 1952.

43 FO 1016-398: Carden, PA, Qatar to Gault, PR, 29 August 1955; FO 371-114707: Shucklough, FO Minutes, 1 September 1955; FO 1016-398: Gault to FO, 15 January 1955.

44 FO 371-114774: Gault to Macmillan, FO, 15 August 1955.

45 FO 1016-184: Weir, PO, Qatar to Laver, PA, Bahrain, 22 March 1952, p. 119; FO 1016-184: Weir to Laver, 8 March 1952, 125–6; FO 371-98324: Hay to Ross, Persian Gulf, Summary of Events, March 1952, 5 April 1952.

46 FO 1016-268: Qatar Diary, 28 September–27 October 1953, no. 194.

47 FO 1016-152: Qatar Diary, 1–15 March 1950, p. 54.

48 FO 371-114774: Bahrain to FO, 25 August 1955.

49 FO 1016-398: Carden to Gault, 4 August 1955.

50 FO 371-120554: Burrows to Walmsley, FO, 24 September 1956, p. 21.

51 FO 371-98330: Fisher, Commanding Officer, Flamingo, Description of Events in Doha, 23–26 June 1952.

52 FO 371-98330: Weir to Pelly, 30 June 1952.

53 FO 371-98330: FO to PR, Bahrain, 28 June 1952.

54 FO 371-104260: Hay to Ross, FO, Persian Gulf, Summary of Events, November 1952, 11 December 1952.

55 FO 371-109805: Burrows to Eden, FO, 12 March 1954, p. 15.

56 FO 1016-398: Carden to Gault, 17 September 1955.

57 FO 371-126995: Burrows to FO, 3 October 1957.

58 FO 371-120541: Burrows to Riches, Monthly Summary, April 1956; 19 March 1956, p. 51.

59 FO 371-126869: Carden to Burrows, 26 January 1957; FO 371-120541: Burrows to Riches, Persian Gulf, Monthly Report, July 1956, 18 August 1956, p. 106; March 1956; 16 April 1956, p. 39.

60 FO 371-120554: Burrows to Lloyd, FO, 22 October 1956, p. 55.

61 FO 371-120541: Burrows to Riches, Persian Gulf, Monthly Report, August 1956; 17 September 1956, p. 114; FO 371-126869: Carden to Burrows, 26 January 1957.

62 FO 371-120554: Burrows to FO, 14 October 1956, p. 39.

63 FO 371-120554: Burrows to Walmsley, 24 September 1956, p. 20; Qatar Diary, Confidential Annex, 1–30 November 1956, 5 December 1956, p. 91; FO 371-126869: Burrows to Lloyd, Persian Gulf, Annual Report, 1956, 24 April 1957, p. 5; Carden to Burrows, 26 June 1957; FO 371-126871: Burrows to Riches, Persian Gulf, Monthly Report, November 1956; 10 January 1957, pp. 9–10.

64 FO 371-120554: Burrows to Lloyd, 22 October 1956, p. 59; FO 371-120677: Qatar Police Regulation 1956, 22 November 1956.

65 FO 371-127021: Carden to Burrows, 30 November 1957.

66 FO 371-82139: Lermitte, Petroleum Concessions Limited, Bahrain to Longrigg, London, 17 April 1950.

67 FO 371-104352: Laver to Rose, FO, 15 April 1953.

68 FO 371-114577: Gault to Broad, FO, Persian Gulf, Monthly Report, September 1955, 17 October 1955.

69 IO R/15/2/30: Keyes to Knox, Reports of Yusif Kanu, 2 August 1914, p. 32.

70 FO 371-82003: Wilton, Administration Report, British Agency, Doha, August–December 1949.

71 FO 371-109442: Hay to Ross, 6 February 1953; FO 371-126872: Qatar Diary, 1–31 May 1957; 1 June 1957, no. 41.

72 Jo Franklin Trout says the shaikhs of Wakra refuse to use license plates as an expression of this opposition. "The oil kingdoms," Pacific Productions, Pacific Mountain Network, 1983, aired on WGBH, Boston, 29 September 1984.

73 FO 1016-145: Qatar Diary, 31 October–15 November 1949, p. 28.

74 FO 371-98324: Hay to Ross, Persian Gulf, Summary of Events, March 1952, 5 April 1952.

75 FO 1016-163: Qatar Diary, 21 April–20 May 1950, p. 2.

76 FO 1016-163: Qatar Diary, 21 April–20 May 1950, p. 2.

77 FO 1016-63: Jacomb to PR, 28 September 1950, p. 17.

78 FO 1016-161: Qatar Diary, July 1951, p. 12; October 1951, p. 28; FO 371-91259: Hay to Furlonge, Persian Gulf, Summary of Events, May 1951, 7 June 1951, p. 123; December 1950, 10 January 1951, p. 148; FO 1016-152: Qatar Diary, 1–15 January 1950, p. 74; FO 1016-63: Jacomb to PR, 28 September 1950, p. 17.

79 FO 371-98324: Hay to Ross, Persian Gulf, Summary of Events, March 1952, 5 April 1952.

80 FO 1016-184: Ali bin Abdalla to Hay, 10 October 1952, p. 29.

81 FO 1016-184: FO Minutes, 27 October 1952, p. 20.

82 FO 371-126869: Burrows to Lloyd, Persian Gulf, Annual Report, 1956, 24 April 1957, p. 5.

83 FO 371-120554: Burrows to Walmsley, 24 September 1956, p. 20.

84 FO 371-120554: Burrows to FO, 15 October 1956, p. 46.

85 FO 371-120541: Burrows to Riches, Monthly Summary, October 1956, 28 November 1956, p. 142; FO 371-120554: Qatar Diary, 1–30 November 1956, 5 December 1956; FO 371-126871: Burrows to Riches, Monthly Summary, December 1956, 25 January 1957; FO 371-126869: Carden to Burrows, 26 January 1957.

86 FO 1016-184: Weir to Laver, 30 April 1952, p. 112.

87 FO 1016-152: Qatar Diary, 16–31 March 1950, p. 50.

88 FO 371-74944: Gethin, Visit to Qatar – 4th to 6th August, in Jakins to Burrows, FO, 18 August 1949.

89 FO 1016-152: Qatar Diary, 22 July–21 August 1950, p. 15.

90 FO 1016-145: Qatar Diary, 30 September–14 October 1949, p. 16.

91 IO R/15/2/143: Jassim bin Mohammad, note enclosed to Prior, 25 September 1944; FO 371-98433: Weir to PA, Bahrain, 22 May 1952.

92 IO R/15/2/143: Hickinbotham to PR, 22 November 1944, pp. 43–4.

93 FO 1016-145: Qatar Diary, 1–15 September 1949, p. 7.

94 IO R/15/2/143: Petition to Hickinbotham, 16 November 1944 from ten Qataris, p. 45; PR to PA, 24 November 1944, p. 49; PA to Shaikh Abdalla, 29 November 1944, p. 53; Jasim Muhammad to PA, 2 December 1944.

95 FO 1016-145: Qatar Diary, 16–29 September 1949, p. 11.

96 FO 371-82003: Wilton, Administration Report, British Agency, Doha, August–December 1949.

97 FO 1016-145: Qatar Diary, 1–15 September 1949, p. 8.

98 FO 1016-61: Gethin to Jakins, 23 August 1949.

99 FO 1016-144: PA, Qatar to Jakins, 22 October 1949, p. 3.

100 FO 371-82003: Wilton, Administration Report, British Agency, August–December 1949; FO 1016-152: Qatar Diary, 1–20 April 1950, p. 31.

101 FO 371-109871: Ewart-Biggs, FO Minutes, 8 April 1954, p. 15.

102 FO 371-104345: Ross to Wall, Bahrain, 10 July 1953.

103 FO 371-98330: Rose, FO Minutes, 6 March 1952.

104 FO 371-109901: Burrows to Fry, FO, 21 June 1954, pp. 66–7.

105 FO 371-82004: Pelly, Bahrain Intelligence Summary, 16–31 January 1950.

106 FO 371-109858: Burrows to Johnston, 29 December 1953, p. 4.

107 FO 371-104265: Ewart-Biggs, FO Minutes, 31 October 1953.

108 FO 1016-398: Carden to Richards, 30 June 1955.

109 FO 371-120554: Translation of an anonymous pamphlet attacking Darwish, May 1956, p. 4; Richards, Bahrain to Samuel, FO, 28 May 1956, p. 3.

110 FO 371-120554: Burrows to Lloyd, 22 October 1956, p. 66.

111 FO 371-120554: Burrows to Walmsley, 24 September 1956, p. 20; Burrows to FO, 14 October 1956, p. 39; FO 371-126869: Carden to Burrows, 26 January 1957; FO 371-120541: Burrows to Riches, Persian Gulf, Monthly Diary, September 1956, 22 October 1956, p. 125; FO 371-126873: Carden, Qatar Diary, 25 September 1957, Confidential Annex.

112 FO 371-126872: Qatar Diary, 5 May 1957.

113 FO 1016-146: Qatar Diary, 31 October–15 November 1949, p. 24.

114 FO 371-120554: Burrows to Lloyd, 22 October 1956, p. 65.

115 FO 1016-145: Qatar Diary, 23–31 August 1949, p. 4.

116 FO 371-109805: Burrows to Eden, FO, 12 March 1954.

117 FO 371-98324: Hay to Ross, Persian Gulf, Summary of Events, 9 May 1952.

118 FO 1016-164: Hay, Note, 24 November 1951, p. 12.

119 FO 371-120541: Burrows to Riches, FO, Persian Gulf, Monthly Report, January 1956, 16 February 1956, p. 16; FO 371-127012: Marshall, PR to Hird, Labour Counsellor, British Embassy, Beirut, 24 January 1957.

120 FO 371-91360: Jacomb, FO Minutes, 28 July 1951.

121 FO 371-74942: Audsley, Chancery, British Middle East Office to FO, 9 April 1949; FO 371-91360: Jakins to PA, Bahrain, 20 January 1951.

122 FO 371-91363: Audsley to Cranston, FO, 10 September 1951: 162 British, 13 Americans, 522 Indians, and 1753 Arabs, 1580 of whom were classified as Qatari, including 328 foreigners with Qatari papers.

123 FO 371-82119: Translation of speech delivered by Saleh Bin Mani, 3 February 1950.

124 FO 371-82004: Hay to Furlonge, Persian Gulf, Summary of Events, 8 April 1950; FO 1016-152: Qatar Diary, 1–15 March 1950, p. 54; FO 1016-28; Qatar Diary, 26 June–28 July 1953, no. 147; FO 371-120541: Burrows to Riches, Monthly Report, Persian Gulf, February 1956, 17 March 1956, p. 28.

125 FO 371-91363: Hay to FO, 21 July 1951.

126 FO 1016-161: Qatar Diary, July 1951, p. 23; FO 371-91363: Haugh, Extract, Qatar Monthly Report, September 1951 and October 1951; FO 1016-161: Qatar Diary, July 1951, p. 31.

127 FO 371-98465: Hay to Greenhill, 8 October 1952; Hay to Sarell, FO, 18 September 1952; FO 371-98424: Agreement between Petroleum Development (Qatar) Ltd. and the Ruler, 1 September 1952.

128 FO 1016-152: Qatar Diary, 1–15 March 1950, p. 54; 16–31 March 1950, p. 50.

129 FO 371-82119: Translation of speech delivered by Saleh Bin Mani, 2 February 1950.

130 FO 371-91360: Fry, FO to Hay, 7 May 1951.

131 FO 371-98464: Weir to Laver, 14 April 1952; FO 371-98324: Hay to Ross, 9 May 1952.

132 IO R/15/2/1829: File of case histories of slaves who reported to the Residency.

133 FO 371-98464: Weir to Laver, 14 April 1952; FO 371-91360: Jacomb to PA, Bahrain, 28 July 1952; FO 371-98464: Hay to Eden, FO, 17 April 1952.

134 FO 371-91360: Jacomb, FO Minutes, 28 July 1951; FO 371-91360: Jakins to PA, Bahrain, 20 January 1951.

135 FO 371-91360: Pelly to FO, 5 February 1951; FO 371-74944: Hay to Bevin, 1 September 1949, p. 7; FO 1016-161: Qatar Diary, July 1951, p. 15.

136 FO 1016-398: Gault to Macmillan, FO, 29 August 1955; Carden to Gault, acting PR; FO 1016-435: Agreement between HH and QPC, 17 August 1955, pp. 1–10.

137 FO 371-98323: Hay to Eden, FO, Persian Gulf, Annual Review, 1951, 15 January 1952.

138 FO 371-109901: Burrows to Fry, FO, 21 June 1954, p. 66.

139 FO 1016-433: Gault to Carden, 14 October 1955.

140 FO 371-114707: Johnston, PA, Qatar to Burrows, 3 March 1955.

141 FO 371-82003: Wilton, Administration report, British Agency, Doha, August–December 1949; FO 371-82004: Hay to Furlonge, Persian Gulf, Summary of Events, March–April 1950; FO 371-98324: Pelly to Ross, Persian Gulf, Summary of Events, June 1952, 10 July 1952; FO 371-114577: Gault to Fry, Persian Gulf, Monthly Report, June 1955, 11 July 1955, no. 34; FO 371-98465: Ewart-Biggs to Hay, 5 October 1952.

142 FO 371-114707: Proclamation, Ali b Abdulla al-Thani to Qatari employees of QPC, 14 August 1955.

143 FO 371-120673: Burrows to Lloyd, FO, 1 May 1956.

144 FO 371-126869: Carden to Burrows, 26 January 1957.

145 The UN summarizes parts of the 1970 census; Economic Commission 1980: 10–9. The 1986 census, unpublished in full, is one source for Qatar, Central Statistical Organization 1987.

146 There are no official figures. Bazarian (1980: 69) estimates 50,000; the London *Times*, 60,000 (12 November 1985: 17).

147 FO 371-74938: Bahrain Intelligence Summary, 16–30 September 1949.

148 FO 371-120554: Burrows to Lloyd, 22 October 1956, p. 55.

149 FO 371-104260: Hay to FO, Persian Gulf, Summary of Events, February 1953, 12 March 1953.

150 FO 1016-268: Qatar Diary, 27 April–26 May 1953, no. 82.

151 FO 371-120541: Burrows to Riches, Persian Gulf, Monthly Report, February 1956, p. 27.

152 IO R/15/2/30: Keyes to Knox, 9 September 1914, p. 45.

153 FO 371-120541: Burrows to Riches, Persian Gulf, Monthly Report, July 1956, 18 August 1956, p. 106; FO 1016-145: Qatar Diary, 1–15 September 1949, p. 7.

154 FO 371-114577: Gault to Broad, Persian Gulf, Monthly Report, August 1955, 9 September 1955.

155 FO 371-126869: Carden to Burrows, 26 January 1957.

156 FO 371-126871: Qatar Diary, February 1957, Confidential Annex.

157 FO 371-126995: Burrows to Shaikh Ali, 20 October 1957.

158 Nasir's problems with the succession have not abated. In 1976 Nasir was attacked in London by three armed men over continuing unsettled family business. Nasir turned up again in a London hospital in 1986 with bullet wounds amid speculation that succession had once again triggered family dissent (*New York Times*, 31 May 1960: 4; 22 June 1976: 41; *Middle East Newsletter*, 19 May 1986: 4).

159 FO 1016-161: Qatar Diary, July 1951, p. 42.

160 FO 1016-145: Qatar Diary, 23–31 August 1949, p. 4; FO 371-120554: Burrows to Walmsley, 25 September 1956, p. 21.

161 FO 1016-184: FO Minutes, 29 October 1952, p. 20.

162 FO 1016-145: Qatar Diary, 31 October–15 November 1949, p. 26; FO 371-104442: Greenhill to Serpell, FO, 17 February 1953.

163 FO 1016-385: Burrows to Hickinbotham, Governor of Aden, 6 September 1954.

164 FO 371-114577: Burrows to Fry, FO, Persian Gulf, Monthly Report, March 1955, 28 April 1955.

165 FO 371-114597: Fry, FO Minutes, 18 March 1955.
166 FO 371-82003: Wilton, Administrative Report, British Agency, August–December 1949; FO 1016-145: Qatar Diary, 16 November–15 December 1949, p. 32; FO 371-91258: Hay to FO, 29 May 1951, p. 66; FO 1016-268: Qatar Diary, 27 February–26 March 1953, no. 46; Qatar Diary, 27 March–26 April 1953, no. 61; FO 371-126935: Gault to Lloyd, 13 June 1957, no. 13; Riches, Confidential memo, Zubara, 1 August 1957.

Select bibliography

Abaidan, Yusif Muhammad. 1979. *al-Mu'assasat al-siyasiyya fi dawlat qatar*. Doha: Ministry of information.

Abdou, Kamal Saleh. 1958. A stranger in Kuwait. *The New Leader*, 41: 16–18.

Abdulla, Saif Abbas. 1974. *Politics, administration and urban planning in a welfare state: Kuwait*. PhD dissertation, Indiana University.

al-Abdulla, Yousof Ibrahim. 1981. *A study of Qatari–British relations, 1914–1945*. Doha: Orient Publishing.

Abu-Hakima, Ahmad Mustafa. 1965. *History of Eastern Arabia: the rise and development of Bahrain and Kuwait*. Beirut: Khayats.

1972. The development of the Gulf states. In *The Arabian peninsula: society and politics*, ed. Derek Hopwood, pp. 31–53. London: George Allen and Unwin.

1983. *The modern history of Kuwait*. London: Luzac and Company.

Abu Saud, Abeer. 1984. *Qatari women past and present*. Burnt Mill: Longman House.

Adams, Michael. 1958. Is Kuwait next on Nasser's timetable? *The Reporter*, 19: 26–8.

Ajami, Riad. 1979. *Arab response to the multinationals*. New York: Praeger.

Alessa, Shamlan. 1981. *The manpower problem in Kuwait*. London: Kegan Paul.

Alrayes, Tarik Mohammad. 1979. *Authority and influence in the government civil service in the state of Kuwait*. PhD dissertation, Claremont Graduate School.

Alsadek, Jihad. 1983. *Simulating lifetime incomes and the impacts of government distributive policies: the case of Kuwait*. PhD dissertation, George Washington University.

Amin, Muhammad Amin. 1984. Muhakamat al-kuwait takshif al-jiha al-haqiqiyya wara'a al-tafjirat. *al-Majalla*, 11–17 February, pp. 16–17.

Amin, Samir. 1974. *Accumulation on a world scale: a critique of the theory of underdevelopment*, trans. Brian Pearce. London: Monthly Review Press.

al-Amiri, Uthman. 1986. Awda ila al-diwaniyyat. *al-Majalla*, 8–14 October, pp. 12–15.

Anderson, Lisa. 1986. *The state and social transformation in Tunisia and Libya, 1830–1980*. Princeton: Princeton University Press.

1987. The state in the Middle East and North Africa. *Comparative Politics*, 20: 1–18.

Anderson, Perry. 1974. *Lineages of the absolutist state*. London: Vergo.

Anthony, John Duke. 1975. *Arab states of the lower Gulf: people, politics, petroleum*. Washington, Middle East Institute.

Arthur D. Little (ADL). 1962. *Economic survey of Qatar (phase 1 – preliminary report)*. Cambridge, MA.

Aruri, Naseer. 1972. Politics in Kuwait. In *Man, state, and society in the contemporary Middle East*, ed. Jacob Landau, pp. 68–90. New York: Praeger.

1980. Kuwait: Sociopolitical developments. *American Enterprise Institute, Foreign Policy and Defense Review*, 2: 44–50.

Assiri, Abdul-reda. 1988. Kuwait's political elites. *Middle East Journal*, 42: 48–58.

Atiyah, Edward. 1956. Oil and nationalism in the Persian Gulf. *The Listener*, 27 September, pp. 448–51.

Attiga, Ali. 1981. How oil revenues can destroy a country. *Petroleum Intelligence Weekly*, 19 October, pp. 1–4.

Baaklini, Abdo. 1982. Legislatures in the Gulf area: the experience of Kuwait, 1961–1976. *International Journal of Middle Eastern Studies*, 14: 359–79.

Barry, Brian. 1975. Review article: political accommodation and consociational democracy. *British Journal of Political Science*, 5: 477–505.

Batatu, Hanna. 1978. *The old social classes and the revolutionary movements of Iraq.* Princeton: Princeton University Press.

Baz, Ahmad Abdulla Saad. 1981. *Political elite and political development in Kuwait.* PhD dissertation, George Washington University.

Bazarian, Carl. 1980. Bahrain and Qatar: economic developments. *American Enterprise Institute, Foreign Policy and Defense Review*, 2: 68–70.

Beblawi, Hazem and Giacomo Luciani, eds. 1987. *The rentier state.* London: Croom Helm.

Bibby, Geoffrey. 1969. *Looking for Dilmun.* New York: Alfred A. Knopf.

Bidwell, Robin, ed. 1971. *The affairs of Kuwait: 1896–1905.* London: Frank Cass.

1982. *The affairs of Arabia: 1905–6.* London: Frank Cass.

Bowen, Richard. 1949. Arab dhows of Eastern Arabia. *American Neptune*, 9: 87–132.

1951. Marine industries of eastern Arabia. *Geographical Review*, 41: 384–400.

1951a. The pearl fisheries of the Persian Gulf. *Middle East Journal*, 5: 161–80.

1952. Primitive watercraft of Arabia. *American Neptune*, 12: 186–221.

Buckingham, J. S. 1829. *Travels in Assyria, Media, and Persia.* London: Henry Colburn.

Calverly, Edwin. 1916. A city of pearls and thirst. *Travel*, 27: 14–44.

1962. Kuwait today, yesterday and tomorrow. *Muslim World*, 52: 39–47.

Cardoso, Fernando and Enzo Faletto. 1979. *Dependency and development in Latin America.* Berkeley: University of California Press.

Carter, J. R. L. 1984. *Merchant families of Saudi Arabia.* London: Scorpion Books.

Celine, K. 1985. Kuwait living on its nerves. *Merip Reports*, 130: 10–12.

Chisholm, Archibald. 1975. *The first Kuwaiti oil concession.* London: Frank Cass.

Cohen, Youssef, Brian Brown and A. F. K. Organski. 1981. The paradoxical nature of state making: the violent creation of order. *American Political Science Review*, 75: 901–10.

Cordesman, Anthony. 1984. *The Gulf and the search for strategic stability: Saudi Arabia, the military balance in the Gulf, and trends in the Arab-Israeli military balance.* Boulder: Westview.

Cottrell, Alvin, ed. 1980. *The Persian Gulf states.* Baltimore: Johns Hopkins University Press.

Daalder, Hans. 1974. The consociational democracy theme. *World Politics*, 26: 604–21.

Daher, Ahmad and Faisal al-Salem. 1984. Kuwait's parliamentary elections. *Journal of Arab Affairs*, 3: 85–97.

Dalyell of the Binns, G. 1938. The Persian Gulf. *Royal Central Asian Journal*, 25: 349–64.
1941. The Persian Gulf. *The Scottish Geographical Magazine*, 52: 58–65.

Daniels, John. 1971. *Kuwait journey*. Luton: White Crescent Press.

Darwiche, Fida. 1986. *The Gulf stock exchange crash: the rise and fall of the souq al-manakh*. London: Croom Helm.

Davis, Eric. 1979. The political economy of the Arab oil-producing nations: convergence with western interests. *Studies in Comparative International Development*, 14: 75–94.

deCandole, E. A. V. 1959. Development in Kuwait. *Royal Central Asian Journal*, 46: 27–34.
1964. Kuwait today. *Royal Central Asian Journal*, 52: 31–7.

deCardi, Beatrice, ed. 1978. *Qatar archaeological report excavations 1973*. Oxford: Oxford University Press.

Declassified documents reference service. 1977, 1978. *Retrospective collection*. Washington: Carrollton Press.

deGaury, Gerald. 1983. *Traces of travel*. London: Quartet Books.

Delacroix, Jacques. 1980. The distributive state in the world system. *Studies in Comparative International Development*, 15: 3–22.

Deutsch, Karl. 1961. Social mobilization and political development. *American Political Science Review*, 55: 493–514.

Dickson, H. R. P. 1956. *Kuwait and her neighbours*. London: George Allen and Unwin.

Dickson, Violet. 1971. *Forty years in Kuwait*. London: George Allen and Unwin.

Dickson, Zahra. 1949. Kuwait and its people. *Islamic review*, 37: 25–7.

Dobson, Meric. 1963. Labour in Kuwait. *Middle East Forum*, December, pp. 27–9.

al-Easa, Juhaina. 1983. Changing family functions in Qatar. *Journal of South Asian and Middle Eastern Studies*, 7: 50–6.

al-Ebraheem, Hassan. 1975. *Kuwait: a political study*. Kuwait: Kuwait University.

Epstein, Edward Jay. 1983. Kuwait: embassy cables. *Atlantic*, 251: 16–19.

Evans, Peter. 1979. *Dependent development: the alliance of multinational, state, and local capital in Brazil*. Princeton: Princeton University Press.

Farah, Tawfic. 1979. Inculcating supportive attitudes in an emerging state: the case of Kuwait. *Journal of South Asian and Middle Eastern Studies*, 2: 56–68.

Farah, Tawfic, ed. 1983. *Political behavior in the Arab states*. Boulder: Westview.

Felber, John, ed. 1962. *Kuwait welcomes commerce*. Newark: International Import Index.

Ffrench, Geoffrey E. and Allan Hill. 1971. *Kuwait: urban and medical ecology*. Berlin: Springer-Verlag.

Field, Michael. 1985. *The merchants: the big business families of Saudi Arabia and the Gulf states*. Woodstock: The Overlook Press.

Finnie, David. 1958. *Desert enterprise: the Middle East oil industry in its local environment*. Cambridge: Harvard University Press.

Frank, Andre Gunder. 1967. *Capitalism and underdevelopment in Latin America*. New York: Monthly Review Press.

Freeth, Zahra. 1956. *Kuwait was my home*. London: George Allen and Unwin.

Freeth, Zahra and Victor Winstone. 1972. *Kuwait: prospect and reality*. London: George Allen and Unwin.

Gause, F. Gregory, III. 1985. British and American policies in the Persian Gulf, 1968–73. *Review of International Studies*, 11: 247–73.

1990. *Saudi Arabia and the Yemens: domestic structures and foreign influence.* New York: Columbia University Press.

Gavrielides, Nicolas. 1987. Tribal democracy: the anatomy of parliamentary elections in Kuwait. In *Elections in the Middle East: implications of recent trends*, ed. Linda Layne, pp. 153–213. Boulder: Westview.

Gerard, Bernard. 1974. *Qatar: a forward looking country with centuries old traditions.* Paris: Editions Delroisse.

Graham, Helga. 1978. *Arabian time machine: self-portrait of an Arab state.* London: Heinemann.

Great Britain, Admiralty, Naval Staff, Naval Intelligence Division, Geographical Section. 1916–17. *A handbook of Arabia*, vol. 1. Oxford: Oxford University Press.

Great Britain, Foreign Office (FO)
FO 371, General Correspondence.
FO 1016, General Correspondence.

Great Britain, India Office (IO)
R/15/1, Political Residency, Bushire, 1763–1947.
R/15/2, Political Agency, Bahrain, 1900–47.
R/15/5, Political Agency, Kuwait, 1904–47.
L/P&S/10–12, Departmental Papers.

al-Haddad, Mohammad. 1981. The effects of detribalization and sedentarization on the socio-economic structure of the tribes of the Arabian peninsula: Ajman tribe as a case study. PhD dissertation, University of Kansas.

Halliday, Fred. 1975. *Arabia without sultans.* New York: Vintage Books.

Hammoud, Hassan. 1986. The impact of technology on social welfare in Kuwait. *Social Service Review*, 60: 52–69.

Harrison, Paul. 1924. Economic and social conditions in East Arabia. *Muslim World*, 14: 163–71.

1924a. *The Arab at home.* New York: Thomas Y. Crowell.

al-Hatim, Abdalla. 1980. *Min huna bada'at al-kuwait.* Kuwait: Dar al-Qabas.

Hay, Rupert. 1955. The impact of the oil industry on the Persian Gulf shaykhdoms. *Middle East Journal*, 9: 361–72.

1959. *The Persian Gulf states.* Washington: Middle East Institute.

Hewins, Ralph. 1963. *A golden dream: the miracle of Kuwait.* London: W. H. Allen.

Hijazi, Ahmad. 1964. Kuwait: development from a semitribal, semicolonial society to democracy and sovereignty. *American Journal of Comparative Law*, 13: 428–38.

Hill, Enid. 1979. The modernization of labor and labor law in the Arab Gulf states. *The Cairo Papers in Social Science*, Monograph 2. Cairo: the American University in Cairo.

Hirschman, Albert, 1970. *Exit, voice, and loyalty: responses to decline in firms, organizations, and states.* Cambridge: Harvard University Press.

Hunter, Shireen. 1986. The Gulf economic crisis. *Middle East Journal*, 40: 593–613.

Huntington, Samuel P. 1968. *Political order in changing societies.* New Haven: Yale University Press.

Ibrahim, Hasan. 1975. *Kuwait: a political study.* Kuwait: Kuwait University.

Ibrahim, Saad Eddin. 1982. *The new arab social order: a study of the social impact of oil wealth.* Boulder: Westview.

International Bank for Reconstruction and Development (IBRD). 1965. *The economic development of Kuwait.* Baltimore: Johns Hopkins University Press.

el-Islam, M. Fakhr. 1976. Intergenerational conflict and the young Qatari neurotic. *Ethos*, 4: 45–56.

   1978. Transcultural aspects of psychiatric patients in Qatar. *Comparative Medicine East and West*, 6: 33–6.

Ismael, Jacqueline. 1982. *Kuwait: social change in historical perspective.* Syracuse: Syracuse University Press.

Ives, Edward. 1773. *A voyage from England to India, in the year MDCCLIV.* London: Edward and Charles Dilly.

Izzard, Molly. 1979. *The Gulf: Arabia's western approaches.* London: John Murray.

al-Jasim, Najat Abdalqadir. 1980. *Baladiyyat al-kuwait fi khamsin aman.* Kuwait: Kuwait Municipality.

Johnson, Paul. 1957. The new role of Great Britain. *New Statesman*, 54: 53–6.

   1958. High noon in Kuweit. *New Statesman*, 56: 105–6.

Johnstone, T. M. and J. C. Wilkinson. 1960. Some geographical aspects of Qatar. *Geographical Journal*, 126: 442–50.

Jones, Geoffrey. 1978. *Banking and oil: the history of the British Bank of the Middle East*, vol. 2. Cambridge: Cambridge University Press.

Jones, Mervyn. 1969. Thrice-worried Kuwait. *New Statesman*, 77: 722–3.

Karl, Terry. 1981. Petroleum and political pacts: the transition to democracy in Venezuela. *Working Papers* 107. The Wilson Center, Latin American Program.

Kelly, J. B. 1958. Sovereignty and jurisdiction in Eastern Arabia. *International Affairs*, 34: 16–24.

   1980. *Arabia, the Gulf and the West.* New York: Basic Books.

Kerr, Malcolm and El Sayed Yassin, ed. 1982. *Rich and poor states in the Middle East: Egypt and the new Arab order.* Boulder: Westview.

Key, Kerim. 1976. *The state of Qatar: an economic and commercial survey.* Washington: K. Key Publications.

Khadduri, Majid. 1967. Political trends in Iraq and Kuwait. *Current History*, 52: 84–9.

Khouja, M. W. and P. G. Sadler. 1979. *The economy of Kuwait: development and role in international finance.* London: Macmillan.

Khuri, Fuad, 1980. *Tribes and state in Bahrain.* Chicago: University of Chicago Press.

Kline, Nathan. 1963. Psychiatry in Kuwait. *British Journal of Psychiatry*, 109: 766–74.

Kostiner, Joseph. 1987. Shi'i unrest in the Gulf. In *Shi'ism, resistance and revolution*, ed. Martin Kramer, 173–86. Boulder: Westview.

al-Kubaisi, Amir. 1981. al-idara al-amma wa al-tanmiyya bi dawlat qatar khilal aqdain. *Journal of the Gulf and Arabian Peninsula Studies*, 7: 43–87.

Kurtz, Richard. 1982. Perceptions of medical clinics in Kuwait. *Journal of Asian and African Studies*, 17: 208–17.

Kuwait, Ministry of foreign affairs. 1981. *Kibar rijal al-dawla wa al-sharikat al-wataniyya al-rasmiyya.*

Kuwait, Ministry of planning. 1987. *Annual statistical abstract.*

Kuwait, Ministry of social affairs. 1958. *taʿdad sukan al-kuwait li-sanat 1957.*

Kuwait News Agency (KUNA). 1981. *Democracy in Kuwait.*

Kuwait Oil Company. 1959. *The story of Kuwait.*

al-Kuwari, Ali Khalifa. 1978. *Oil revenues in the Gulf emirates.* Boulder: Westview.

Lackner, Helen. 1978. *A house built on sand: a political economy of Saudi Arabia,* London: Ithaca Press.

Lawson, Fred. 1983. State of Qatar. In *World encyclopedia of political systems and parties,* ed. George Delury, vol. 2, pp. 856–9. New York: Facts on File.

1985. Class and state in Kuwait. *Merip Reports,* 132: 16–32.

Lees, G. M. 1928. Qatar peninsula. *Geographical Journal,* 71: 464.

Lenczowski, George. 1960. *Oil and state in the Middle East.* Ithaca: Cornell University Press.

Lerner, Daniel. 1958. *The passing of traditional society.* New York: Glencoe Free Press.

Liebesny, Herbert. 1956. Administrative and legal development in Arabia: the Persian Gulf principalities. *Middle East Journal,* 10: 33–42.

Lienhardt, Peter. 1975. The authority of shaykhs in the Gulf: an essay in nineteenth-century history. In *Arabian Studies,* eds. R. B. Serjeant and R. L. Bidwell, vol. 2, pp. 61–75. London: C. Hurst and Company.

Lijphart, Arend. 1969. Consociational democracy. *World Politics,* 21: 207–25.

Lindt, A. R. 1939. Politics in the Persian Gulf. *Royal Central Asian Journal,* 26: 619–33.

Linz, Juan and Alfred Stepan, eds. 1978. *The breakdown of democratic regimes.* Baltimore: Johns Hopkins University Press.

Lorimer, John Gordon. 1908–15. *Gazetteer of the Persian Gulf, Oman, and Central Arabia.* Calcutta: Superintendent, Government Printing. Republished 1970. Westmead: Gregg International Publishers.

Mahdavy, Hossein. 1970. The patterns and problems of economic development in rentier states: the case of Iran. In *Studies in the economic history of the Middle East,* ed. M. A. Cook. Oxford: Oxford University Press.

el-Mallakh, Ragaei. 1979. *Qatar: development of an oil economy.* London: Croom Helm.

1981. *The absorptive capacity of Kuwait.* Lexington: Lexington Books.

Marouf, Nawal. 1982. Administrative development in Kuwait. *Arab Journal of Administration,* April, pp. 30–53.

McCutcheon, Shaw. 1983. Sheik chic: Kuwait cruising with the Arab high-rollers. *Motor boating and sailing,* 151: 42–7.

Meiring, Desmond. 1979. *A foreign body.* London: Constable.

Melamid, Alexander. 1953. Political geography of trucial Oman and Qatar. *The Geographical Review,* 43: 194–206.

Melikian, Levon. 1981. *Jassim: a study in psychosocial development of a young man in Qatar.* London: Longman.

Melikian, Levon and Juhaina al-Easa. 1981. Oil and social change in the Gulf. *Journal of Arab Affairs,* 1: 79–98.

Migdal, Joel. 1987. Strong states, weak states: power and accommodation. In *Understanding political development,* eds. Myron Weiner and Samuel P. Huntington, pp. 391–434. Boston: Little Brown and Company.

Miles, Samuel. 1919. *The countries and tribes of the Persian Gulf.* London: Harrison.

Monroe, Elizabeth. 1954. The shaikhdom of Kuwait. *International Affairs,* 30: 271–84.

1964. Kuwayt and Aden: a contrast in British policies. *Middle East Journal*, 18: 63–74.

Moore, Jr., Barrington. 1967. *Social origins of dictatorship and democracy: lord and peasant in the making of the modern world*. Boston: Beacon Press.

Moorehead, John. 1977. *In defiance of the elements*. London: Quartet Books.

Muna, Farid. 1980. *The Arab executive*. London: Macmillan.

al-Musa, Abdalrasul Ali. 1981. *al-Tatawwur al-umrani wa takhtit fi al-kuwait: 1952–1980*. Kuwait: al-Kazima.

Muslim students following the line of the imam. n.d. *Documents from the U.S. espionage den: U.S. interventions in the Islamic countries: Kuwait*. Tehran: n.p.

Mylrea, Stanley. 1917. Kuwait, Arabia. *Muslim World*, 7: 118–26.

Nafi, Zuhair. 1983. *Economic and social development in Qatar*. London: Frances Pinter.

al-Nafisi, Abdalla. 1978. *al-Kuwait al-ra'i al-akhar*. London: TaHa Advertising.

Nakhleh, Emile. 1977. Labor markets and citizenship in Bahrayn and Qatar. *Middle East Journal*, 31: 143–56.

1980. Political participation and the constitutional experiments in the Arab Gulf: Bahrain and Qatar. In *Social and economic development in the Arab Gulf*, ed. Tim Niblock, pp. 161–86. London: Croom Helm.

al-Naqeeb, Khaldun. 1976. *Changing patterns of social stratification in the Middle East: Kuwait as a case study*. PhD dissertation, University of Texas at Austin.

1978. Social strata formation and social change in Kuwait. *Kuwait University Journal of the Social Sciences*, 5: 236–71.

Nettl, J. P. 1968. The state as a conceptual variable. *World Politics*, 20.

9th June studies. 1974. *The United Arab Amirates and Qatar: pro-imperialist oil-producers in the Gulf*, ed. and trans. Gulf committee. London: Russell Press.

Nore, Petter and Terisa Turner, eds. 1980. *Oil and class struggle*, London: Zed.

Nyrop, Richard, *et al.* 1977. *Area handbook for the Persian Gulf states*. Washington: US Government Printing Office.

O'Donnell, Guillermo, Philippe Schmitter, and Laurence Whitehead, eds. 1986. *Transitions from authoritarian rule: prospects for democracy*. Baltimore: Johns Hopkins University Press.

Oil for underdevelopment and discrimination: the case of Kuwait. 1978. *Monthly Review*, November, pp. 12–21.

al-Othman, Naser. 1984. *With their bare hands: the story of the oil industry in Qatar*, trans. Ken Whittingham. London: Longman.

Owen, Roderic. 1957. *The golden bubble*. London: Collins.

Pal, Dharm. 1945. British policy towards the Arabian tribes on the shores of the Persian Gulf (1864–1868). *Journal of Indian History*, 24: 60–76.

Palgrave, W. G. 1865. *Personal narrative of a year's journey through central and eastern Arabia (1862–1863)*. London: Macmillan.

Pelly, Lewis. 1863. Remarks on the tribes, trade, and resources around the shore line of the Persian Gulf. *Bombay Geographical Society Transactions*, 17: 32–162.

Peterson, J. E. 1977. Tribes and politics in eastern Arabia. *Middle East Journal*, 31: 297–312.

1988. *The Arab Gulf states: steps toward political participation*. New York: Praeger.

Qatar, Advisory council. 1981. *Majlis al-shura fi sutur*, prep. Qusai al-Abadala.

1982. *Qa'imat al-sharaf*.

Qatar, Central statistical organization (CSO). 1987. *Annual statistical abstract.*

Qatar, Department of legal affairs. 1975. *Majmuʿat qawanin qatr: 1961–75* (4 vols.).

Qatar, Ministry of information. 1973. *Qatar into the seventies.*

    1976. Speeches and statements by His Highness Sheikh Khalifa Bin Hamad al Thani.

    1980. *Turath qatr wa thaqafatuha al-muʿasira.*

    1982. *Qatar year book 1980–81.*

    1982a. *Majmuʿ at khutub wa bayanat: 1971–81.*

Qatar, the developing Gulf sheikhdom. 1969. *Orient* 10: 45–9.

al-Qinaʿi, Najat Abdalqadir al-Jasim. 1982. *Taʾrikh sinaʿat al-sufun fi al-kuwait.* Kuwait: Kuwait Association for the Advancement of Science.

al-Qudsi, Sulayman. 1981. Pre- and post-fiscal distributional patterns in Kuwait. *Middle Eastern Studies,* 17: 393–407.

Riggs, Fred. 1966. Bureaucrats and political development: a paradoxical view. In *Political development and social change,* eds. Jason Finkle and Richard Grable. New York: John Wiley and Sons.

Rihani, Ameen. 1930. *Around the coasts of Arabia.* London: Constable and Company.

Rostow, Walt. 1960. *The stages of economic growth: a non-communist manifesto.* Cambridge: Cambridge University Press.

al-Rumaihi, Muhammad. 1975. Harakat 1938 al-islahiyya fi al-kuwait wa al-bahrain wa dubai. *Journal of the Gulf and Arabian Peninsula Studies,* 1: 29–68.

    1983. *Beyond oil: unity and development in the Gulf.* London: Al Saqi.

Rush, Alan. 1987. *Al-Sabah: history and genealogy of Kuwait's ruling family, 1752–1987.* London: Ithaca Press.

Sabah, Mohammed. 1978. *A critical analysis of inflation in Kuwait (1971–1976).* Senior Thesis, Claremont Men's College.

Sabah, Y. S. F. 1980. *The oil economy of Kuwait.* London: Kegan Paul International.

Sadik, Muhammad and William Snavely. 1972. *Bahrain, Qatar, and the United Arab Emirates: colonial past, present problems, and future prospects.* Lexington: D. C. Heath.

al-Sadun, Jasim. 1977. al-Awamil al-muʾashira fi takafaʾa al-dakhal (dirasat ʿan al-kuwait). *Journal of the Gulf and Arabian Peninsula Studies,* 3: 79–115.

Salame, Ghassan, ed. 1987. *The foundations of the Arab state.* London: Croom Helm.

Salameh, Ghassan. 1986. Hangover time in the Gulf. *Merip Reports,* 139: 40–3.

al-Salim, Hadayat Sultan. n.d. *Ahmad al-Jabir: raʾid al-nahda al-haditha fi al-kuwait.* Kuwait: n.p.

Samore, Gary. 1983. *Royal family politics in Saudi Arabia (1953–1982).* PhD dissertation, Harvard University.

Sanmiguel, Victor. 1978. *Pastor in Kuwait: 1966–1978.* Essex: Kevin Maynew Limited.

Sapsted, David. 1980. *Modern Kuwait.* London: Macmillan.

Selected documents of the international petroleum industry: peoples Libyan Arab jamahiriya and Qatar, pre-1966. 1983. Buffalo: William Hein and Company.

Shabon, Anwar. 1981. *The political, economic and labor climate in the countries of the Arabian peninsula.* Philadelphia: Wharton School, Industrial research unit.

Shamma, Samir. 1959. *The oil of Kuwait.* Beirut: the Middle East Research and Publishing Center.

Shaw, Ralph. 1976. *Kuwait.* London: Macmillan.

Shehab, Fakhri. 1965. Public sector plays unique economic role. *Emergent Nations*, 1: 158–9.

Shiber, Saba. 1964. *The Kuwait urbanization*. Kuwait: Government Printing Press.

al-Shihab, Yusif. 1980. *al-dalil al-tijari al-kuwaiti*. Kuwait: al-Shihab Bureau.

Skocpol, Theda. 1979. *States and social revolutions*. Cambridge: Cambridge University Press.

1982. Rentier state and Shi'a Islam in the Iranian revolution. *Theory and Society*, 11: 265–83.

Smith, Richard Austin. 1957. The greatest oil king of them all. *Fortune*, 55: 162–78.

Staley, Eugene. 1933. Business and politics in the Persian Gulf. *Political Science Quarterly*, 48: 367–85.

Stark, Freya. 1937. Kuwait. *The Geographical Magazine*, 5: 385–98.

Stepan, Alfred. 1978. *The state and society: Peru in comparative perspective*. Princeton: Princeton University Press.

Stoakes, Frank. 1972. Social and political change in the third world: some peculiarities of oil-producing principalities of the Persian Gulf. In *The Arabian peninsula: society and politics*, ed. Derek Hopwood, pp. 189–215. London: George Allen and Unwin.

Stocqueler, J. H. 1832. *Fifteen months pilgrimage through untrodden tracts of Khuzistan and Persia*. London: Saunders and Otley.

Sweet, Louise. 1964. Pirates or polities? Arab societies of the Persian or Arabian Gulf, 18th century. *Ethnohistory*, 11: 262–80.

al-Thakeb, Fahed and Joseph Scott. 1981. Islamic law: an examination of its revitalisation. *British Journal of Criminology*, 21: 58–69.

Thomas, Bertram. 1932. *Arabia felix*. New York: Scribner's.

Tilly, Charles, ed. 1975. *The formation of national states in western Europe*. Princeton: Princeton University Press.

Trimberger, Ellen. 1978. *Modernization from above: military bureaucrats and development in Japan, Turkey, Egypt, and Peru*. New Brunswick: Transaction Books.

United Nations. 1972. *United Nations inter-disciplinary reconnaissance mission*, vol. 2, *Qatar*. Beirut.

United Nations, Economic commission for western Asia. 1980. *The population situation in the ECWA region: Qatar*. Beirut.

United States, American consulate, Kuwait. 1960. Economic summary of Kuwait: 1959. Foreign Service Despatch 237, 1 February.

United States, Department of state. 1987. *Background notes: Qatar*.

United States, US Embassy, Kuwait. 1982. Leading Kuwaiti companies, directory of directors as at 31 December 1981.

Unwin, P. T. H., comp. 1982. *Qatar*. Oxford: Clio Press.

al-Uthman, Nasir Muhammad. 1980. *al-sawāʿid al-samr: qisat al-naft fi qatr*. Doha: al-dawha al-haditha.

Villiers, Alan. 1948. Some aspects of the Arab dhow trade. *Middle East Journal*, 2: 399–416.

1969. *Sons of Sinbad*. New York: Charles Scribner's Sons.

Viorst, Milton. 1988. A reporter at large: out of the desert. *The New Yorker*, 16 May, pp. 43–74.

Waterbury, John. 1984. *The Egypt of Nasser and Sadat.* Princeton: Princeton University Press.

Weiner, Myron. 1987. Political change: Asia, Africa, and the Middle East. In *Understanding political development*, eds. Myron Weiner and Samuel P. Huntington, pp. 33–64. Boston: Little, Brown and Company.

Wilkinson, J. C. 1983. Traditional concepts of territory in South East Arabia. *The Geographical Journal*, 149: 301–15.

Wilson, Rodney. 1983. *Banking and finance in the Arab Middle East.* Byfleet, Macmillan.

Zahlan, Rosemarie Said. 1979. *The creation of Qatar.* London: Croom Helm.

1981. The Gulf states and the Palestine problem. *Arab Studies Quarterly*, 3: 1–21.

Zureik, Elia. 1981. Theoretical considerations for a sociological study of the Arab state. *Arab Studies Quarterly*, 3: 229–57.

Index

Ruling family members (shaikhs) are alphabetized by first name, all others by family name.

Cambridge Middle East Library